Teenage Troubles

Teenage Troubles

Youth and Deviance in Canada
Second Edition

Julian Tanner
University of Toronto

NELSON

™

THOMSON LEARNING

Australia • Canada • Mexico • Singapore • Spain • United Kingdom • United States

Teenage Troubles: Youth and Deviance
in Canada,
Second Edition

by Julian Tanner

Editorial Director and Publisher:
Evelyn Veitch

Executive Editor:
Joanna Cotton

Marketing Manager:
Don Thompson

Developmental Editor:
Toni Chahley

Production Editor:
Bob Kohlmeier

Production Coordinator:
Hedy Sellers

Copy Editor:
Ruth Chernia

Proofreader:
Sarah Weber

Art Director:
Angela Cluer

Cover Design:
Peggy Rhodes

Cover Image:
John Terence Turner/FPG Photos

Compositor:
Susan Calverley

Indexer:
Edwin Z. Durbin

Printer:
Webcom

Canadian Cataloguing in Publication Data

Tanner, Julian
Teenage troubles : youth and deviance in Canada

2nd ed.
Includes bibliographical references and index.
ISBN 0-17-616817-6

1. Juvenile delinquency – Canada.
2. Juvenile delinquents – Canada.
I. Title.

HV9108.T35 2001   364.36'0971
C00-933045-3

Contents

CHAPTER 6   *She's a Rebel? Female Deviance and Reactions to It*   **178**

Preface

At the heart of much public discussion about crime and other social problems is a concern with the misbehaviour of young people. This is perhaps most evident in headlines that warn us about escalating rates of juvenile crime and in political rhetoric that sees the solution to the problem of crime in the reform of the juvenile justice system. Public views of the troublesome character of youth, however, extend beyond any narrow conceptualization of criminal conduct. Many elements of contemporary youth culture, including hip-hop or heavy metal music, raves, video arcades, and spectacular styles of dress are widely seen as reflecting, stimulating, or resulting from the social problems that plague adolescents.

In this volume, I provide a critical review of much of what is known about youth crime and deviance. The scope of the analysis is broad and directs the reader's attention to a set of topics both traditional—how much youth crime is there and what are its causes?—and new—are girls becoming more violent and aggressive? What happens to delinquents when they grow up? How should we best understand squeegee kids? Are schools catalysts for violence? Are young people the forgotten victims of crime?

Drawing on a range of empirical studies and theoretical viewpoints (starting with, though not limited to, subcultural theory), the book calls into question much of the conventional thinking about youthful misbehaviour. It challenges, for instance, the view that the behaviour of young people today is significantly worse than it was in the past and suggests that the study of youthful deviance is about both the determinants of rule-breaking behaviour and the social reaction to that behaviour. It also warns of, *pace* Columbine, the dangers of over-reacting to youth problems.

The opening chapter focuses upon the social construction of youth problems and the sources and nature of popular images of deviant youth. Chapter 2 concerns itself with the reality of youth deviance as measured by both official and unofficial counts and explorations of crime and delinquency. I provide a largely descriptive account of patterns of adolescent deviance in Canada, as well as a brief review of what is known about crime that is directed against adolescents—victimization, in other words.

Chapter 3 begins by documenting the chequered history of subcultural theory from its original inception in the United States in the 1920s and 1930s through to its more recent manifestation in the United Kingdom. I also look at several attempts to integrate subcultural theory into other sociological theories of delinquency.

The theories outlined, I then examine in Chapters 4 and 5 the main arenas in which adolescent subcultures emerge and where patterns of deviance and victimization are acted out. These are the high school and the street.

As you will soon discover, students of crime and delinquency have considered females as an afterthought. Most theory and research on delinquency and deviant youth culture has been based on assumptions made about male behaviour and experiences. Chapter 6 confronts the problem of distorted images of female delinquency, examines attempts to explain its patterns and incidence, and explores how female deviants have been dealt with by the criminal justice system.

In Chapter 7 the definitional questions that have informed the introductory chapter are revisited: why and how do societies like Canada respond as they do to the behaviour of the young? The focus here is upon the intense debate surrounding the introduction of the Young Offenders Act, shifting philosophies of juvenile justice, and different attempts to reduce levels of juvenile crime. In a short concluding chapter I review the main ideas and themes that have been the focus of this book.

Having said something about the subject of this book, I should also indicate what it is not about, and what it does not contain. I have deliberately refrained from writing a "sociology of delinquency," let alone *the* sociology of delinquency. By that I mean that the book does not pretend to provide a comprehensive overview of all the theories and research currently available on delinquency and typically covered in large textbooks on the subject. There are many topics conventionally included in texts of this sort that I have paid very little attention to—the relationship between age and criminality, or religion and delinquency, for example. Preferring not to write another tome on well-trodden themes, I chose instead to focus on a relatively small number of key issues central to the behavioural and definitional aspects of youth deviance.

I hope that this book will inform, and that it will also encourage the reader to think critically about adolescent crime and deviance and the policies intended to prevent or control these behaviours.

ACKNOWLEDGMENTS

A number of people have helped me, directly and indirectly, in the production of this book. First of all, I owe a tremendous debt of gratitude to all the people at what is now called the University of East London (Barking Regional College of Technology when I was there) who provided me with an excellent undergraduate education. Thank you Barrie Newman, Mike Brake, Andrew Cornwall, Alan Watson, David Chalmers, Eric Baker, Sabby Sagan, and all the rest. They, and later on Graham Murdock at the University of Leicester, stimulated and supported my academic interests in sociology and beyond; to this day they remain my mentors. Tim Hartnagel has played a similar role since I arrived in the New World.

I would also like to express my appreciation of Vince Sacco and Les Kennedy, who originally encouraged me to write this book and navigated me through the first edition. Thanks to the reviewers, whose insightful comments helped in many ways to make this book more useful: Stephen Baron, University of Windsor; Kathryn Campbell, University of Ottawa; Peter D. Chimbos, Brescia College, University of Western Ontario; and, again, Vince Sacco, Queen's University. Thanks also to all the people at Nelson Thomson Learning, especially Toni Chahley this time around, for their support and encouragement, and to Ruth Chernia, who contributed an accomplished copy edit.

My belated introduction to the wonderful world of computers has meant that Audrey Glasbergen has not had to type innumerable drafts of this second edition. Nonetheless, she has contributed to the final product in many ways, both large and small.

Finally, a few more immediate and personal debts: I am grateful to my parents for their help and support over the years—it is certainly easier writing about delinquents than to suffer the consequences of having become one; my friends in both Canada and Britain; and, most of all, Rhonda and Alexa, who make life worth living.

Julian Tanner
University of Toronto

Deviant Youth: The Social Construction of Youth Problems

INTRODUCTION

Where were you when you first heard about the shootings at Columbine High School in Littleton, Colorado, on April 20, 1999? I was at home in front of my television set, expecting to be informed about the latest developments in Kosovo. But instead of learning more about ethnic violence in the faraway Balkans, I was vicarious witness to scenes of carnage from the more familiar setting of a North American high school. The protagonists? Two masked and heavily armed male students. Their victims? Twelve of their fellow students.

Very quickly, media coverage of the event moved from reportage of the basic facts to putative explanation. A wide range of possible causes were identified and discussed at length: media violence, particularly the violent nature of much popular culture; an emergent "Goth" subculture (specifically the "trench coat Mafia"); parental neglect; the overlooking of "obvious" warning signs of trouble ahead by parents, teachers, and local law enforcement agents; and the easy availability of lethal firearms.

What happened at Columbine had the immediate effect of concentrating the public mind on the dispositions and behaviour of young people. Indeed, for many people, but especially adults, the name "Columbine" has become a one word summation for a wide range of deeply held fears about the collective condition of contemporary youth. In particular, Columbine is taken as evidence that today's young people are more violent and aggressive than their predecessors.

However, it may surprise you to find out that this is how the young have frequently been viewed by their elders. Social surveys consistently indicate that crime, and particularly violent interpersonal crime, ranks prominently among the features of modern life that people find least attractive; a disproportionately large amount of this anxiety focuses upon the behaviour of adolescents. No other social group receives as much negative attention as the young. They are judged variously as troubling and troubled (and sometimes both simultaneously: troubling *because* they are troubled). Newspaper and television reports fuel these fears with stories of squeegee kids, violence in schools and at rock concerts, drug use at "raves," and so on. Although the particular deviant motif varies—bike gangs yesterday, Goths today—what remains constant is the tarnished view of youth that is portrayed.

The story that the unrelenting media coverage tells is of high and increasing incidents of juvenile crime, the explanation (and blame) for which is sought in a wide range of factors: too much of the wrong sort of leisure, divorced parents, working mothers, "deadbeat dads," the erosion of "family values," the lack of discipline in schools, too few jobs, and a reluctance to adequately punish young offenders. What also runs through these accounts— and this is typified by the response to Columbine—is the assumption that the behaviour of modern youth is much worse than the behaviour of youth has ever been in the past, and that Canada is beginning the new millennium with a new and unique set of youth problems. In this regard, a Toronto *Globe and Mail* headline proclaiming "Another outbreak of street gang fighting has reawakened citizens to the extent of the problems these young people present" is instructive.

What incident do you imagine is being described here? A clash between rioters and police on Yonge Street in Toronto in the aftermath of the original trial verdict in the Rodney King case in Los Angeles? An outbreak of swarming at a suburban shopping mall? Both are reasonable guesses, but both are wrong. The headline is from an editorial in *The Globe and Mail* from January 1949—over fifty years ago. The street fighters in question were, in fact, boys— the Junction Boys, a then-prominent gang based in Toronto's west end. Their delinquent activities included car theft, breaking and entering, liquor offences, street brawls, and inciting riots (with baseball bats) in communities other than their own. Politicians and newspapers explained and deplored their behaviour in terms of broken homes, declining moral standards, and—this was in the days before television, don't forget!—violent gangster movies.

The 1949 *Globe and Mail* editorial was resurrected by journalist Colin Vaughan to introduce, in the same newspaper, his own more recent commentary on youth gangs in Toronto (1992). The title of his article, "Everything old seems new again, to teens," sums up his thesis: for all its apparent novelty, contemporary teenage behaviour is not much different from that of the past.

Vaughan points out that the idea that Canada's largest city has until recently been immune to crime ("Toronto the Good") is a myth. From the beginning Toronto has had its fair share of gang conflicts. In support of his argument he describes the Jubilee Riots of 1875, when Protestant Orangemen attacked Irish Catholic immigrants on city streets, and recalls the notorious Christie Pit Riots of 1933 when, toward the end of a long, hot summer, young Jews were set upon by juvenile fascists (members of the Swastika Club). Fighting fanned out along Bloor Street as both sides called in reinforcements. A sequel of sorts took place in 1965, when a neo-Nazi rally at a downtown park was protested.

Gang fights in Toronto have not been restricted to ethnic conflicts. For instance, the Halloween riots of 1945 began when the police arrested a few troublemakers and ended after a crowd of seven thousand besieged a west-end police station. The outbreaks of trouble between youths and police that occurred fairly regularly on the last day of the Canadian National Exhibition should also be remembered. And, lest you gain the impression that Toronto alone experiences youth riots, cast your mind back to the disturbances that have occurred in recent years in Montreal and Vancouver after, respectively, Stanley Cup victories and defeats.

But back to Colin Vaughan: he is not alone in seeing basic similarities between contemporary teenagers and their predecessors. The British criminologist Geoffrey Pearson reached a similar conclusion and made it the starting point for his own investigation of the nature of the "youth problem" in the United Kingdom. His book, entitled *Hooligan* (1983), begins with an examination of contemporary (mid-1970s) press coverage of youth (mis)behaviour and finds a now-familiar concern with a juvenile crime problem that seemingly has no precedent, the prescribed solution for which is sought in stiffer punishments for young offenders. Furthermore, the troubled present is compared with an apparently more tranquil past. Contemporary media commentators and politicians were able to recall a time—roughly twenty years earlier—when young people were not out of control, schools were still able to exert authority over the young, family values were intact, parents were more willing and able to supervise their children, police were not handcuffed by petty bureaucratic rules, and the courts were able to administer appropriately severe punishments.

Intrigued by this rosy view of the 1950s, Pearson then examines newspaper coverage of youth behaviour from that time. And what do you imagine he finds? Virtually the same concerns and arguments expressed in roughly the same language! In the 1950s juvenile crime was seen as a new and disturbing problem; the youth of the nation was being corrupted by post-war affluence, and so forth. Again, there was a harking back to a time, twenty years earlier, when young people had not been a problem. Proceeding in this manner, Pearson delves further and further back into British history, trying to find a time when youthful deviance was not a source of anxiety. Always the crime-free golden age is reckoned to be twenty years prior to the present and therefore remains a perpetually elusive utopia.

What are the sociological implications of Pearson's observations? First, and most obviously, anxieties about the delinquent activity of youth have a long pedigree. There is very little that is new about our current concerns with raves, squeegee kids, swarming, youth gangs, or violence in schools. As we shall see, our Victorian forebears were scarcely less concerned about unsupervised and uncontrolled youth on the streets than we are today. Second, the myth of the good old days influences our thinking about and prescriptions for contemporary juvenile offenders: if delinquency was once less of a problem than it is now, today's problems can be solved by doing what they did yesterday. The usual assumption is that juveniles were punished more harshly in the past and that is the reason why delinquency was less of a problem (Bernard, 1992, p. 13). Third, studying reactions to delinquent behaviour is as important a task for students of crime as studying the behaviour itself. This is partially a matter of acknowledging that how we respond to youth—what we celebrate, tolerate, or condemn—tells us much about society's moral boundaries. But more importantly, studying our reactions to delinquency alerts us to the fact that objective social conditions alone do not give rise to social problems such as crime and deviance.

Over the past several decades sociologists have pondered the nature of social problems and the reality of the threat that they pose to society. The traditional argument is that delinquency is a problem because the antisocial behaviour of adolescents is dangerous and damaging to persons and property within the community. This might be called an objectivist approach to social problems. The focus of deviance is upon norm-violating behaviour, particularly behaviour that is evaluated negatively because of the harm and injury that it causes.

From a second, more recent perspective, delinquency is a problem because it has been defined or labelled as such by some people. This is referred to as a constructionist approach to social problems, and its proponents believe

> that our sense of what is or is not a social problem is a product, something that has been produced or construed through social activities. When activists hold a demonstration to attract attention to some social condition, when investigative reports publish stories that expose new aspects of the condition, or when legislators introduce bills to do something about the conditions, they are constructing a social problem. (Best, 1989, p. xviii)

MEDIA PORTRAYALS OF YOUTH DEVIANCE

The way in which the mass media present news stories about youth is an obvious example of the process described above. As Pearson's study suggests, media reports on youth invariably focus on disreputable behaviour, a preoccupation confirmed by another British study. A content analysis of a sample of national and local newspapers revealed that the vast bulk of youth stories had a negative orientation in that they concentrated disproportionately on deviant activities (Porteous and Colston, 1980, cited in Muncie, 1984).

Although no equivalent Canadian study has been conducted, two researchers have reported on a brief review of the *Toronto Star* during the first week of December 1990. They found that on each day of the week, at least one story managed to link youth with crime. And as you would probably have guessed, the incidents that these stories dealt with did not include the pilferage of Mars bars from 7-Eleven stores or other trivial offences. They focused instead upon spectacular but atypical crimes of violence, such as drive-by shootings (Corrado and Markwart 1992). A more recent, and detailed, examination of the Canadian print media's coverage of youth crime found a similar focus: over a three-month period, the vast majority (94 percent) of stories involved cases of violence (Sprott, 1996).

Needless to say, youth gangs are a particularly attractive topic for news organizations. For an example of how they get reported on, we can again turn to the *Toronto Star*, which in the fall of 1998 mounted an extensive three-part investigation of what it saw as a growing problem in Canada's largest city.

The series, by reporter Michelle Shepherd (1998), was prominently displayed—it was, literally, front-page news—and began with the claim that there are "more than 180" youth gangs operating in Toronto. Where did this seemingly high number come from? Not from official data-gathering agencies: neither Statistics Canada nor police departments across the country categorize criminal incidents according to whether they are "gang related." Nonetheless, it does appear that Shepherd relied heavily on police information for her story. But one problem with this source is that police officers are only provided with vague legal guidelines regarding the dimensions of gang behaviour. Bill C-95, for instance, advises that a gang entails "five or more individuals engaged in criminal activity." However, according to the *Globe and Mail* (1998, November 2), police also define a youth gang as "two or more persons engaged in antisocial behaviour who form an allegiance for a common criminal purpose, and who individually or collectively are creating an atmosphere of fear and intimidation within a community."

In the absence of more precise and generally agreed upon criteria about what constitutes gang activity, different commentators are free to come up with their own best estimates regarding the nature of teen gangs. Furthermore, the creation by the police of special youth-gang units means that such bodies have a vested interest in discovering gang activities. Doing so justifies their own activities and budgets. The often close relationship between local police sources and crime reporters leads to generous estimates of the size and scope of the problem at hand (Chibnall, 1977). Indeed, if a gang can be said to exist with as few as two members, the antisocial behaviour in question is not specified, and the criteria for "fear and intimidation within a community" are a matter of judgment, it is not difficult to see how the "more than 180" might be arrived at and why citizens might be scared of the teenagers in their neighbourhoods.

Similarly, the essentially loose and discretionary criteria employed in gang spotting can lead to the misidentification (and misinterpretation) of casual and informal small group activity among adolescents as "gang-related behaviour." For instance, are we to understand that the numerous small cliques of kids who hang around smoking outside high schools or the bunch of kids who act up on the bus or subway on the way home from school are engaged in gang activity? If the police decide to define such behaviour in gang terms, and issue warnings and make arrests, then the size and scope of the gang problem is only going to get bigger.

But the reporter did not use only police sources for her story; she also collected information from students themselves in the form of questionnaires completed outside school premises. Again, the focus was upon, among other things, gangs. Students were asked whether there were gangs in their school and, if so, did they belong to one? Over half of the respondents affirmed a gang presence in their school and 10 percent reported gang membership.

The problem with these questions is that they are predicated on the assumption that the reporter asking the question and the students answering them are in agreement about how we define gang behaviour. Is gang activity and gang membership limited to robbing and stealing, dealing drugs, and violent and aggressive behaviour or does it also include hanging out with your friends, playing sports, or going to parties and clubs together? Since the content of gang behaviour was not specified in the question, it is hard to know what meaning to attach to the information supplied by respondents.

Overall, the theme of Shepherd's *Toronto Star* series was that there is a crime problem getting out of control; that official statistics suggesting otherwise were misleading; that school boards were deliberately suppressing information about youth-gang activity; and that although Toronto was not yet like Los Angeles, this was the (downward) direction in which things were heading: "Blood and Crips. The chilling gang names have never meant much north of the border. Now they do" (Shepherd, 1998).

The message of escalating gang activity in Toronto was not conveyed just by facts and figures, however. Information was also relayed visually in the form of a computer-enhanced, full-colour map, entitled "Toronto youth gang territories," which detailed the geographic location of each of the 180 named gangs. I suggest that this illustrated guide to youth-gang operations in Toronto has the effect of making teenage gangs appear more numerous, organized, predatory, and geographically diffuse than they really are. The other likely effect of this visual presentation is an increased fear of youth crime, about which I will have more to say in a moment.

An earlier, more extensive and systematic analysis of Canadian print media reportage of gang activity has been carried out under the auspices of the Ministry of the Solicitor General (Fasiolo and Leckie, 1993). The authors analyzed daily news stories about gangs over a four-month period from July to October 1992, focusing on how gangs were characterized in the Canadian print media. They found that 77 percent of stories emanated from five cities: Vancouver, Montreal, Calgary, Ottawa, and Toronto. Rather than being precipitated by any specific event, gang stories in all regions of the country began life as part of a generally growing sense of concern about the gang problem in Canada.

Content analysis included the type of gang mentioned in news stories. Here there were regional variations: for everywhere except Quebec, the most frequently cited type was the Asian gang. In Quebec, the concern about gangs was not related to any specific racial group. The researchers also looked at details of gang activity as identified in news stories. They found that while gangs were associated with a broad sweep of criminal activity, their most common ventures were related to drugs, homicide, and extortion.

The origins or causes of gangs were not mentioned in the majority of stories. However, if and when explanations of rising gang activity were discussed or alluded to, the two most commonly occurring precursive factors were, tellingly, immigration and the state of the economy. It seems likely, therefore, that, at least in English-speaking Canada, concern about Asian gangs is ultimately linked to race and immigration.

Supplementing the quantitative analysis with a qualitative reading of the news stories, the researchers identified a number of recurring themes and patterns. Although this is seldom made explicit, the news stories imply that gangs are a new and growing problem. Their depiction as a modern phenomenon emerges in a number of ways. First, they are seen as a consequence of profound social changes and economic uncertainties in modern society. Second, and related, they are viewed as a product of changing social values that are held responsible for increasing youth violence. Occasionally, the claim that gangs are a new phenomenon is given a statistical reference; for example, the *Ottawa Citizen* claimed on October 17, 1992, that although as recently as two years previously there had been no youth gangs in the nation's capital, there are now thirteen.

According to the newspaper sources, gangs are not only new, they are also widespread. This assertion does not, however, relate well to actual patterns of youthful behaviour. Further, police action may actually contribute to the incidence of gangs. One newspaper article describes how a police department set up a telephone hotline to abort the emergence of youth gangs that existed in the community at that time. As Fasiolo and Leckie (1993) point out, such preventative action is more likely to stimulate gang activity than to deter it, a theme that I will be returning to. The qualitative analysis also reveals that gangs are depicted as a threat to society, a belief highlighted in the headlines used to introduce the accompanying stories.

The final ingredient found in the vitriolic coverage of gangs in Canada is the focus on race. Most gangs are distinguished in media reports according to their racial or ethnic composition. This tendency results in polarized images of "us" (the law-abiding majority) and "them" (a minority of racially distinctive youthful gangsters), particularly when blanket terms are used—such as the constant reference to Asian gangs. The authors quote a vivid example from an editorial in the *Calgary Sun:*

> For only when *they* [Asian gangs] live in fear that *our* investigators will almost certainly uncover *their* nefarious deeds, *our* courts will certainly find *them* guilty, and *our* prisons await *them*, will *they* stay away from *our* shores. *We* must let the purveyors of these obscenities know that *their* filth is not welcome in *our* city or in *our* province. (Fasiolo and Leckie, 1993, p. 25; emphasis in original)

What makes this practice of identifying Asian gang activity so insidious is that there is no corresponding tendency to link the criminal activities of Caucasian youth to their racial or ethnic origins.

The commonsense view about the relationship between the mass media and youth crime is that the journalists who write the stories that attract our attention in the newspaper or on the nightly newscasts are simply recording events as they unfold. According to this argument, media accounts about youth crime provide a more or less faithful reflection of an objectively existing social problem (Muncie, 1984; Surette, 1992). However, media organizations do much more than just report the facts. Whether they realize it or not, journalists shape how their readers, viewers, and listeners feel and think about the behaviour of youth. Research on media institutions indicates that the news that we consume is the result of a selection process. Items for inclusion in news reports compete for time and space; stories about deviant youth have an advantage in this competitive process because they are deemed highly newsworthy (Muncie, 1984).

In his study of law-and-order news, the British sociologist Steve Chibnall (1977) identified a number of informal criteria (or rules) that are used regularly by journalists as the basis for story selection. These include visible and spectacular incidents and possible political and sexual connotations. Chibnall's study also suggests that similar decisions are made about how crime stories are to be presented: how many photographs are going to accompany a story and which ones, what headlines are going to be used, and so forth.

One common strategy is to introduce a story with a dramatic example. Here is an illustration used by Joel Best from the *Los Angeles Times* and concerning a gang intervention program in that city:

> Everything about him said it was no big deal: How he kicked back in his chair. How he tossed his blue gang-rag on the table in the interrogation room. Threatening to kill a woman—so what?

The woman was a sixth-grade teacher. The suspect, the case-hardened veteran sitting across from Detective Jeffrey Greer, was 11 years old.

"I thought that was, like, the worst," Greer remembered thinking. (Morrison 1988, I-1; quoted by Best, 1989, p. 1)

This is what journalists refer to as a "grabber." As Best says, it captures the reader's attention by connecting, in this example, the broader problem of "gang warfare" to the specific image of a remorseless pre-adolescent. As he also points out, the message being relayed to the reader is not that this case is typical, rather, it is literally a worst-case scenario. Readers are given a sense of the growing magnitude of the youth-gang problem—things are getting worse because criminals are getting younger.

These comments are not meant to suggest that the media invent or fabricate news stories about youth deviance, or that the problems of delinquency and crime would suddenly stop if journalists stopped writing about them (Muncie, 1984, p. 20). Rather, the main point to be made about the reporting and presentation of youth stories is that they exaggerate and sensationalize events and situations, often presenting atypical cases as representative and, in so doing, they construct a problematic image of youth that does not always correspond to actual behaviour.

If media reports had no effect upon how audiences view deviance, these details would be interesting but of no real consequence. But research does suggest that media presentations of crime issues affect public perceptions of the criminal justice system. For instance, surveys conducted for the Canadian Sentencing Commission found that members of the public overestimated the amount of crime in Canada, believed that rates of recidivism are higher and that maximum sentencing penalties are lower than they really are, and underestimated the severity of penalties routinely administered (Corrado and Markwart, 1992).

Tellingly, the majority (95 percent) of respondents also revealed that they derived their knowledge about crime in Canada predominately from the mass media. The commission also found—as have several American studies—that violent crime is overrepresented in news stories about crime. In fact, stories reporting that by the time a young person graduates from high school, he or she will have been witness to "x" number of both real and fictional stabbings, shootings, murders, and so forth have become something of a cliché. *Time* magazine, in a cover story on "Our Violent Kids" (June 12, 1989), has put that figure in the United States at two hundred thousand (Acland, 1995, pp. 14, 147).[1] Violent crime is actually more likely to appear in print and broadcast items than in real life! This has a predictable effect: the

Canadian public believes that crimes of violence form a much higher proportion of the total volume of crime than they really do (Roberts and Doob, 1990). Similarly, when members of the public are asked to evaluate the efficacy of the Young Offenders Act and the state of the youth justice system, they tend to do so in terms of worst-case incidents that receive extensive coverage, rather than more typical but less newsworthy cases (Sprott, 1996). The public's reliance on the news media for information about crime therefore intensifies its fear of crime, promotes negative evaluations of the criminal justice system, and encourages support for more punitive crime-control policies (Surette, 1992).

YOUTH, MORAL PANICS, AND DEVIANCY AMPLIFICATION

By this stage it will probably not surprise you to discover that the mass media have been held responsible for creating particularly exaggerated fears about youth problems, fears that have been referred to as "moral panics" (Cohen, 1973). Stanley Cohen coined this term after witnessing clashes between rival groups of "mods" and "rockers" on the beaches of England in the mid-1960s and analyzing media interpretations of those events. Media coverage was, in fact, intense, driven by a combination of fear, anxiety, and moral outrage about what this episode said about the condition of the British nation.

Cohen concluded—like Pearson after him—that many of the claims made about delinquent youth had been made before and were, in fact, part of a repetitive cycle in which the mass media were heavily implicated:

> Societies appear to be subject, every now and then, to periods of moral panic. A condition, episode, person or group of persons emerges to become defined as a threat to societal values and interests; its nature is presented in stylized and stereotypical fashion by the mass media; the moral barricades are manned by editors, bishops, politicians and other right-thinking people; socially accredited experts pronounce their diagnoses and solutions; ways of coping are evolved or (more often) resorted to; the condition then disappears, submerges or deteriorates and becomes more invisible.
>
> Sometimes the object of the panic is quite novel and at other times it is something which has been in existence long enough, but suddenly appears in the limelight. Sometimes the panic passes over and is forgotten, except in folklore and collective memory; at other times it has more serious and

long-lasting repercussions and might produce such changes as those in legal and social policy or even in the way the society conceives of itself. (Cohen, 1973, p. 9)

According to Cohen, societies suffer from moral panic attacks at times of profound, but scarcely understood, social change, when established values and beliefs are believed to be threatened. "Folk devils"—witches in seventeenth-century New England, mods and rockers in mid-twentieth-century (old) England—are identified as external threats to established values and institutions against whom "normal society" can unite and rally.

Moral panics frequently involve youth because their successful socialization into conformist behaviour is made problematic by their susceptibility to antisocial influences. These influences tend to occur when the major agencies of socialization (the family, the established church, the school system) appear to be breaking down, when young people seem to be out of control. In Cohen's analysis, for instance, the fights between the mods and the rockers were seen by media commentators as a consequence of too much affluence, too much leisure, and the end of compulsory military training (national service). Post-war changes had weakened the influence of traditional authority (as vested in family, school, and religion), and gang fights at seaside resorts were one highly visible result.

As the case of the mods and rockers shows, in Britain the deviant and delinquent behaviour of working-class youth is most likely to inspire moral panics, particularly if their activities include violence and aggression. Often the frightening and discreditable activities of youth are traced back to the corrupting influences of popular entertainment and culture—an argument that has a long pedigree (Sacco and Kennedy, 1994, p. 215).

In Victorian times, it was believed that crime melodramas available in cheap theatres would induce imitative behaviour among their young working-class audiences. In the course of the twentieth century, rising rates of youthful crime have been linked at different times to the spread of horror and crime comics, dime-store novels, gangster movies, rock 'n' roll, and, more recently, slasher films (or, as the British call them, "video nasties"). However, the most common, recent focus is television. Our concern with Ninja Turtles and Mighty Morphin Power Rangers or, less obviously, *The Simpsons* or *South Park,* reflects a prevailing belief that the mass media exert a powerful and negative effect upon a young and impressionable audience, resulting in high rates of youthful crime, particularly violent crime (Murdock, 1982; Barrat, 1986). This argument was, of course, much in evidence after Colombine, when it was suggested that movies such as *Heathers* and *The Basketball Diaries* had triggered imitative "copy-cat" killings. (Incidentally, identical concerns were expressed thirty years ago when Stanley Kubrick's cinematic adaptation of Anthony Burgess's novel *A Clockwork Orange* was first released.)

Similar moral panics about youth have been produced in North America.[2] Here, however, race has been the catalyst more often than class. It is often minority youth who have been assigned the folk devil role, setting in motion both heavy-handed policing and suspect media accounts. One early example can be found in what became known as the Zoot Suit Riots that took place in Los Angeles in the early 1940s.

The Zoot suit was a clothing style popular in that period among young Mexican-Americans, often referred to as Chicanos. The style consisted of wide-shouldered, long jackets; pleated baggy pants; long watch chains; double-soled shoes; and wide, flat hats. In 1942, a young Chicano male was killed in a gang fight at the Sleepy Lagoon, a popular nightclub. The media responded by giving extensive coverage to the dangers of Zoot suit gangs and their Chicano members. The police responded by arresting twenty-two gang members, seventeen of whom were convicted of conspiracy to murder. To prevent further instances of Zoot suit–inspired mayhem, police instigated sweep arrests of young Mexican males.

Police and media activity thus created an environment hostile to racially and stylistically distinctive youth, in particular fomenting the idea that Zoot suits indicated membership in violent Mexican gangs. Publicly defined as a threat to law and order, young Mexicans thereafter became a popular target for attacks from Anglo servicemen on leave in the city. These culminated in the Zoot Suit Riots—a series of short but intense battles between white servicemen and Hispanic youth.

Were the teenaged Zoot suiters the serious problem that media reaction and police behaviour made them out to be? Not according to the social scientists of the day, most of whom interpreted the collective street-corner activity of young Mexican males as a typical response to the "normal" problem of growing up poor and disadvantaged in American society. In this regard they were not substantively different from the young European immigrant gang members studied by Frederick Thrasher in Chicago a generation before (1937). These earlier gangs faded away when the various ethnic groups from which they were drawn entered the mainstream of American life. At the time of the Zoot suit episode there was little reason to believe that Mexican-Americans would not follow the same assimilative route. The Zoot Suit Riots, therefore, had little to do with the objective problems faced or posed by Mexican youth, and a lot to do with how this group was viewed by the dominant Anglo population in Los Angeles.

Race may similarly be playing a role in fuelling contemporary Canadian concerns about youth crime. Expressed in varying degrees of explicitness as the belief that young blacks, particularly Jamaican males, commit a disproportionately large amount of both violent and drug-related crime, these fears may reflect the sort of societal changes that Cohen identifies as stimulating moral panics.

Applying Cohen's argument to Canadian society, it can be noted that, historically, this country was predominately peopled by immigrants from the United Kingdom and the largely white nations of Western Europe. However, since the 1960s the Canadian population has become progressively less racially and ethnically homogenous, a trend that periodically kindles debate and soul-searching about national identity and unity. According to this argument, a growing inclination to link youth crime to race is symbolic of broader uncertainties about the impact of new-comers or cultural and racial outsiders on the fabric of Canadian society (for evidence of this development, refer back to the extract from the *Calgary Sun* on page 9).

This is not to say that the activities of black youth are irrele-vant to this process. Contemporary "claims-makers"[3] are responding to something, just as their Victorian predecessors were when drawing attention to the behaviour of (white) street youth in large cities (Frith, 1985). For many citizens and the police, the sight of what appears to be large numbers of black youth hanging out together, publicly playing music that they find incomprehensible (rap or hip-hop or jungle), and wearing strange clothes is frightening and hightens fears of "black crime." These fears may be responsible, at least partially, for the fact that young black males are more likely than other groups to be stopped, par-ticularly when driving a car, by police in Toronto (Wortley, 1996). Although the police would doubtless argue that they have good legal reasons for harbouring suspicions about the conduct of young black males, members of the black community counter— sardonically—by claiming that those who are stopped are guilty only of "driving while black."

An interesting study pertinent to popular perceptions of black and white youth has recently been undertaken in the United States. It focuses upon how major news organizations have chosen to represent two of the more prominent and reviled forms of contemporary rock music and the subcultures that they have spawned: "heavy metal" and "rap" (Binder, 1993).

Two particular events have served to bring heavy metal and rap to the public attention. In 1985 the U.S. Senate conducted hearings into the nature of rock music lyrics, particularly those found in heavy metal. The highlight of those hearings was the testimony of a group of "Washington wives," led by Tipper Gore (wife of then-senator Al Gore). Presenting themselves as the Parents Music Research Center, they saw it as their duty to alert senators to the dangers and harm of rock lyrics that increasingly invoked themes of pornography, violence, devil worship, suicide, and drug use.

Roughly five years later similar claims were being made about rap music. This time the event that served as a catalyst was the successful prosecution in a Florida court of the rap group 2 Live Crew. Their album *As Nasty as They Wanna Be* was judged obscene. Again, debate was stimulated about the harmful effects of lyrics in contemporary pop music.

Despite a similar concern with the deleterious effects of harmful lyrics, there are important differences in media formulations of the dangers posed by heavy metal and rap. On the basis of a content analysis of major American news outlets, Binder concludes that whereas the (negative) effects of heavy metal are depicted as being largely individual or personal in nature, rap music is construed as a threat to the social fabric as a whole. Given that the two "outlaw" genres have a similar preoccupation with sex and violence and transmit an anti-authority message, why is there a differential media response to them?

Part of the explanation lies in the more explicit nature of the lyrics of rap. The language is more offensive (in the use of "hard" swear words) and offensive usage occurs more frequently. Also, rap music is more likely to allude to aggressive street-cultural themes—including violence against the police. Heavy metal, by way of contrast, is more likely to deliver (relatively) innocuous messages against parents and teachers. The inference is that whereas heavy metal is toying with youthful rebellion, rap is an expression of the real thing: an authentic "communiqué from the underclass" (quoted in Binder 1993, p. 763).

A black underclass, I might add. Rap is construed as a more dangerous problem than heavy metal because of the perceived racial characteristics of the audience base for the two musical forms. The guiding assumption of media workers is that the producers and, more importantly, the consumers of rap are black—principally black adolescent males. The prime consumers of heavy metal are, conversely, assumed to be white—primarily white adolescent males.[4] Rap is depicted as a more grievous threat because those most keenly identified with it are seen as more threatening to society as a whole.

Whether other members of the community—such as police officers—share the view that black rappers constitute a more serious social problem than white heavy metallers is not explored by Binder in her research, nor does she deal with the possible effects of media definitions (or "frames") on those designated as dangerous or threatening. However, other research has found that media-based campaigns directed at youth problems sometimes have an effect opposite to the one intended: instead of curbing youth deviance, they intensify it. In sociological terms, this process is known as "deviancy amplification" (Wilkins, 1964; see also Becker, 1963).

Stanley Cohen drew on this concept when discussing media coverage of the mods and rockers. He argues that the presentations of deviant youth as folk devils attracted additional thrill-seeking youth to the battles on the beach. Similarly, adolescents who previously had only weak ties to the two groups may have had their subcultural identifications strengthened by the intensity of the media presentation, as well as by the increasing police surveillance.

In similar terms, it might be argued that the *Toronto Star*'s investigation of youth gangs gave nascent gangs in the area much free publicity that aided recruitment. The same coverage may also have jolted scared students into forming their own gangs in order to counter the gang activity that they had read about in the *Star* or encouraged them to start bringing weapons to school for self-protection. (At least one young correspondent to the letters page pointed out that she had only learnt that there were gangs in her school after she had read the newspaper.) Finally, the media attention given the first anniversary of the Colombine shootings was probably responsible for a rash of threats of similar violence in several high schools across the country. What better way for rebellious students to disrupt the routine of high school life?

But this is speculation. Other research has more substantively explored the connections between youth, moral panic, and deviancy amplification. One such study was carried out in Phoenix, Arizona, by Marjorie Zatz (1987). Again, it involved the gang activities of Chicano youth. The thrust of her analysis is that the police department and the local media were more responsible than Chicano youth for the gang problems in Phoenix. Media and police reaction, in fact, made the problem worse, resulting in a rapid increase—from five or six to over a hundred—in police estimates of the number of gangs in the city.

Zatz identifies three main factors in explaining the escalating concern about gangs in Phoenix: (1) the vested interest of the police department in securing more funds in order to "fight crime" more adequately; (2) the perception that Mexicans and Chicanos were fundamentally different from the Anglo population; and (3) a common belief that Chicano youth gangs are violent. A fourth element might also be added: media outlets need large audiences—a requirement that is easily met by providing stories about ethnic gangs.

Zatz is persuaded that no real increase in gang delinquency had occurred in Phoenix because an examination of official police and court statistics revealed no significant differences in levels or types of offences between gang members and a control group of non-gang juvenile offenders. However, although there was little objective basis to beliefs about growing gang activity, the media and police responded in a way that convinced many people that Phoenix was confronted with a serious gang problem.

Another example of how the deviancy amplification process can work has been provided by a study conducted in Scotland. Glasgow is a tough city, and one of its toughest housing estates is called Easterhouse. Media reports throughout the 1950s and 1960s depicted the Easterhouse youth gangs as the toughest in Glasgow, a portrayal that was taken by gangs in other parts of the city as a challenge. As a result, gangs from all over Glasgow gravitated to Easterhouse in the hope of pressing their own claims for supremacy.

Although the Easterhouse gangs did not necessarily concur with their media image of toughness, they were forced to defend it when confronted by other groups. In the process of responding to external threats, therefore, they reinforced their existing deviant identity (Armstrong and Wilson, 1973). More recent Canadian research similarly indicates that youth groups often become delinquent when obliged to defend themselves in the course of conflictual interactions with other groups in public spaces (Kennedy and Baron, 1993). However, the most straightforward way in which the deviant activities of adolescents may be intensified is through the direct intervention of control agents (teachers, social workers, police officers). Although it is by no means the case that labelling always heightens deviant commitments (for a skeptical view see Gove, 1975), some research supports this basic contention.

As Binder's study of rap and heavy metal suggests, popular music has often been singled out as a corrupter of youth. Although the evidence supporting this belief is weak at best, this has not prevented various communities in the United States from acting upon it. One of these communities is Orange County, California, where special programs have been developed by both private and public agencies for dealing with adolescents who have become involved in perceived deviant subcultures associated with rock music. The subcultures in question centre on punk and heavy metal.

To combat the pernicious influence of punk and metal, a quasi-official organization called Back in Control (BIC) has the authority to insist that troubled youth who listen to and identify with deviant rock subcultures go through a process of "de-punking" and "de-metalling." In addition, the BIC group has published *The Punk and Heavy Metal Handbook,* which categorizes the harms incurred by listening to this music. The BIC also recommends early intervention on behalf of "at-risk" youth to increase their prospects of rehabilitation. To that end, members of the local police department have been enrolled in preventive exercises: they give lectures to various audiences in the community about the dangers of rock music, and how to spot the telltale signs of moral degeneration (T-shirts, black clothing, and punk jewellery, for instance). More decisively, youth counsellors and probation officers who come in contact with adolescents attired in punk or metal clothing use their clients' appearance as a basic cue in the intervention process.

Not only were the consumers of punk and metal regarded as deviant, their participation in the respective subcultures was viewed as a sign of psychological disturbance, a label that carried quite severe consequences for those so defined, as Rosenbaum and Prinsky (1991) have shown. They constructed a series of hypothetical situations and vignettes based on juveniles over-identified with punk and metal subcultures and presented them to hospital officials who were then invited to make recommendations about how to best treat the teens. Representatives of ten (83 percent) of twelve psychiatric hospitals responded by suggesting that the symptoms of mental illness were significantly serious to warrant medication.

As the researchers point out, this sort of reaction is taking place at a time when there has been a growing emphasis upon de-institutionalization—treating troubled kids informally, rather than bringing them into contact with criminal justice agencies. Heavy metal and punk kids in Orange County are, on occasion, institutionalized on the basis of their appearance and for activities—listening to rock music—that may be deviant, but are certainly not delinquent. Court personnel, in conjunction with hospital officials, are labelling as delinquent behaviour that is conspicuous by its absence from the criminal code (Rosenbaum and Prinsky, 1991, p. 534).

The researchers conclude by interpreting their findings in terms of a central tenet of the labelling perspective (discussed more fully in Chapter 3): the process of defining adolescents as delinquent on the basis of the clothes that they wear or their tastes in rock music may transform mild deviants into more serious ones. Without the active intervention of control agents and their imposition of a negative label, the developing adolescent might simply grow up and out of punk and metal styles.

It is also worth noting how previously neutral items of clothing can very quickly acquire highly deviant connotions. Before Columbine, few people noticed nor cared that some adolescents wore long trench coats to school. Since Colombine, trench coats have been banned from high schools across North America, and those students who continue to wear them have found themselves suspended.

Likewise, members of the Gothic subculture—hitherto a small and inconspicuous presence in most high schools—reportedly have suddenly become the focus of negative attention from both media sources and more immediate control agents—teachers and peers. Almost instantly, wearing a trench coat and listening to Goth rock became a marker of criminal status, an intimation of violent and aggressive tendencies. The process of deviance amplification thus involves elements of blaming, scapegoating, and demonizing.

Another popular focus for moral panic is drug use, the recurring nature of which is evident in current concerns about raves. Ecstasy is the problematic drug this time around, with a few high-profile incidents precipitating claims of widespread ecstasy-related deaths. But before ecstasy there were similar concerns about the growing use of crack-cocaine. Again, far from reducing it, media coverage may end up promoting the very behaviours that are condemned. Two American researchers have proposed that dramatic news stories about new and exotic substances such as crack serve as unpaid advertising for desperate or adventurous youth previously inclined to indulge in risk-taking behaviour (Reinarman and Levine, 1989). They observe that the language used to condemn crack—"cheaper than cocaine," "better than sex," an "intense rush"—does not necessarily deter those young people already interested in drug use. They tell the story of one mature university student who read an account of crack in *Newsweek* magazine, in which the drug was compared with medieval plagues and the attack on Pearl Harbor. As the student tells it:

> I had never heard of it until then, but when I read it was better than sex and that it was cheaper than cocaine and that it was epidemic, I wondered what I was missing. I questioned why I seemed to be the only one not doing the drug. The next day I asked some friends if they knew where to get some. (Treback, 1987, p. 7, quoted in Reinarman and Levine, 1989, p. 131)

Drug use has also been used to answer why moral panics occur when they do. One persuasive answer to this question has been provided by Ben-Yehuda (1986) in his analysis of a moral panic involving Israeli adolescents that occurred in May 1981. He notes initially and significantly that there was no factual basis to repeated claims made at that time about a sudden epidemic of drug use among high school students in Israel. (Several surveys conducted over the previous decade had shown no increase in the use of psychoactive drugs.) If the objective conditions did not justify widespread concern about drug use, what factors were primarily responsible for the drug crisis of May 1982? Ben-Yehuda argues that the panic was fabricated—not merely amplified—by the Israeli police, who had two reasons for doing so. Firstly, in the "fight against crime" they wanted more resources and what better way to demonstrate this need than to claim an epidemic of teenage drug use? Secondly, they needed to direct public attention away from an embarrassing incident in which it had been revealed that false testimony in a trial following a drug operation had put seventy people in prison. Moreover, a key witness claimed that, under pressure from the police, he had framed young drug users. The police therefore required anxiety about widespread drug use among Israeli youth to deflect public attention away from their botched operation.

As Ben-Yehuda points out, drugs are a common focus for moral panics because young people do use them, and they have become symbolically associated with depravity, decadence, promiscuity, resistance to adult authority, and—as a cumulation of all the above—crime and delinquency.

But recreational drug use has always been viewed in this way. Why did the Israeli drug scare occur in 1982 and not in, say, 1981 or 1983? Ben-Yehuda's explanation focuses upon the activities and interests of key law enforcement agents and officials at a particular point in time. In effect, he shows that moral concerns can on occasion serve non-moral interests. Likewise, I would not be the first person to suggest that law enforcement agencies and officials stand to benefit from the current panic about raves: additional funding in the war against drugs can more easily be secured and the expansion of police activities more easily be justified in the train of media stories about the dangers of ecstasy use (Jenkins, interviewed in the *Globe and Mail,* May 24, 2000).

Commercial interests may also have played a role in the timing of the *Toronto Star*'s exposé of youth gangs, refered to earlier (Shepherd, 1998). Why did it profile this story when it did—at a time when youth crime rates were actually declining? (Evidence of this downward trend will be documented in the next chapter.) Was it coincidental that the series appeared just before a new national daily newspaper, the *National Post,* began publishing?

Did the *Toronto Star* decide to highlight youth gangs—a topic with proven reader interest—in anticipation of a circulation war with a new competitor? A columnist in the employ of the *Toronto Star* has suggested as much (DiManno, 1998). Moreover, this would not be the first time that newspaper wars have influenced the timing and intensity of the crime stories they run, as the following item reveals.

Lorenzo Boyd robbed eleven banks in the Toronto area between 1949 and 1952. He became the most infamous criminal of the immediate post-war era for two main reasons. Firstly, because criminals of that vintage did not rob banks in "Toronto the Good" at gunpoint. In another words, there was a real and objective basis to concerns about increasingly violent crime in the city. Secondly, the gang received blanket coverage from the two big daily newspapers: the now defunct *Toronto Telegram* and the *Toronto Star*.

According to a recent book by Brian Vallee (1997), the criminal enterprise of Boyd and his "gang" (the later robberies were conducted with no more than five associates, the earlier ones were solo efforts) was "blown out of all proportion" (p. 11) because of an ongoing circulation war between the two newspapers, each of which was producing up to eight daily editions devoted to the exploits of the Boyd Gang. As a result, Boyd's reputation was ensured—although, as Vallee ironically acknowledges, he is now best (collectively) remembered as a folk hero rather than as a notorious criminal or folk devil.

Although most panics about youth focus on behaviour that is perceived as threatening the social order, some emerge as expressions of concern about self-destructive behaviour. For instance, certain types of rock music known as Gothic rock (the Jesus & Mary Chain, the Cure)—have been charged with encouraging suicide—a claim that, in at least one instance (Judas Priest) has resulted in a court case.

What these stories and events reveal, I think, is the growing importance of a "youth-in-crisis" perspective on social problems (Acland, 1995). Although it is unlikely to replace the older concerns about youth and public disorder, its emergence reveals growing empathy with the difficulties facing contemporary young people growing up without prospects for decent jobs. The threat posed by youth, has, as it were, turned inward. There is much talk about a "lost generation," exhibiting high levels of depression, suicide, and suicide pacts (Gaines, 1991). Needless to say, the murder–suicides at Colombine High School fit easily—in terms of both the behaviour itself and the extensive media coverage given it—within this crisis paradigm.

Indeed, some commentators have recently begun to suggest that young people are now growing up in a "risk" society. Although it has a number of sources and referents, this argument has become associated with the German social theorist, Ulrich Beck (1992). He proposes that a wide range of economic, social, and cultural changes are transforming human societies, that the old institutions and social constructs are unable to affect social norms and cultural expectations, and that many of the certainties of life have been removed and replaced by a state of "risk."

Many parts of this argument apply to, or can be made to apply to, the experiences of the young. For instance, it is claimed that the transition from school to work has become increasingly problematic because of global changes in the nature of economic life (Krahn and Lowe, 1997; Marquard, 1998). In the Maritime provinces, for example, sons can no longer anticipate following their fathers into the fishing industry; more generally, a good education no longer guarantees a good job.

Although young people today have more choices than earlier generations, they also face more constraints. More importantly, the old markers of class and gender that traditionally guided young people toward, or away from, particular futures, have lost their determinative influence. Decision making—which career to pursue, what sort of education to get, if and when to get married and have children—is becoming not only riskier but also more individualized.

This thesis has not gone unchallenged. Growing up has never been easy—indeed, the various difficulties involved with doing so have given rise to over fifty years of "youth culture," as we will see in a moment. Is the process really harder now than throughout the 1930s or during and just after the Second World War? Is it really the case that class and gender (or race, for that matter) have lost their ability to shape life chances or lifestyle choices?

These criticisms notwithstanding, the influence of Beck's ideas has been such that researchers have started to ponder the range of "risks" that young people encounter in the course of their daily lives (Furlong and Cartmel, 1997). Indeed, as far as young people and deviance is concerned, risk has been interpreted quite literally in terms of victimization and the dangers that both it and offending pose to the successful attainment of adult status.

The strategic position that young people occupy in social imagery about crime and deviance—in particular, the idea that they are both "troubling" and "troubled"— also means that their behaviour is regularly used as a barometer of, or cipher for, the moral health or sickness of the community (Cohen, 1973; Gilbert, 1986; Davies, 1990). In fact, along with the military (the battle against teenage crime; boot camp for teenage thugs; crackdown on crack), medicine provides most of the popular and emotive metaphors for the interpretation of adolescent deviance. Hence repeated reference to the "epidemic" of juvenile crime.

The murder in February 1993 of two-year-old James Bolger by two ten-year-old boys near Liverpool in England produced many news items headlined by medical imagery. One that was reprinted in the *Toronto Star,* for instance, read "British toddler's death symbolizes a wider sickness." The wider sickness in question was the moral torpor of the British nation; the incident bode badly (to say the least) for the future of British society. Because youth represent the future, they become the sounding board upon which the deeper fears, and less frequently, hopes, of adults are projected.[5] The more recent Colombine incident has, of course, been used in much the same way.

However, the danger of imbuing the behaviour of the young with important symbolic meaning is that it leads to images of adolescent deviance that do not always correspond with reality, as will be seen in the next chapter. Simply being young and hanging out with friends on the street or in a shopping mall is often enough to generate negative stereotyping or a deviant label. But appearances are sometimes deceiving; the facts are that most young people are not in serious conflict with society, do not hold values that clash with those of the parental generation, and do not engage in the types of deviance that adults find most troubling.

This is periodically confirmed by social surveys, one example of which is Bibby's investigation of the social attitudes of Canada's teenagers (Bibby, 1985). On a wide range of issues—what they value, what they enjoy, their religious beliefs, occupational ambitions, sexual mores—teenagers are revealed to be utterly conventional in their choices and preferences, expressing views that their parents would not find outrageous. In fact, these findings exemplify a more general point: most children are remarkably like their parents and are "distinguished from one another, and by the same variables, as are adults" (Campbell, 1969, p. 877).

THE INVENTION OF ADOLESCENCE AND DELINQUENCY

If, as I am suggesting, there is a gap between the perception and reality of adolescent deviance, what factors have encouraged the view that youth is a particularly difficult and problematic stage in the life cycle? Why do images of trouble and deviance colour so many people's understanding of adolescence?

The answer to these questions can be found in changes in the economic and social organization of society that have occurred over the past two hundred or so years that have had the cumulative effect of removing the young from adult society. The problematic image of modern youth is a consequence of their emergence as a separate and distinct age-based social category.

Given the contemporary preoccupation with the transgressions, both real and imagined, of juveniles, it is hard to conceive of a time when the young were not so collectively burdened with the stigma of deviance. Yet the fact is that before the middle of the nineteenth century they were rarely a subject of public concern. For instance, the word "adolescence"—so much a part of contemporary discourse about the young—was rarely used outside of scientific writings before the turn of the century (Kett, 1971, p. 97). Modern assumptions about youth—particularly the idea that young people are naturally inclined toward rebellion and nonconformity—are of relatively recent vintage; their origins can be traced back to the modern world created by the industrial revolution of the eighteenth and nineteenth centuries. Prior to that time no clearly defined intermediate stage between childhood and adulthood existed. The classic statement on this issue has been provided by Philippe Aries (1962). His research on pre-industrial Europe found no significant distinction drawn between childhood and other forms of pre-adult status. Terms such as "youth" and "adolescence" were in currency but corresponded more closely to contemporary notions of young adulthood than to an intermediary phase in the life cycle. Similarly, in classical antiquity (ancient Greece and Rome) the term "youth" was employed to describe healthy, productive persons rather than a category of individuals no longer children but not yet adults. In Europe, before the eighteenth century, children entered the adult world of work and leisure at a considerably earlier age than they do in our own time; moreover, the different age groups were more closely integrated than they are today. Medieval French children, for instance, often worked alongside adults from the age of seven onward. This egalitarian participation in economic activity extended into non-work time as well. Children were present at, and participated in, all the great ceremonies and rituals of the life cycle—including death—to a degree that would be unheard of today. Children were treated, in effect, as little adults as indicated by their dress, games, and legal status. Similarly, when they broke the law and were caught by the authorities, the chronologically young were responded to in the same (or a similar) punitive manner as adult offenders. They neither were treated more leniently nor placed in separate juvenile prisons. The law recognized no meaningful distinction among violators on the basis of age, hence there was no legal designation of delinquency.

What changed all of this? The short answer is that human societies became increasingly age differentiated as a result of the industrial revolution. The connection between the two events is sometimes made quite explicit, as in Frank Musgrove's observation that "the adolescent was invented at the same time as the steam engine" (Musgrove, 1964, p. 33).

When Musgrove talks about adolescence being "invented" or when sociologists discuss the social construction of youth, what they mean is that those intermediate age-based categories that we now take for granted and use more or less interchangeably did not exist on any grand scale prior to the transformations ushered in by the industrial revolution.

At the risk of oversimplifying what was a very complex process, two key transitions associated with industrialization have relevance for arguments about the social construction of adolescence and delinquency: the transitions from an agriculturally based economy and society to an industrial one and from home-based work (the cottage system) to the factory system.

Early versions of the factory system depended upon the relatively simple labour power provided by men, women, and children. However, the development of increasingly sophisticated machine technology, cheaper and more productive than human muscle power, eventually led to the displacement of large numbers of workers; the subsequent labour surplus resulted in plunging wage rates. In the face of competition for scarce jobs from cheap child labour, male factory workers, through their trade unions, campaigned to restrict the employment of children in the mines and factories. A similar goal was simultaneously sought by other individuals and groups, albeit for very different reasons. Humanitarian reformers opposed the hiring of children on the grounds that the conditions and terms of employment in the factory system were sufficiently harsh and exploitative that the young should not be subjected to them. This alliance of male industrial workers and humanitarian reformers secured the passage of legislation that checked the use of child labour. As the nineteenth century progressed, the streets of major Canadian, American, and European cities were, therefore, increasingly filled with the unemployed young, now displaced from the production system.

In order to survive, they needed to steal. The urban milieu facilitated reaching this objective by bringing the impoverished young into contact both with their potential victims and with other youth with whom they could forge predatory networks. What subsequently became recognized as juvenile delinquency was originally property crime committed on city streets by young, working-class males directed against upper-class adults. For the first time in history, thanks to industrialization and urbanization, property crime had become the main form of criminal activity in society; and most of it was committed by young people (Bernard, 1992). This is not to suggest that all of the activities of nineteenth-century street youth were criminal. Working (selling newspapers and matches and so on) and playing were more important. Although there were many vagrants and petty thieves illegally working the streets, many daily activities, such as gambling, buying, and selling, blurred the distinction between legitimate trading and crime—a pattern that exists to this day in parts of London, England (Foster, 1990).

Nonetheless, the work and leisure activities of street youth disturbed middle-class observers—reformers, clergymen, journalists—who deplored the morally corrupting lifestyle in which they were engaged. The introduction of compulsory education was one means of controlling street urchins and providing the sort of moral training and direction that was lacking in their home lives.

These concerns were particularly acute in Canada because Great Britain had utilized this country as a dumping ground for the orphans and destitute of its own cities. Between the 1860s and 1920, Britain exported ninety thousand children to Canada (Bean and Melville, 1989). Their presence was something of a mixed blessing. On the one hand, they solved a perennial problem facing Canadian farmers—the shortage of cheap labour. Although it is doubtless the case that some children's lives were improved immeasurably by their involuntary migration to the New World, many others were ruthlessly exploited. They often worked a sixteen-hour day on isolated homesteads, were badly abused, and never saw their families or native country again. As one contemporary participant put it, "Adoption, sir, is when folks gets a girl to work without wages" (Sutherland, 1976, p. 10).

However, the economic advantages of cheap labour were offset by law-and-order considerations. These labourers' origins as members of an impoverished underclass made them particularly vulnerable to the lure of the criminal life. Likewise, their early experiences rendered them a source of contamination, spreading criminal values throughout Canada's major cities. As the expert witnesses of the day put it:

> "The importation of children taken from the reformatories, refuges and workhouses of the old world" the commissioners concluded, was "fraught with much danger … calculated, unless conducted with care and prudence, to swell the ranks

of the criminal classes in this country." They strongly recommended that if the practice were to continue "such precautions be taken" as would "effectually prevent the bringing into this country of children of parents known to be criminal," or of children who had "spent their whole lives in an atmosphere of vice and crime" and were "so saturated with evil" and know "so little of good." In 1892 the federal inspector of penitentiaries argued that "these street Arabs" speedily returned "to their old habits, on arriving in Canada, and, as a consequence, became a burden and an expense upon the taxpayers of the Dominion in our reformatories, goals, and penitentiaries." (Sutherland, 1976, p. 30, quoting from Report, 1891, pp. 215, 432–51, 738–42, 540, 729; Canada, 1893, p. vii)

Quite clearly, the fear was that foreign immigration and urban blight would generate an epidemic of crime. Working-class parents—as well as foreign migrants—were at fault because they willingly exposed their children to the allures and dangers of the street. Curtailing and curing the discomforting behaviour of children and youth from questionable social and physical environments became a priority.

From roughly 1883 onward, reformers became more and more convinced that committing young offenders to common lock-ups was counterproductive—such institutions were little better than schools for crime. Determined to prevent boys and girls from graduating to the "burdensome ranks of paupers, drunkards and criminals" when they grew up, they argued for separate penal institutions for juveniles (Sutherland, 1976, p. 91).

It is important to emphasize that the concerns of the reformers were by no means restricted to young people who had actually broken the law. Other juveniles also deemed at risk from the corrupting influences of city streets included the neglected (waifs and beggars) and the destitute (orphans). The influence of the reformers was such that as the nineteenth century drew to a close the state became increasingly inclined to intervene on behalf of all problem children, irrespective of whether they had committed an illegal act. Children of the street and those from broken homes and orphanages were treated as if they were young offenders, more specifically as "pre-delinquents." The future course of juvenile justice legislation in Canada, as elsewhere, was predicated on expansive assumptions about what constituted "delinquent behaviour."

THE JUVENILE DELINQUENTS ACT OF 1908

The official history of juvenile delinquency in Canada begins in 1908. Following similar legislative initiatives in the United

States and Great Britain, the first piece of legislation pertaining specifically to juveniles was passed in that year. The Juvenile Delinquents Act had the deliberate effect of legislating the distinction, which we now take for granted, between adult and young offenders. A separate juvenile court and a probation service were two of its most enduring features.

The legislative intent of the reformers was twofold. First, the legislators felt that treating old and young criminals alike was inhumane: the indiscriminate use of harsh punishment violated, to use the modern parlance, the civil rights of the young. Second, reacting to juvenile offenders as hardened criminals and placing them in adult prisons extinguished any possibility of reform. Unlike adult criminals—who were largely beyond redemption—there was still hope that inner-city street youth could be saved. On the one hand, therefore, the young were seen as being particularly prone to crime and deviance but, on the other hand, they were viewed as being most amenable to reform.

Applying these ideas resulted in legislation that targeted not only a diverse set of conditions—law-breaking, pauperism, and dependency—but also a wide range of prohibited acts. The Juvenile Delinquents Act in Canada, and its counterpart in other parts of the English-speaking world, ensured that young people got in trouble with the law for a much larger number of offences than did adult offenders. Although some youth crime was the same as adult crime (robbery, assault, theft), there were other offences for which young people, and young people alone, were liable to arrest, punishment, and treatment (Frith, 1985). These latter violations are known collectively as status offences. They included the consumption of alcohol, truancy, running away from home, refusal to obey parents, having delinquent friends, and the use of profanity—activities that were illegal solely because the individuals who engaged in them were underage.[6] The broad scope of what counted as delinquency is evident in revisions to the original act, passed in 1924. According to the law, a delinquent was

> any child who violates any provision of the Criminal Code or of any Dominion or provincial statute, or of any by-law or ordinance of any municipality, or who is guilty of sexual immorality or any similar form of vice, or who is liable by reason of any other act to be committed to an industrial school or juvenile reformatory under the provisions of any Dominion or provincial statute. (quoted in West, 1984, p. 33)

The age of minimal legal responsibility was kept at seven, and the upper age limit (that is, the age at which a young offender became an adult offender) varied according to province: sixteen in Ontario, Alberta, New Brunswick, Nova Scotia, P.E.I., the Yukon,

Saskatchewan, and the Northwest Territories; seventeen in British Columbia and Newfoundland; and eighteen in Manitoba and Quebec. The most severe sentence the juvenile court could impose was institutionalization in a training school where the emphasis was upon discipline and character training. It is also worth noting that, along with a broad definition of delinquency, judges were granted considerable discretion regarding the punishment that wrongdoers should receive, the severity of which was determined not by the seriousness of the offence but by the "needs" of the offender—as decided by judges and probation officers (West, 1984).

From the perspective of a constructionist approach to youth problems, the reformers and journalists responsible for the original juvenile justice legislation were claims-makers (Best, 1989). They apprised politicians of the conditions facing young people on city streets, persuaded them that young criminals constituted a new and distinctive law-and-order problem, and crusaded for a solution in specific juvenile justice legislation.

Although most sociologists accept this account of the origins of juvenile justice legislation—and thus to some extent accept the constructionist perspective on social problems—there is some disagreement as to whose interests the Juvenile Delinquents Act in Canada really served, or how altruistic the sponsors of the new legislation really were. An influential skeptic on this issue is Anthony Platt (1969), who coined the term "child-savers" to describe the architects of American juvenile justice legislation.

Platt notes that the first juvenile court in the United States (1899) was largely the creation of upper-class white women, often the wives and daughters of prominent industrialists who composed the political and business elite of Chicago. These women, like their husbands, were both conservative and wealthy, and able to employ plenty of servants to take care of housework and look after their children. Bored and with time on their hands, they solved their personal dilemma, according to Platt, by focusing upon the problems of the poor, particularly poor street youth. Because they were conservative, they sought to do so in ways that did not destabilize the existing distribution of power and privilege. On Platt's reading of the situation, the child-saving movement was a nineteenth-century attempt to control the behaviour of troublesome youth without fundamentally rearranging the structure of wealth and opportunity in American society. It is a view, however, that has not gone unchallenged: the motives of the Canadian reformers responsible for the Juvenile Delinquents Act have been defended by Sutherland (1976) and Corrado and Markwart (1992); while Platt's refusal to acknowledge the role of competing interests in the formulation of the legislation has been criticized by Hagan and Leon (1977).

In 1984 the Juvenile Delinquents Act was replaced by the Young Offenders Act. In May 1998 the federal government announced plans for another overhaul of the youth justice system. The historical trajectory of the legislative response to juvenile offenders in Canada will be discussed at greater length in Chapter 7. For the moment, though, it is important to note that the Juvenile Delinquents Act for the first time officially recognized the wrongdoings of the young as a distinctive social problem requiring special legislative intervention.

ADOLESCENTS, DELINQUENCY, AND YOUTH CULTURE

Although the history of delinquency begins with nineteenth-century street youth, the concerns aroused by their public behaviour quickly spread to include all adolescent activity. In the view of prominent Victorian opinion makers, the nature of adolescence made all young people susceptible, or vulnerable, to the lures of delinquency.

From the beginning, adolescence has never been merely a transitional stage between childhood and adulthood. It has invariably been seen as a time of turmoil and conflict. Academics writing at the turn of the century are primarily responsible for this viewpoint. These experts—mainly psychologists and psychiatrists—were of the opinion that every young person flirted with delinquency because rebellion was a natural and universal characteristic of this intermediary stage in the life cycle.

The person most closely identified with this interpretation of adolescence was a prominent pioneer psychologist, G. Stanley Hall, a man much influenced by the work of Charles Darwin and his thesis regarding the biological evolution of the species. Hall argued that just as the human species as a whole passed through a series of stages in its development, so too did each individual human being. The human species and its individual units thus evolved through conditions of early animal primitivism into refined, civilized, mature entities. Paralleling Darwin's designation of an intermediate stage in the evolution of the species, Hall identified a similar phase in individual development: adolescence, a time of *sturm und drang* (storm and stress) that Hall felt corresponded to an equally unstable and tumultuous phase in the development of human civilization. Hall similarly allowed the biological doctrine of recapitulation to mould his views on the origins of juvenile delinquency, which he saw as the outcome of a clash between the "savage" inclinations of youth and the civilizing influences of society (Kett, 1977, p. 255).

His prognostications unleashed a series of books on the adolescent years and inspired a coterie of experts prepared to counsel on the problem of youth. His assertions about the "natural" sources of adolescent rebellion were quickly and eagerly embraced by the educators and welfare workers of the day and had a significant effect upon the development of a justice system that caters specifically to the needs of those who are no longer children but not yet adults. Moreover, and not coincidently, Hall's storm and stress model of adolescence influenced subsequent debate about rising juvenile crime, the effects of popular entertainment, and the relationship between the two (Murdock, 1982, p. 64).

Hall and the psychologists who followed him operated with a view of adolescence that concentrated on the inborn inclination of young people toward problematic behaviour. Although they focused upon structural and cultural factors rather than individualistic ones—adolescence was a social as well as a personal experience—the early sociologists shared the same problem-centred view of their subject matter.

In the 1940s sociologists began to draw attention to the growing importance of a separate, sub-society of adolescence; the premier American sociologist of the day, Talcott Parsons, referred to this "society within a society" as a "youth culture" (1942). Parsons was the leading light of the then-dominant sociological paradigm of functionalism. However, it was left to other sociologists working within the same functionalist paradigm to enlarge upon the origins and nature of youth culture. The fullest flowering of the functionalist view was provided by S. M. Eisenstadt (1956). For Eisenstadt, youth culture was an outcome of disruptions in the transition from childhood to adulthood, characteristic of industrial society, and manifested as generational differences and conflicts. Some elaboration of these complexities is in order.

Functionalists view social institutions as a set of interrelated parts that contribute to the smooth functioning of the whole. Hence, the function of the family is to equip children with an understanding of the basic norms of society, and the function of the educational system is to prepare the young for their future occupational roles. Successful fulfillment of the tasks allocated to society's various component institutions leads to strong social integration; weak integration leads to conflict. Intergenerational conflict is seen as a consequence of a poor fit—weak integration—between age groups and society. Weak integration, and hence generational conflict, is seen as being particularly pronounced in advanced industrial societies because of the problematic nature of the transition from childhood to adulthood.

Pre-industrial or traditional societies avoid conflict of this sort for two main reasons. First, the journey into adulthood is smoothed because adult work skills are acquired at an early age. Children typically work alongside their parents or other adult members, learning the job skills that they will themselves use when they attain adult status. The informal acquisition of job skills and knowledge not only blends work and educational worlds, it also keeps parents and children in close physical and emotional proximity. A simple division of labour and limited job tasks ensure both an easy transition into adult work roles and a continuity of experience between the generations. Second, pre-industrial societies confer full adult status upon the young via a specific ceremony—a rite of passage—that denotes the shedding of childhood and a subordinate status and its replacement by adulthood, with its full range of rights and responsibilities. Moreover, this formal and public acknowledgment of social adulthood corresponds to biological adulthood; full adult status is accorded to the individual at more or less the same time that he or she reaches puberty.

Industrialization has ruptured the transitional process because an increasingly complex and constantly evolving division of labour has meant that appropriate job skills cannot be taught informally in the bosom of the immediate family. As a result, the preparation for future adult work roles has been transferred from the nuclear family setting to specialized educational institutions.

The elongated training period required for occupational roles and the absence of a ritual that publicly acknowledges the arrival of adulthood are seen as creating ambiguities and uncertainties for the young regarding their role and status in society. Their exclusion from adult work roles and subsequent confinement in a separate educational institution has cultivated a collective sense of marginality and distinctiveness.

It is the gap between what the family is no longer capable of delivering (occupational skills and training) and what an increasingly complex economy requires (specialized and extended periods of occupational training in educational institutions) that gives rise to autonomous youth groups. As one interpreter of Eisenstadt's functionalist argument has expressed it: "Peer groups are the bridge between childhood and adulthood when society is complex enough that attainment of full adult status cannot be insured in the family unit" (Campbell, 1969, p. 838).

Other factors have only served to make youth groups and youth culture even more important in the years following the Second World War. First, the massive increase in the birth rate after 1945—the "baby boom"—meant that the young made up an increasingly large proportion of the total population. In Canada the ten years between 1951 and 1961 saw the number of fifteen-to nineteen-year-olds in the population increase by over a million (Owram, 1996, p. 145). Second, and as one would expect, the baby boom had a huge impact on the schools, colleges, and universities of most Western nations. More young people were spending increasing amounts of time in the education system, where they interacted more or less exclusively with their peers. The common, age-specific character of their experiences engendered a collective self-consciousness regarding their distinctive location in society.

These feelings were, in turn, reinforced by another increasingly ubiquitous influence: the machinations of a growing teenage leisure industry that was not slow to realize that the young constituted a new and largely untapped market. For the first time ever, consumer goods, services, and entertainment—movies, magazines, and, in particular, popular music—were pitched specifically at the expanding youth population. Appealing to what were felt to be universal age-specific needs, emotions, and experiences, the youth-oriented leisure industries helped nurture a view of the young as a unique, distinctive, and homogeneous social category, united in their tastes and interests.

Some sociologists, following Parson's lead, saw in the cumulative effect of these changes the rise of what has been referred to as an "adolescent society." James Coleman describes the gulf between the larger society and the modern high school student:

> "Cut-off" from the rest of society [and] [w]ith his fellows, he comes to constitute a small society, one that ... maintains only a few threads of connection with the outside adult society ... separate subcultures exist right under the very noses of adults—with languages all their own, with special symbols, and most importantly, with value systems ... that lead away from those goals established by the larger society. (Coleman, 1961, pp. 3, 9)

In his account of what was happening in high school, Coleman reveals a preoccupation with the same set of concerns that informed Stanley Hall's earlier view of adolescence. That is, he is stressing the factors that encourage adolescent rebellion and identifying sources of conflict between the generations. The adolescent society is one in which sport and entertainment take precedence over scholarship and teens are bound together by shared concerns about popularity and conspicuous consumption.

According to Coleman's structural functionalist argument, American teenagers were becoming rapidly involved in a classless culture of youth, the deviant qualities of which stem from its usurpation of adult values and standards. Coleman's study epitomized an increasing willingness in the 1950s and 1960s to connect images of youth to forms of rebellion that were explained by the common experience of age. However, alongside this conception of generational conflict were older fears of delinquency. There was a concern that a school-based youth culture is informed by essentially delinquent values and activities—that involvement in youth culture leads inevitably to delinquent outcomes.

For many adults, the preoccupations of youth—new music, new fashions, new dances, fast cars, fast food—spell trouble: more and more "ordinary" adolescents "looked and behaved like juvenile delinquents" (Gilbert, 1986, p. 17). High school was where ordinary adolescents ("teenagers") were increasingly forced to rub shoulders with the more obviously delinquent. As clear-cut distinctions between deviancy and conformity started to break down, the term "teenager" (invented at about the same time as "youth culture," in the 1940s) became increasingly interchangeable with, and indistinguishable from, delinquency. This development is nicely illustrated by an (apparently) popular joke of the time in which one suburban housewife tells another, "My husband was two hours late getting home the other night. Oh, my God, I thought, the teenagers have got him" (Murdock and McCron, 1976, p. 18).

As James Gilbert points out, what gave these fears added substance was the fact that, beginning in the 1950s, fewer working-class and minority youth were dropping out of school. In Canada, 1954 marked the first time that more than 50 percent of fourteen- to seventeen-year-olds were in school; by 1960, 66 percent of this age group were students (Owram, 1996, p. 145). No longer, therefore, were the traditional folk devils confined to the mean streets and neighbourhoods of the inner cities where they had first emerged in the nineteenth century: delinquent values and networks had now found a place in high school, where they exerted a pernicious influence on ordinary teenage culture (Gilbert, 1986).

Gilbert, in fact, offers an analysis of cyclical concerns about juvenile delinquency in the United States that is very similar to the British-based arguments of Cohen and Pearson. He proposes that American apprehensions about delinquency reached new levels of intensity in the 1950s. Mass culture was, once again, singled out as the guilty party: it was believed that crime comics (as well as Hollywood movies) were responsible for rising rates of juvenile crime.[7]

A subcommittee of the U.S. Senate, chaired by Estes Kefauver, was struck to investigate the growing delinquency problem. The committee concurred with the assessment of psychologist Frederic Wertham, author of the influential book *The Seduction of the Innocent* (1953), that comic books were corrupting American adolescents. Public concern about crimino-genic effects led the comic book industry to adopt a code of ethics.

Like Cohen, Gilbert argues that public apprehension about delinquency in the 1950s was out of all proportion to the known facts. The American fear of delinquency was at its highest when its incidence was comparatively low. On the other hand, in the 1960s, when the rate of juvenile crime did escalate rapidly, the level of societal concern was much less intense. (Doug Owram has made a similar observation about Canadian society. He suggests that adults became more accommodating to youth culture in the 1960s—tolerating, if not exactly endorsing it—at just about the moment that the crime rate was starting to rise again [Owram, 1996, p. 157]). So what explains the gap between the fear of delinquency in the 1950s and the severity of the problem at that time?

Gilbert suggests that the comic book episode was symptomatic of wider concerns in the 1950s about the harmful effects on American adolescents of a cleverly marketed, commercial youth culture. New and unfamiliar forms of mass cultural expression (television, radio, rock 'n' roll) betokened an era of unprecedented teenage freedom: parents became increasingly anxious about losing control over their children through the influence of the mass media.

Parallels between Gilbert's work and Pearson's discussion of the hooligan problem in British history have also been noted by Brannigan (1987). He argues that moral panics about youth and delinquency grew out of post-war changes that saw adult society losing confidence in its ability to control the cultural activities of its teenage offspring. In the United States, in particular, it was felt that teens' developing financial independence (a major source of which was discretionary income from part-time jobs) was creating a ready market for youth culture, the content and behavioural directions of which parents were ill equipped to manage.

Gilbert was not, however, the first person to notice similarities between delinquency and youth culture. David Matza had earlier (1961) made a similar observation, but with an important twist: rather than encouraging or facilitating delinquent activity, the growth and spread of youth culture has moderated the scope and seriousness of adolescent deviance.

His starting point is the by now familiar one that the aforementioned conditions of modern life make young people prone to rebelliousness of various sorts. Although delinquency is its most recognizable and most enduringly threatening form, it is not the only one; student radicalism and bohemianism are other types that have occasionally proven attractive to largely middle-class youth.

However, Matza's thesis is that only a small number of adolescents engage in serious deviancy. The majority of young people are either not deviant at all, or engage in what he calls conventional versions of deviant youth traditions. Matza holds that delinquency (along with radicalism and bohemianism) are subterranean traditions in American life, and that youth culture is little more than a cleaned-up, less serious form of the delinquent tradition. What delinquency and youth culture share is a similar spirit: a commitment to a leisure ethic rather than a work ethic; a disdain for the regularities and routine of school and work; and a general striving for excitement, thrills, and kicks. Where they differ is that youth culture stops short of serious illegality in pursuit of these goals. In practical terms, this means that the consumption of alcohol, sexual experimentation, and partying is okay, but that stealing, robbery, and physical assault are not—which brings us to the hub of Matza's argument. He concedes that for some adolescents involvement in youth culture serves as a preparation for more serious delinquent careers; but for most, it has a preventative and restorative effect.

Although delinquency is generally understood as illegal behaviour committed by young people, there is no similar agreement about the conceptualization and meaning of youth culture. What it comprises, whom it involves, and why vary according to cultural context. Although this book is not about such comparisons, it is interesting to note some differences between North American and British youth culture. One important contrast involves geographic mobility (a theme taken up again in Chapter 3). Canadian and American adolescents have significantly greater access to cars and this significantly broadens the scope of their everyday leisure routines. At the same time, British teenagers have the same need to escape parental controls and spend time with friends. This they accomplish—according to Sarah Thornton, a British-based American sociologist writing about "club cultures" in the 1990s—through a more active patronage of music-oriented dance clubs, often located in city centres, close to public transportation routes (Thornton, 1995).

More generally, British youth culture revolves around popular music, whereas North American teenagers are more consistent moviegoers. Hollywood makes movies for and about American teenagers; there are sufficient cultural similarities between the United States and Canada for those films to be enjoyed equally by Canadian adolescents (Owram, 1996). American films are, however, of less interest to British teens. Furthermore, the much smaller British movie industry does not cater to the domestic youth market—there are few British "teen-pics" (Thornton, 1995). But music is another story entirely. Both respectable and deviant youth culture in Britain is dominated by popular music as a source of style and identity in a way that has no parallel in North America.

CONCLUSION

I began this chapter by reversing the sequence in which youth deviance is usually looked at by focusing upon societal reactions to delinquent and deviant behaviour. By concentrating upon the media coverage of and moral panics surrounding young people, I am making the following point: when youth are talked about as being deviant or a social problem (or both), it is not just particular patterns of aberrant behaviour that are described, but also a set of largely adult responses to that behaviour. The study of youth deviance, therefore, has two components: the study of norm-violating behaviour and social reactions to that behaviour. These two by no means mutually exclusive concerns make up what were identified earlier as objectivist and constructionist approaches to social problems research. I will explore both approaches.

In behavioural terms, there is little doubt that industrialization has changed the patterns of young people's lives and their experiences of work and leisure. Employment has become less prominent as a life experience, while schooling has become more important. These changes have created both opportunities and motivation for deviant behaviour: more time for recreational activities, more time for experimenting with illicit adult pleasures of sex and drugs, and more frustrations caused by the constraints of high school. The vagaries and angst of adolescence make deviants of all or most of us at some time or another during the long transitional phase between childhood and adulthood. All, or most of us, try our hand at smoking, drinking, maybe even a bit of shoplifting at this time. However, most of us only do these things occasionally, limit our indiscretions to relatively trivial activities, and give up on them pretty quickly as adulthood, in the form of a job, marriage, or parenthood, looms on the horizon. Not all adolescent deviance is like this, of course. Some of it is serious—in the personal and social harm it causes—and some of it is done repeatedly. In this book the answers to the important behavioural questions about youth deviance are sought in a variety of theories, most importantly, though not exclusively, in subcultural theory, which makes sense of deviant activity as a collective enterprise entered into as a response to the problems of growing up in a fundamentally unequal society.

NOTES

1. The inference contained in these headlines, of course, is that witnessing violence on the television or at the movies increases the prospects of real-life violence. However, while there is little doubt that adolescents and children are constantly exposed to media violence, there is considerably less agreement about what this exposure means for adolescent behaviour. Here are some reasons why I am skeptical about claims that the mass media makes any significant direct contribution to real life violence.

   First, young Canadians and Americans are exposed to much the same kinds of media programming, and yet the United States has significantly higher crime rates—particularly violent crime rates. Similarly, European youth watch many of the same violent movies (though probably fewer of them) and enjoy much the same kinds of music and yet have much lower rates of violent crime than their North American counterparts. Second, all theories of media influence concentrate on violent crime, but crimes of violence are not common among young people (as will be revealed in Chapter 2). Thus, even if the media effects on teenage violence and aggression are real and substantial, we are left wondering why a steady consumption of violent movies and anti-authority rock songs and videos has produced mainly minor property crimes (Sacco and Kennedy, 1998, pp. 272–73).

   Third, as I have emphasized throughout this chapter, popular culture has routinely been blamed for the ills of society, particularly adolescent violence. In this regard, it is worth remembering that the most murderous gang of the twentieth century was the Nazis, the leaders of which were highly cultured men who enjoyed the music of Wagner and Beethoven and other classical German masters. Does anybody ever claim that their genocidal behaviour was caused by their preferences for high culture (Morrison, 1997)?

2. Though not as regularly as in the U.K. It has been suggested that moral panics are an endemic feature of British life because of the highly competitive nature of the British newspaper industry. A large number of national daily newspapers vie for readers by deliberately provoking controversy over moral issues (Thompson, 1998).

3. Claims-making refers to the process whereby social problems get identified by key individuals and groups, who then seek public support for the claims that they make about both the problem and ways of rectifying it (Best, 1989).

4. I say "assumed" because, according to evidence presented by Binder, large numbers of suburban white youth form part of the audience for rap. Indeed, since she completed her study, rap has increasingly become a mainstream taste, as popular with white as black adolescents. It is a moot point as to whether it has now lost its dangerous edge. More on this topic in Chapter 3.

5. On this point, see McRobbie (1994). She argues that in the weeks and months following the videotaped abduction and murder of James Bolger, the British press significantly increased the amount of

attention that they paid to the crimes of young people. At the same time, concerns about the inadequate legal provisions available to judges when sentencing young criminals began to emerge, followed by claims that certain types of family structure—in particular, the one-parent family—is responsible for the new wave of juvenile crime. The parenting skills of teenage mothers were brought into question, as well as the morality of having children without the support of a father and breadwinner (McRobbie, 1994, pp. 199–200).

6. As will be discussed in Chapter 7, status offences have been formally eliminated from the new Young Offenders Act. However, it still appears that young offenders, particularly female ones, are subject to judicial intervention for a much broader range of wrongdoings than are adults (Bell, 1994; Chesney-Lind, 1997).

7. For an account of how crime comics were seen as fostering delinquency in Canada in the years before, during, and after the Second World War, see Augustine Brannigan (1986).

The Reality of Youth Problems: What Do We Know about Deviant and Delinquent Youth and How Do We Know It?

INTRODUCTION

The focus of the last chapter was on the public perception of youth problems—a perception largely driven and relayed by the mass media and other high-profile claims-makers. The goal of the present chapter is to examine the reality of these problems as captured by official data-gathering sources (the police and courts) and the results of sociological investigation.

Most mass media accounts of "youth problems," particularly crime and delinquency, are made persuasive by the use of data compiled by the police, the courts, and other official governmental agencies. Dramatic and provocative headlines are quickly followed up by statistics derived from these official sources. Statistics provide a quantitative dimension to the scope of the problem; generally speaking, the larger the numbers, the higher the rates; the more rapid the increase, the worse the problem is deemed to be. Significantly, individuals and groups with an agenda regarding youth crime, drug use, dropping out, and so on, invariably make recourse to statistical information when organizing and presenting their claims. An avalanche of statistics therefore lends authority to the claims-making process (Best, 1989; Jenkins, 1992; Felson, 1998).

Moreover, every important theory of deviant behaviour relies for its veracity upon information on offences and offenders collected by or on behalf of the government. It is important, therefore, to know something about the data that are thus generated and how they are collected.

Of course, data are not available on every aspect of youth deviance; no official report is kept, for instance, of the number of adolescents who irritate and shock adults by dying their hair green,[1] shaving their heads, or listening to the more threatening forms of rock music (I'm thinking here of performers such as Eminem or Limp Bizkit rather than, say, Ricky Martin or Hanson). Government agencies do not as a rule gather information on these largely symbolic (or expressive) forms of adolescent deviance. Instead, they concentrate their attention (and money) on more serious forms of adolescent misbehaviour—crime and delinquency (or, as it increasingly seems to be called, "youth crime"), and alcohol and drug use. We will follow suit.

YOUTH CRIME IN CANADA: THE OFFICIAL STATISTICS CONSIDERED

In Canada—as elsewhere—the government agencies primarily responsible for collecting data on crime and delinquency are the police and the courts. An initial examination of the official statistics apparently confirms everybody's worst fears: youth crime is a large and intractable problem.

Since 1962 the basic count of criminal infractions in Canada has been provided by a system of uniform crime reports. According to an arrangement originally pioneered in the United States, police departments across the country file information on the crimes of which they are aware —"crimes known to the police" in the official parlance. This system is designed to produce consistent, comparable, and national crime statistics.

According to Uniform Crime Reporting (UCR) statistics for 1999 (Tremblay, 2000), 99 746 youths between the ages of twelve and seventeen were charged by police with a criminal code offence—roughly 5 percent of Canada's youth population (Savoie, 2000). These young offenders contribute significantly to the overall amount of crime recorded in Canada: in 1997, 23 percent of those charged with a criminal code offence were in this age group (*A profile of youth justice in Canada*, 1998). In the estimation of Keith Marron, the author of a popular examination of youth crime in Canada, one juvenile in twenty is arrested by the police at some time during her or (more likely) his adolescence (Marron, 1992).

Moreover, this pattern has existed for a very long time. Irrespective of whether overall rates of crime are high or low in a particular time or place, young people—those in their teens and early twenties—will disproportionately be found to be responsible (Bernard, 1992, p. 22). As many adults fear, crime is very much a young person's game (Hartnagel, 1992). So much so, in fact, that some commentators have designated the age basis of crime as a universal invariant and the single most important fact about crime requiring explanation (Hirschi and Gottfredson, 1983; Gottfredson and Hirschi, 1990).

The data indicate that arrests begin in early adolescence, steadily increase throughout the teenage years, and then start to taper off when individuals reach their twenties. In 1997, in Canada, 45 percent of young persons accused of crime were sixteen or seventeen, 38 percent were fourteen or fifteen, and 38 percent were either twelve or thirteen (*A profile of youth justice in Canada*, 1998). American data indicate that the bulk of all offenders are under twenty-five, while the peak age for arrests is nineteen; these sources also show that the peak age for property offences is the late teens, while violent offenders are more likely to be in their early twenties (Empey, 1982).

Canadian UCR data similarly reveal that it is older adolescents and young adults who are most likely to commit violent offences, while the criminal behaviour of younger adolescents is more likely to be restricted to property offences and minor acts of violence (*A profile of youth justice in Canada*, 1998).

But age is only one part of the official youth crime story. Crime is not simply or mainly a pursuit of the young: it is primarily a prerogative of young males. In 1999, for instance, 77 percent of twelve- to seventeen-year-olds charged by police were male (Tremblay, 2000). Again, this gender difference is a feature of all industrialized societies, and it is particularly pronounced with regard to violent crime. The gender gap in juvenile crime has, however, narrowed slightly over the past several decades. There is more about this trend in Chapter 6.

Uniform crime reports and data from youth court surveys also tell us something about the types of illegal activity that young people participate in. Simply put, the vast bulk of youth crime involves property offences—arson, breaking and entering, motor vehicle theft, false pretences, forgery, fraud, possession of stolen property— rather than the crimes of violence that attract so much media attention. As shown in Table 2.1, in 1999, nearly half (49 percent) of young offenders in Canada were charged with property crimes, compared with 21 percent charged with violent offences. The rest were charged with "other" criminal code offences (Tremblay, 2000).

TABLE 2.1

Youth 12 to 17 Charged by Police by Type of Offence, Canada, 1999

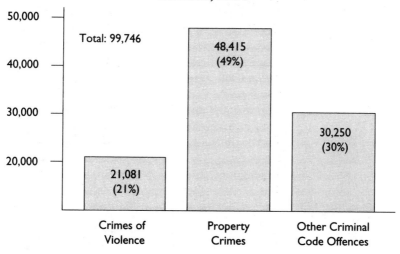

Source: Tremblay, 2000, in *Juristat* 20, no. 5 (Statistics Canada), Catalogue No. 85-002.

A more detailed picture of the nature of youthful property offending is provided by 1997 UCR data. Overall, theft made up 29 percent of all charges, 23 percent were for thefts under $5000, 5 percent for motor vehicle theft, and 1 percent for theft over $5000. Breaking and entering was the second most common offence, involving 14 percent of all youth charged (*A profile of youth justice in Canada*, 1998). By and large, these are not crimes of great complexity or sophistication in planning or execution; nor were the losses very large. No less significantly, young people are more likely to commit property crime than are adults. According to 1999 figures, 49 percent of youth crime involves property offences, compared with 35 percent of adult crime (Tremblay, 2000). Conversely, adults are more likely to perpetrate violent offences, which make up 30 percent of all adult crime; by comparison, violent offences make up 21 percent of all youth crime.

And what of violent youth crime? Police statistics indicate that assault—specifically common assault—is its principal manifestation. In 1997, 13 percent of all youths charged were charged with common or major assault and young persons charged for those offences comprised 71 percent of those charged with a violent offence. Furthermore, common assault is the least serious type of assaultative crime; of those youths charged by police with assault, nearly three-quarters were charged with common assault.

Overall, while the official record certainly supports popular perceptions of the pervasiveness of youth crime, it does not substantiate the attendant claim that most of it is of a violent, predatory nature. Clearly, statistical evidence of mundane property crime contradicts the persistent media image of widespread teenage violence.

However, this does not necessarily settle the issue in favour of a more moderate view of youth crime, since it is generally acknowledged that police and court reports are not an unblemished guide to delinquent activity. In particular, the official count of crime includes only a small proportion of the delinquent behaviour that actually takes place. One of the best-recognized problems with official statistics is that they understate the occurrence of illegal behaviour. (For people already concerned about high levels of youth crime, this is not a comforting thought.) The official count of crime published in Statistics Canada documents is of "crimes known to the police"—that is, official statistics include only incidents of which the police are aware.

The police become aware of delinquent episodes in two main ways: either members of the public report violations to them or the police detect infractions themselves. Contrary to the impression given by television cop shows, the former is more important than the latter. According to one well-known American study, only about 10 percent of crime is actually detected by police officers. In the vast majority of cases, the police only become involved in crime because members of the public draw their attention to it by reporting their own experiences as victims or observers of crime (Black and Reiss, 1970). Most policing is, therefore, reactive rather than proactive.

This dependence upon the public for information about crime leads to selective reporting and statistical distortions. The most obvious manifestation of this problem is underreporting: most texts on crime and delinquency like to emphasize that official counts of crime underestimate its real or actual incidence because many illegal acts are not reported to the police or are not detected by them.

There are numerous reasons why people choose not to share their knowledge of crime with the police. Many of these have been revealed in what are called victimization surveys in which members of the public are invited to discuss their experiences as victims of crime. They include the fact that people are sometimes distrustful of the police and doubt their competence in catching criminals or tracing stolen property. Sometimes victims feel intimidated by offenders, particularly if they know them. On other occasions victims are inclined to view the incident as too trivial to warrant contacting the police. Finally, victims may not even realize that they have become a victim of crime, assuming instead that a stolen wallet or purse has been lost, for instance.

There are fewer surveys of adolescent victimization than of adult victimization. However, those that have been conducted indicate that adolescents don't report for much the same reasons as adults—with the addition of two extra teen-specific motivations. First, research in Edinburgh, Scotland, by Anderson, Kinsey, Loader, and Smith (1994) and preliminary findings from an ongoing study in Toronto (Tanner and Wortley, 2000) reveal that high school students are often reluctant to report incidents to parents and police (although not to friends) if they have been victimized at times or in places declared off limits by parents: doing so could result in a curtailment of their leisure activities. Second, our research suggests that among adolescents strong norms exist against snitching on one's classmates—a prescription not simply reducible to fear of retaliation (although that is certainly part of the reason for not reporting).

However, even if crimes are reported to the police or the police detect incidents themselves, there is still no guarantee that an arrest will be made or a charge laid. The police may decide that the incident was insufficiently serious to merit an arrest or they may respect the wishes of the complainant and—depending on the gravity of the offence—not press charges (Black and Reiss, 1970).

MORE YOUTH CRIME OR LESS?

The large number of criminal incidents that go unobserved, unreported, undetected, and, therefore, unrecorded means that the official statistics always underestimate the true volume of crime in society. And because so much actual crime and delinquency is omitted from police and court records, it is difficult to provide authoritative answers to questions about changes in youth crime rates over time. Statistical estimates of youth crime are based upon some combination of actual ("real") adolescent behaviour and the reporting and recording of that behaviour. The problem is that all three elements are subject to variation that can affect statistical outcomes (Liska, 1987).

What happens, for example, if, for whatever reason, the public becomes more willing to report delinquent incidents to the police or the police become more successful at uncovering crime and recording it? Quite simply, rates of crime and delinquency will increase, which gives substance to claims about a growing youth crime problem! However, this increase may have occurred independently of any aggregate change (for better or worse) in teenager behaviour. Although official statistics often suggest that youth crime rates are increasing, perhaps it is only reporting by citizens and detection by police officers that have increased.

Indeed, it is conceivable that evidence of rising youth crime is the result of a self-fulfilling prophecy—a prediction that causes behaviour that makes the prediction come true (Merton, 1968). If people believe than today's adolescents are more inclined to violent crime than their predecessors, then they are more likely to make their suspicions and misgivings known to the police. In turn, citizens are likely to hold these beliefs because the newspapers that they read and the television programs that they watch have alerted them to the growing problem of youth crime.

Similarly, police departments have expanded, embraced technological gadgetry and become more professional. As a result, their ability to catch young offenders has improved. Perhaps, too, the police are increasingly willing to treat crime reports from the general public more seriously. If any one or more of these developments have occurred, then we can anticipate an increase in teenage crime, regardless of whether teenagers are committing more crime (cf. Liska, 1987, p. 17).

Official statistics on violent youth crime can be used to illustrate some of these possibilities. Between 1987 and 1997, police data indicate that the rate of violent youth crime had doubled; 1998 figures indicate that the rate of young people charged with violent crime is 77 percent higher than in 1988—a much sharper increase than for adults (6 percent) (Savoie, 1999.)

On the face of it, these statistics point to a sudden and very dramatic decline in the behavioural standards of Canadian youth over this period. But although it is possible that something of this sort did happen, it is not very likely. What is rather more probable is that factors that we discussed earlier were responsible for the increases in violence registered in the police and court reports. In particular, people are now more sensitive to the problem of youth violence than they have been in the past, and this may be influencing their definitions of what is violent behaviour and their willingness to report it to the appropriate authorities. Take, as a more specific example, the issue of violence in schools, presented by the news media as a new and disturbing problem.

However, what may be changing is not the conduct of kids in school but the response of teachers and school boards to that behaviour. Having learned of a growing social problem with youth crime, they are less inclined to deal informally with troublesome students. So instead of handing a detention to the protagonists in a schoolyard fistfight, the police are called in and an assault charge is laid. Indeed, where zero-tolerance policies are in place, school personnel may well have little choice in this matter: they are required to make criminal incidents known to the police. Paradoxically, therefore, a growing intolerance of violence and aggression leads to more systematic recording of its occurrence. As Empey has noted, "adolescent misbehaviour that might have been ignored in the past now becomes a matter of public record" (1982, p. 104). I will have more to say about both patterns of school violence and responses to it in Chapter 4.

Similarly, since the police tend to respond to citizen complaints about deviant behaviour rather than proactively seek it out, the deployment of police resources is strongly influenced by the wishes, concerns, and priorities of the general public. One consequence of high levels of public concern about serious youth crime is the establishment, in most major Canadian cities, of youth-gang units. It does not stretch the imagination too far to deduce that the creation of special gang units will increase the amount of youth crime detected, and hence recorded, in the official statistics. Similarly, in a climate of concern about youth crime, the police will be more inclined to arrest than discharge the juveniles whom they encounter on the street, and Crown counsels more willing to prosecute and judges more disposed to institutionalize the young offenders brought before them.

Nor does this exhaust the possible ways in which the official data can give a misleading impression of the nature of, and changes in, violent behaviour. There is also the manner in which violent crime gets categorized, and, thereby, officially defined, by Statistics Canada.

A wide range of offences is included under the rubric of violent crime, ranging in seriousness from homicide to common assault. And although homicide is plainly a more serious crime than common assault, it also occurs considerably less often. For instance, in 1998–99, 22 percent of all cases heard in youth courts in Canada involved violence. Of this 22 percent, 45 percent involved minor assault—as we have seen, the least serious form of violent crime—compared with less than 1 percent for murder, attempted murder, and manslaughter, the most serious type of violent crime (Carrière, 2000).

What should also be emphasized is that most of these violent incidents do not involve knives or firearms. Despite the concern about the spread of these weapons among young people, their use is not common. The 1998 crime statistics show that a weapon was present in only 14 percent of violent incidents involving an accused youth, and that a knife was far and away the most frequently employed weapon (48 percent), compared with firearms at 13 percent. Most incidents classified as violent result in common assault charges under which any injuries incurred are due to physical force (that is, punches and kicks) rather than guns and knives.

And what does minor or common assault look like when statistics are turned into real events? Remember the incident a few years back involving hockey star Eric Lindros at a Whitby nightclub that was heavily reported in the Canadian media? He was charged with, though subsequently acquitted of, assault after dousing a young woman on the dance floor with beer. Without wishing to minimize the victim's discomfort, it is unlikely, to say the least, that being soaked with beer is what immediately comes to mind when people worry about violent crime. Yet barroom fracases of this sort routinely enter Statistics Canada classifications as violent criminal behaviour. The Lindros case is illustrative of the extent to which minor incidents are allowed to dominate even serious violent crime categories.

No less importantly, these are the sorts of incidents that in the past citizens might not have bothered the police with; or, if such incidents were reported to them, the police might have decided not to act on the information received, preferring instead to handle the case informally. However, in the present climate, with a heightened sensitivity to crimes of violence, people are more willing to report and the police more likely to record such incidents. And all the evidence suggests that the upward climb in youth violence from the mid-1980s to the early 1990s is mainly attributable to the proliferation of common assault charges—the rate in 1997 being 119 percent higher than in 1987.

What is being proposed here is that official measures of crime are susceptible to shifting societal norms and values that influence what gets reported by the public, investigated by the police, and prosecuted by the courts. However, this is less of a problem with serious crimes like homicide because few of us need convincing that killing other people is morally wrong; we are therefore willing to report such incidents to the police. Moreover, dead bodies are (relatively) difficult to hide for any length of time and are therefore (relatively) easy to detect. The official statistics are consequently more accurate (because they are more complete) for homicide than for other crimes. For this reason, homicide statistics are generally regarded by criminologists as the best—the most reliable and valid—measure of changing crime rates in society. And what do the official statistics tell us about the incidence of, and trend in, youth homicide?

Murder is, first of all, rarely committed by offenders of any age. However, it is particularly uncommon among young people. Statistics Canada data reveal, for instance, that in 1997, of the

434 persons charged with homicide, only 54 (12 percent) were under eighteen. These 54 individuals constitute a very small proportion (less than 0.1 percent) of young people charged with a criminal act in 1997 (*A profile of youth justice in Canada*, 1998). In 1998, a total of 56 youths were charged with homicide, 13 percent of all persons charged with the crime (Savoie, 1999). Second, although the homicide rate among young people has fluctuated over the past decade, it has not steadily and consistently increased (Sprott and Doob, 1998); nor are murderers becoming younger—another commonly expressed fear about youth crime. Despite the vast amounts of media and public attention, homicide is not, and has never been, a characteristic feature of youth crime in Canada.

Ironically, although the public remains concerned about rising youth crime, the most recent official—that is to say police and Court—data chronicle the opposite trend: a decline in both youth and adult crime rates. It is a decrease that holds for all offence categories combined, as well as for separate property and violent crime categories, and 1999 was the eighth consecutive year of decline. The downward direction began with property crime rates at the end of the 1980s, and has subsequently been duplicated with regard to violent crime rates. It is unlikely that the teenage population of Canada suddenly and collectively raised its behavioural standards as the new millennium beckoned. And although changes in reporting and recording may have contributed to the decrease, it is more probable that other factors and processes are afoot.

Part of the explanation is clearly demographic: there is a smaller proportion of young males in the population. As we have just seen, this is the group who commit the most crime. Accordingly, when there are large numbers of them in the population, crime rates will go up. For instance, between 1962 and 1978 there was a 24 percent increase in the number of fifteen- to twenty-four-year-old males in Canada—and a 158 percent increase in the crime rate. But when there are fewer young males in the population—as is currently the situation—crime rates go down. This is not a phenomenon unique to Canada: similar patterns of demographically driven decline are observable in the United States, Great Britain, and several European nations.

Other public policy experts also suggest that more young people have begun to heed warnings about the dangers of early school leaving, and are therefore staying in school longer, returning to school, or becoming involved with various initiatives to help them find and keep jobs. These endeavours, it is argued, diminish motivation and opportunities for crime.

Sources more closely identified with the police emphasize a different set of explanations. They insist that tougher, or at least more proactive, policing has reduced crime. They also cite improved community–police relationships for creating safer and more orderly neighborhoods.

That said, not everybody is convinced that crime rates really are going down. In fact, many people believe the very opposite and accordingly report becoming more fearful of crime. As we saw in the last chapter, public perceptions of crime are shaped not by recourse to statistical information (or even personal experience), but by what people see, hear, and read in the mass media. Nor are police representatives or community leaders necessarily prepared to support statistically based conclusions about crime trends, preferring instead more anecdotal evidence that tells of a bad situation that is becoming progressively worse because of, for instance, budget cutbacks that have prevented the hiring of more police officers or because of the continuing failings of the Young Offenders Act. Another strategy is to concede that although overall youth crime rates may be declining, violent youth crime is increasing.

Those who adopt this position are usually not academics. But there are exceptions. For example, Thomas Gabor has recently (1999) suggested that, on the one hand, the worsening qualities of contemporary youth crime are not necessarily accurately captured and contextualized in UCR statistics and, on the other, that criminologists should be prepared to embrace more diverse data sources, including impressionistic ones, when evaluating youth crime. He argues that the more impressionistic sources—media reports and information from school and criminal justice officials, for example—tell us that youth crime either has increased or turned into something much nastier than it used to be.

One of the benefits of using several data sources, as he sees it, is that they would permit a "representation of the facts" more consistent with public beliefs about youth crime. He is thus prepared to validate newspaper stories of frequent swarming incidents, and school principals' and trustees' assessments of rising levels of school violence and victimization on the grounds that, since a lot of people believe that this is what is happening, it must be true.

This is a curious argument and, not surprisingly, he has been quickly rebuked for it. Doob and Sprott (1999) point out that there are all manner of strongly held beliefs that are not in fact accurate: for instance, the fact that blood letting was once believed to be a cure for a range of ailments does not mean that it actually had that effect. Likewise, the fact that people believe that youth crime has become quantitatively and qualitatively worse does not, independent of any further evidence, make that view correct.

In answering Gabor's call for a more catholic range of informational sources, Doob and Sprott draw attention to several (American) surveys that address the "more and worse" view of youth crime. The data that they review indicate, for instance, that in the six 'years between 1992–93 and 1997–98, there was no discernible upward trend in fatal school shootings in the United States. Similarly, the best available longitudinal research on self-reported victimization among American high school students fails to support claims of a steady climb in such incidents. Similarly, they find no evidence of any increase in the numbers of students bringing weapons to school.

On the other hand, whether we are talking about 12 percent or 14 percent of students having been victimized in the past school year, the proportions seem high, as Doob and Sprott emphasize. But—and this is crucial for claims about the worsening nature of youth crime—we do not know if these are high numbers by the standards of the past because information on adolescent victimization was not collected in earlier eras.

YOUTH AS VICTIMS

Ironically, for all the attention given to the issue, there is one aspect of youth crime that hitherto has been underreported in the news media. When people contemplate the problem of teenage violence, they think about violent acts committed by adolescents. However, this focus encourages us to lose sight of the fact that young people are also disproportionately the victims of violent crime and, indeed, of crime more generally.

Beginning in 1988, a number of police departments in Canada expanded the scope of information collected under the auspices of the UCR system. In this revised survey, additional information is gathered about the victims of violence and some of the circumstances of their victimization. Although not necessarily representative of Canada as a whole, these data provide some surprising facts about the victims of teenage crime.

For example, adults, who are the quickest to express fears about violent youth crime, are not its principal target. Instead, the prime victims of violent youth crime are other youth (aged between twelve and seventeen), particularly males. In 1998, over half (52 percent) of all victims of youth crime were other young people. By contrast, adults made up 37 percent of the victims of youth violence. Elderly people, defined as those over fifty-five in the 1998 statistics, are simultaneously the most fearful of youth crime and least likely victims of it. They comprised only 2 percent of the youth crime victims in that year (Savoie, 1999).

On the basis of these figures, it might be expected that young peoples' extensive experience of violent victimization would be met with sympathy and concern. However, prospects for a compassionate response are muted by the knowledge that those who perpetrate violence against young people are often other young people—and that victims often know their assailants, mainly as acquaintances (as in 60 percent of the cases investigated in 1998). In addition, there is information, mostly of American origin from large and representative victimization surveys, indicating that young offenders and young victims often share the same characteristics. They are often single males, for instance, and have class and racial backgrounds in common. Indeed, victims and offenders are not infrequently the same people! This overlap means that young people, in general, are not seen as "good" victims because they are not always "innocent" victims. (On this issue, see Felson, 1998). Some research has revealed that involvement in delinquency is the best predictor of experiences of victimization (Lauritson, Laub, and Sampson, 1992).

THE LOCATION OF YOUTH VIOLENCE

The revised UCR system also sheds some light on the location of violent youth crime, as documented by victims. Media coverage and public perception suggest that a large percentage of crime takes place in schools. However, findings from 1998 indicate that more youth-initiated violence occurs in public places, such as parks, parking lots, streets, and transit systems (35 percent of incidents); than in the home (24 percent) or school (also 24 percent) (Savoie, 1999).

As far as school crime is concerned, the same source (1998) indicates that 10 percent of all criminal incidents occur at a school and that roughly half (51 percent) of these incidents are violent. However, what the data do *not* reveal is whether the crime that takes place at school occurs during the school day or not. American survey evidence—to be discussed in Chapter 4—suggests that significant amounts occur after school hours.

The same official data sources also indicate that there are important differences in *where* youths and adults are victimized. UCR data for 1997 show that whereas adults are most likely to experience violent crime at home (53 percent), young people are more likely to encounter it on the streets (32 percent), or in other public and commercial places and institutions (28 percent). These differences almost certainly reflect the more public and collective nature of youth routines—journeying to and from school and going out in the evening and on weekends together. Significantly, other victim survey evidence indicates that, despite high levels of victimization, young people are considerably less fearful of crime than adults (*Juristat*, 1994, pp. 13, 14).

These observations have been developed into a theory of crime—the routine activity theory—that focuses upon everyday routines and activities that direct people toward, or away from, criminal encounters. For instance, is young peoples' predilection for risky leisure responsible for both their high rates of offending *and* victimization? This is one of the questions informing research on adolescent leisure lifestyles and crime that I am currently conducting with Scot Wortley (Tanner and Wortley, 2000).

Our discussion of police and court statistics reveals them to be far from perfect measures of crime. However, none of the comments that I have made about them is very novel. Indeed, most students of adolescent deviance are only too aware of the limitations of the official data sources. These people have responded to the defects in two main ways: they have tried to improve the quality of the official statistics, and they have sought to ease their reliance upon them by developing additional means of collecting information.

SELF-REPORT STUDIES

The best-known and most regularly used of these additional measures are self-report studies. Respondents—often adolescents, often in a school setting—are invited to report, either in a questionnaire or an interview, on a range of offences that they have committed, regardless of whether these offences have brought them to the attention of the police or courts. Respondents might therefore be asked about their involvement in property crime ("How many times in the past year have you taken something from a store without paying for it?"), vandalism ("How many times in the past year have you damaged or destroyed on purpose property that did not belong to you?"), or violence ("How many times in the past year have you beaten up someone so badly that he or she probably needed a doctor?"). Self-report instruments have also been used extensively to probe adolescents' use of both legal and illegal drugs ("How often do you drink beer, wine, or other alcohol? How often do you smoke marijuana or hash?"). In addition, respondents are asked to provide information about their social characteristics—such as sex, age, race, and parental background.

Self-report studies are important for three main reasons. First, they provide information on the number of persons—usually young persons—who have committed deviant acts and how often they have done so. Second, they force an abandonment of the idea that adolescents can be divided into "delinquent" and "non-delinquent" categories and the attendant assumption that the latter are unsullied by deviant involvements. They therefore encourage an alternative conception of delinquency as a continuous variable, ranging from the most committed or involved to the least committed or involved. Third, they permit comparison between adolescents who have been officially defined as delinquents and those who have not. Self-report studies, therefore, provide a check on the representativeness of those adolescents who become officially delinquent (Hood and Sparks, 1970, p. 46).

This last point is particularly pertinent because the recognition that the official police and court statistics include only a small proportion of offenders and offences invites uncomfortable questions about how typical those juveniles are who are arrested by the police and prosecuted and sentenced by the courts. Some skeptics argue that police statistics more accurately reflect the biases of police officers than the deviant behaviour of particular youths or youth groups. According to this argument, if poor kids or those from racial minorities are arrested more frequently than rich, white kids from the suburbs, it is because police officers discriminate against them and not because members of these groups commit more delinquency.

A similar argument has been made in reverse with respect to girls and delinquency: it is believed that females are more likely than males to benefit from discretionary policing. For example, when confronted with a sea of hostile teenage faces in a shopping mall, the police will arrest male troublemakers, while letting the girls off with a warning. According to this argument, lower female delinquency rates may be attributable to more lenient or chivalrous treatment by police and judges.

Some objections have been raised to using self-report studies as a research technique. Possibly your first reaction is to ask who is going to admit, either on a questionnaire or to an interviewer, that he or she has engaged in behaviour that could have resulted in trouble with the law? Critics of self-report techniques claim that they are bedeviled with problems of concealment: people have little vested interest in providing accurate details of their wrongdoings to strangers, and will not, as a result, provide them with honest answers. Moreover, concealment is not always done purposely or deliberately: human memory is notoriously imperfect, and even obliging adolescents are not always able to accurately recall details of the misdemeanours in which they have been involved. Ironically, the validity of self-report surveys is threatened by the opposite problem as well: anonymous questionnaires present a golden opportunity for boastful adolescents to construct or enlarge upon their deviant identities and delinquent careers. Thus, while some adolescents might feel under pressure to keep their delinquencies secret, others might be tempted to exaggerate the scope and intensity of their delinquent activities.

Needless to say, criminologists are aware of these possibilities and have devised ways and means of validating the findings from self-report studies. Some of these "validity checks" on self-report data are quite ingenious. They include comparing self-report information with police and court dossiers on known offenders, having the friends of those surveyed assess the honesty of the answers given, and subjecting respondents of self-report surveys to lie detector tests (Box, 1981).

To a degree that may be surprising, self-report studies stand up remarkably well to these and other tests of validity. For all but the most serious forms of delinquent behaviour, they are a valid and reliable guide to adolescent deviance. I will return to the "seriousness" issue. For now, I want to concentrate on the main conclusions of self-report studies.

Overall, they show that delinquency is considerably more common than revealed by the official records. Large numbers of young people admit to acts for which they could have been arrested by the police and sentenced by the courts. Indeed, it would be hard to find a self-report survey that did not show that a majority of adolescent respondents had not, at one time or another, used public transportation without paying, pilfered chocolates or gum from a store, drunk alcohol, or been involved in a fight. Delinquency is therefore not the preserve of some sinister minority of the adolescent population. Indeed, in a purely statistical sense, it is quite normal behaviour! Although this finding is not likely to make Canadian parents sleep any more easily at night, it should also be emphasized that self-report studies reveal serious and frequent delinquency to be rather more rare. Although most adolescents admit to some illegalities, only a relatively small number acknowledge persistent and/or serious wrongdoing—and they are the ones who are most likely to become officially delinquent. Similarities between the officially guilty and the hidden delinquents notwithstanding, the two groups are not identical in terms of their delinquent activities.

What do self-report studies tell us about the social characteristics of hidden delinquents and how do hidden delinquents compare to those wrongdoers who are "known" to the police and courts? Studies using police and court data have repeatedly demonstrated that, in addition to age, gender and social class are two of the strongest correlates of delinquency. Thus, delinquency is often seen as an urban, male, working-class phenomenon. To what extent is this depiction challenged by, as Hood and Sparks (1970) put it, "the confessions of the respectable?" Let us look at gender.

Self-report studies indicate that female adolescents confess to less delinquency than male adolescents but commit the same sort of offences—primarily minor property crime. They therefore provide little support for the once popular notion that female delinquents are primarily involved in status offences and prostitution. According to self-report surveys, gender-based variation in delinquency stems more from the volume of activity than its content. Both the official measures and self-report data are in broad agreement that delinquency is characteristically a male phenomenon, although the size of the gender gap is larger in studies based on police and court data than in those that rely on self-report techniques (Box, 1981). I will have more to say about female delinquency and deviance in Chapter 6.

What about social class? Is it the case that working-class adolescents are more involved in delinquency than middle-class ones? This issue has been fiercely debated in criminological circles. Generally speaking, studies that use official statistics as their data source are more likely to find a strong inverse relationship than those based on self-report techniques. Indeed, self-report studies commonly find no significant relationship between social class and delinquency (Tittle and Meier, 1990; Tracy, 1987; Braithwaite, 1981).

An early Canadian example of what was to become a pattern is Edmond Vaz's examination of delinquency in four Canadian communities. The frequency of delinquent activity was no more pronounced among lower-class adolescents than among middle- and upper-class ones (Vaz, 1966).

The common inability of self-report studies to find much evidence for greater working-class than middle-class involvement in delinquency has prompted some commentators (for example, Tittle et al., 1978) to conclude that the relationship between class and delinquency is a myth and recommend that class be removed from consideration as one of the theoretically important determinants of delinquency. Others (for example, Box, 1981) have taken it as evidence that the official statistics are inaccurate and biased, and are confirmation of the suspicion that the police discriminate against working-class adolescents.

There is, however, another no less plausible interpretation, namely, that self-report schedules and the official statistics tap different domains of behaviour and that the discrepancy between the measures is more illusionary than real (Hindelang, Hirschi, and Weis, 1979, 1981). In essence, the argument is that serious delinquents and their serious delinquencies are not reached by self-report instruments.

Most self-report studies, as we have seen, target students who are in attendance at high school. As a result, those adolescents who habitually skip classes or who have discontinued their education completely will not be included in the sample. Since it is likely (some would say highly likely) that the skippers and the dropouts are more seriously delinquent than those with a stronger commitment to schooling, their absence from the sample means that hard-core delinquents will be underrepresented in self-report studies. More to the point, there is reason to believe that chronic offenders are more likely to come from the sorts of disadvantaged backgrounds that sociologists are likely to regard as "working-class" or "lower-class."

However, it is not just hard-core delinquents who are excluded from self-report studies; also missing are the questions that ask about "serious" types of delinquent activity. The reason for this, say Hindelang, Hirschi, and Weis (1981), is that researchers believe it unlikely, even on anonymous questionnaires, that respondents will readily admit to serious crimes, such as armed robbery, murder, and rape. Therefore, they omit questions about them. Through a process of self-censorship, the architects of self-report surveys ensure that most of them inquire about relatively minor delinquency only. And common, nonserious delinquency may be unrelated to social class.

Even serious delinquency revealed by self-report studies often turns out, on close examination, to be relatively harmless. Here, for example, are the delinquent activities of an adolescent categorized as belonging among the most serious 10 percent of young criminals in a very well-known self-report study conducted in the United States:

> ... [at age twelve] he and a friend had knocked down a tent in a neighbor boy's backyard—the aftermath of an earlier mud-throwing fight.
>
> That winter, he had shoplifted gum a few times from a neighborhood store.
>
> On turning thirteen, he had begun to lie regularly about his age to cashiers at movie theaters.
>
> In June, 1961, he had shoplifted a cartridge belt from a hardware store and later gave it to a friend.
>
> The month after, he had taken an address book from a department store.

In the summer of 1961, he and a friend had helped themselves to several beers from his friend's refrigerator.

In late August, 1961, he and another friend had twice raided an orchard not far from R's home, taking ripe pears and unripe apples and grapes. They ate the first, and threw the rest at various targets.

In September, 1961, he had lifted a hunting knife from a sporting-goods store just for something to do. "We took it back the next day, snuck it back in."

He regularly carried a hunting knife under his jacket, "for protection" when he went collecting Friday nights on his paper route. (Gold 1970, p. 30; cited by Hindelang, Hirschi, and Weis, 1981, p. 91)

It is hard to see how these mild misadventures indicate serious delinquency—yet these are the sort of activities that result in this designation in self-report surveys. As Hindelang and his colleagues say about the questions asked in these surveys, "more serious refers to the upper part of a very limited seriousness range" (Hindelang, Hirschi, and Weis, 1979, p. 997).

Some discussions of self-report studies assume or infer that were the police to be made aware of hidden delinquency, they would automatically arrest and charge the offenders. Such is not the case, however. Some misconduct is so trivial—stealing apples from a neighbour's yard, for example—that many people, including police officers, will choose to ignore it or deal with the offence informally.[2] The inclusion in self-report surveys of events and incidents that few people, the police included, find serious, reduces the chances of class becoming a significant correlate or predictor of the more serious delinquent activity represented (indeed overrepresented) in official statistics.

Because most self-report surveys are overly weighted with questions about relatively non-serious delinquent behaviour, social class often fails to emerge as a significant source of variation in delinquent behaviour. Were they to include items of seriousness equivalent to those found in Criminal Code classifications, Hindelang et al. (1979; 1981) argue, significant class differences would become more apparent.

Some of the better and more recent self-report studies have taken account of these criticisms: they do, for instance, include "street" as well as "school" youth in their samples and they do include measures of serious crime. Not coincidentally, they also report findings that show—like studies based on official crime data—an inverse relationship between social class and criminality. The appropriate correctional measures, in other words, reconcile apparently contradictory findings regarding the connections between class and crime (Hagan and McCarthy,

1997). For the most part, though, serious delinquents and their serious delinquencies are probably still underrepresented in most self-report surveys, particularly those conducted in large urban centres in the United States. Thus, although self-report surveys have eased the criminologist's dependence upon official data sources, the spread of these instruments has had the effect of minimizing the continuing importance of traditional predictors of serious delinquency, such as class and—in the United States— race. This is particularly ironic because it is happening at a time when we might have anticipated that those variables would be of growing significance.[3]

Global recession and restructuring have resulted in rising levels of unemployment, homelessness, and poverty—just the sort of changes that might be expected to intensify deviant subcultural activity among the young and marginal (see Chapter 5). However, the effect of these structural inequalities rarely registers in self-report findings. No wonder that some commentators have suggested that the popularity of self-report studies has allowed street gangs and other manifestations of serious subcultural delinquency to remain hidden from view. (See, for example, the collection of articles in Huff, 1990.) Moreover, the apparent decline of serious subcultural delinquency has affected the course of theoretical developments in criminology. In so far as self-report surveys fail to find class (or racial) differences in delinquent involvements, explanations that focus upon the inequalities associated with these variables have been abandoned in preference to theories that emphasize the personal bonds and attachments of adolescence. Here I am referring to control theory and its more recent variant, self-control theory, both of which will be discussed more fully in the next chapter.

SELF-REPORTED VICTIMIZATION

As previously noted, there are fewer studies of youth victimization than adult victimization. However, much of what we know about young people's experiences of victimization has come from self-report surveys in which respondents are asked questions about the things that have been stolen from them and the hurts and injuries that have been inflicted upon them.

Some surveys, including the one that I am currently conducting with Scot Wortley, make a point of inquiring about crimes committed *and* crimes suffered among both school and street samples. Asking both sorts of questions allows researchers to conclude that many teenage victims of crime are also perpetrators of crime. Just why there is such an intimate connection between offending and victimization is one of the important questions we hope to answer with our research.

Preliminary results from our study reveal that, as with offending, there is a large amount of "hidden victimization" taking place. Individuals who are not in school—who are dropouts or street youth or both—have significantly higher rates of victimization than school students, and some of those adolescents who are most fearful of crime and most likely to feel unsafe in a variety of contexts are those who have the least contact with crime as either victims or offenders. They are also the individuals, not coincidentally, who are most closely controlled by parents or guardians.

Although self-report surveys do uncover much hidden offending (and victimization), they also fail to convey the collective quality of adolescent deviant involvement. Delinquency is often conducted in groups and, sometimes, in gangs—a reality not well monitored by individuals probing into backgrounds, traits, attachments, and motivation (Horowitz, 1990, p. 54). Self-report surveys, in other words, decontextualize delinquent acts—a problem only overcome, it is suggested by some, by the willingness of researchers to go where the delinquents go.

WHERE THE ACTION IS: OBSERVATIONAL STUDIES AND THEIR LIMITATIONS

The critics of self-report studies, who also tend to be critical of the official statistics, often advocate direct observation as the best means of gathering valid and reliable information on deviant and delinquent subcultures.

Observational studies, or ethnographies, have probably played a larger part in research on delinquent gangs and deviant youth subcultures than other areas of crime and deviance. Many of the pioneering investigators of subcultural deviance and delinquency have used this method. See, for example, Frederick Thrasher's exhaustive study of youth gangs in Chicago in the 1920s (1937), and William Whyte's detailed account of working-class Italian-American street culture in pre–Second World War Boston (1955).

More recently, there has been something of an ethnographic revival in the sociology of deviance, inspired by dissatisfaction with both the official statistics and self-report surveys. A partial listing of recent ethnographic studies would include Hagedorn's study of youth crime and youth gangs in Milwaukee (1988); Moore's examination of subcultural deviance among Mexican youth in Los Angeles (1991); Padilla's account of the Diamonds, a Puerto Rican gang based in Chicago (1992); Sullivan's research on growing up working-class in three New York City neighbourhoods (1989); Paul Willis's celebrated analysis of how working-class kids in Britain get working-class jobs (1977); and Jay MacLeod's replication of that study in an unnamed American city (Boston?) (1987). And virtually all of what we know about rap, hip-hop, and rave subculture (and club culture more generally) we owe to ethnographic research (for example, Bennett, 1999; Thornton, 1995; Weber, 1999).

Ethnographic studies of youth deviance result from two principal approaches: participant and non-participant observation. In the former, the researcher takes part in the behaviour that he or she is trying to explain. Examples of this approach include Canadian studies of the punk subculture in Victoria (Baron, 1989b), an outlaw motorcycle gang in Edmonton (Wolf, 1991), and skinheads in Calgary (Young and Curry, 1997). On other occasions, researchers have observed, but not participated in, the deviant action. Gordon West's study of young male thieves in Toronto is an example of this strategy (1978, 1979).

Observational studies have a number of advantages. First, members of delinquent youth cultures may be unwilling, and perhaps unable, to fill out questionnaires, the stock-in-trade of survey researchers. Second, researchers are more likely to capture the rich detail of adolescents' cultural activities by observation than by relying on questionnaires. As two critics of early subcultural research note, many studies "fail to include much of what is cultural about subculture" (Fine and Kleinman, 1979, p. 7). Surveys may be a good way of collecting information about violent offending among skinheads or patterns of illicit drug use among ravers, but they do not tell us very much about the lifestyles of skinheads or ravers. Third, studying deviant youth in their "natural settings" may enhance the reliability and validity of the findings. Fourth, surveys have produced insights and hunches that have subsequently been tested using larger data sets and quantitative methods. An excellent recent example is Hagan's examination (1993) of the connection between youth crime and unemployment, in which he draws his hypotheses largely from the ethnographies that I have just cited, most notably the work of Mercer Sullivan.

On the other hand, observational studies also have their drawbacks. Limited resources mean that sample sizes are often very small, and what is gained by intense scrutiny of a small number of cases may be lost by the narrow focus of the coverage. In particular, generalizations about broad patterns of adolescent conformity and deviance are problematic when based on only a small number of observations. (See, for example, Willis, 1977.)

Participant observation can also make unusual demands upon researchers. On occasion, the obligation to take part in the action requires the researcher to adopt a possibly alien lifestyle or embrace a new set of routine activities. For instance, while researching small-time delinquents in Liverpool, England, in the 1970s, Howard Parker acknowledged that he had to drink more beer than he would normally choose to do (Parker, 1974, p. 219). Overconsumption of alcohol sometimes made the writing of field notes difficult.

Field research can also be dangerous. Street youth are often involved in criminal activity. The decision to investigate the criminogenic conditions of inner-city street life brings the participant observer into situations that invite police attention or threaten his or her physical well-being. Steve Baron has described some of the difficulties he experienced in investigating street youth in Edmonton (1994). Sometimes the individual being interviewed by Baron would be approached and threatened (with both words and weapons) by other street youth for reasons connected to drug quality and/or quantity. Baron himself was invited to watch a "skinner" (rapist) receive street justice for his offences, an invitation he declined. Having gained the confidence of his informants, Baron was then faced with the tricky task of not betraying that confidence by refusing to take part in their criminal activities or endorsing their moral hierarchies: for instance, talking to a black youth earned him the enmity of white skinheads with whom he had earlier made contact.

A more cerebral problem, the tension between the participative and observational components of the ethnographic role, has been commented upon recently by Thornton, in light of her investigation of the rave subculture (1995). She notes that, as a participant, the researcher is expected to view the unfolding action sympathetically, essentially from the point of view of the group members. But as an observer, greater detachment is required, along with a more neutral recording of those same events.

There is also the possibility that the presence of an observer may alter the patterns of behaviour of subcultural participants: punks or skinheads or bike gang members may act very differently when they know they are being watched. Finally, there is a variant of the problem that Thornton identifies: the researcher may misinterpret the situation and events that he or she is observing and participating in. This problem is particularly acute when expressive deviancy is involved. Much of the deviant status of high-profile youth groups, such as punks, skinheads, and rappers, derives as much from their collective appearance as from their actual behaviour. The question for researchers therefore becomes one of teasing out the meaning of particular hairstyles, forms of clothing, and musical choices and of understanding how these signs and symbols relate to attitudes and behaviour. Some students of youth subcultures have been willing—some might say too willing—to construe cultural artifacts as statements of youth revolt; for example, to see in the shaved heads and work boots of English skinheads the seeds of youthful resistance to attacks, both real and imaginary, upon working-class communities.

Deciphering the meaning of style is fraught with difficulties, and researchers who have tried to do so are open to the accusation that they allow their sympathies for and identifications with disadvantaged youth groups to colour the interpretations that they make of adolescent deviance (Frith, 1985, pp. 310, 319; Davies, 1990). I will discuss this issue further in the next chapter.

Finally, we should acknowledge that many social investigators of youth deviance use more than one method of data collection. For example, Hagan and McCarthy not only administered surveys to homeless youth, they also observed their street culture and interviewed participants (1997). Weber, when investigating the rave scene, combined ethnographic observation with interviews (1999). The research on adolescent leisure, crime, and victimization that I am involved in with Scot Wortley employs quantitative survey research methods and more qualitative focus group sessions. These (not isolated) instances of methodological pluralism indicate that many researchers view different data gathering techniques as providing complimentary rather than alternative interpretations of social reality.

CONCLUSION

Virtually all of the important claims made about youth deviance— its prevalence, frequency, severity, forms, and changes therein— depend first of all upon the quantity and quality of the data collected by the police and courts—what are commonly referred to as official data sources. In addition, all of the important theoretical initiatives in criminology are bound by the need to explain the facts of delinquency as documented by the official statistics.

Pursuing the available statistics tells us that young people commit a disproportionately large number of the crimes known to the police. Although this knowledge can be seen as justification for public fears about youth crime, it has to be emphasized that the offences typically committed by young people are not the serious, violent ones of popular imagination, but minor property crimes. This pattern is not new—it has existed since the middle of the nineteenth century—nor is it being altered by any significant long-term increase in violent youth crime.

More often than not, therefore, the public image of youth crime does not conform to statistical reality, as recent comparisons of the findings from public opinion polls that probe fear of crime and criminal victimization with police reported crime statistics show. Exercises of this sort demonstrate that although the fear of crime is increasing, the reported crime rate is actually declining and has been doing so for the past eight years. Although some might be tempted to construe this as evidence of public irrationality, others end up questioning the accuracy of the official counts of crime. There is no shortage of critics willing to contest the reality of crime as portrayed in the official data sources.

Dissatisfaction with the omissions and distortions of the official statistics has led to the development of self-report studies. They quickly confirmed what many suspected: numerous delinquent incidents remain undetected by the police, and a large proportion of the adolescent population has committed an illegal act. However, they also show that most adolescents are neither repeat offenders nor engaged in serious wrongdoing. Moreover, comparisons of "official" and "hidden" delinquents allow us to conclude that the police are most likely to arrest and charge, and the courts most likely to prosecute and convict, the most persistent and serious young offenders.

Similarly, both the official statistics and self-report techniques indicate that those most involved in delinquency—that is, repeat offenders or those who commit the most serious offences—are more likely to be male than female and working class than middle class in origin. However, self-report surveys do not always reveal strong class-based differences because hard-core delinquents are not always represented in high school–based sample surveys and, even if they are, they are not asked questions about their truly serious wrongdoings. Hence, it has largely been left to ethnographic field studies—observational research—to document the group characteristics of the seriously delinquent and, increasingly, the seriously victimized. Although their numbers are small, and therefore unrepresentative of all adolescent deviance, there is little doubt that the disadvantages and deprivations associated with class and—particularly in the United States—race are responsible for the formation of delinquent youth subcultures.

Finally, it has to be recognized that the questions raised in this chapter about the nature and extent of youth crime and whether delinquency rates are increasing over time are predicated on the assumption that the involvement of the young with crime, particularly violent crime, is solely as offenders. Such is not the case, however. Evidence is starting to accumulate that shows adolescents are more likely to be the victims of violent crime than they are to be the perpetrators of it. And this observation can be used to make what is, perhaps, a more important point about the relationship between age, class, and criminality. An exclusive focus on adolescents as the creators of delinquent acts not only neglects their sufferings as victims but also deflects our attention from the considerably more serious criminal behaviour of corporations that manufacture cars they know to be faulty, pollute the environment, evade corporate tax payments, or pay insufficient attention to health and safety regulations, thereby endangering and killing employees. Research reported on by Steven Box (1983), among others, leaves little doubt that the adult agents of corporate crimes are responsible for considerably more injury than the mundane street crime of adolescents. And whereas young delinquents are overwhelmingly of working-class origin, the former are no less overwhelmingly drawn from the more advantaged segments of the community.

NOTES

1. Or blue, in the case of the Edmonton student who was prevented from attending her grade 9 graduation ceremony because of her choice of hair colour. She and her parents are now in the process of suing those responsible for the decision: her former principal and the local school board (*National Post*, August 7, 1999, p. A6).
2. One reason why, of course, is that the youth court counts of official delinquency are smaller than police ones. Young people charged by the police may be spared a court appearance because they have been diverted to what are referred to as alternative programs—community service and so forth. As a rule, efforts are made to reserve the youth court for the most serious and persistent offenders. Hence the lighter volume of cases it deals with in comparison to police departments.
3. Canada, unlike the United States, does not officially record information about the racial characteristics of offenders (or their victims); there is currently considerable debate as to whether the American example should be followed in this country. (For an extended discussion of this issue, see the special edition of the *Canadian Journal of Criminology* [1994], 36, no. 2.)

   American statistics indicate that racial minorities are overrepresented in the official counts of crime. Black youths are, for instance, more likely to be arrested than white youths, particularly for violent street crime (Siegel and Senna, 1994, pp. 56–60). Does this mean that young blacks are more criminal than young whites or merely that blacks get arrested for behaviour for which a white person would receive a caution?

One way of resolving this issue is to follow the example of several American researchers and compare correlations between delinquency and race in official data and self-report studies. The results seem to suggest that, regardless of the slightly larger number of delinquent behaviours reported on by black as compared to white youth, the former are considerably more likely than the latter to be arrested. Although some commentators interpret this finding as evidence of discriminatory policing, others insist that racial differences in serious delinquency registered in official statistics are real and cannot be explained away by either a version of labelling theory (see the next chapter) or racial arguments (blacks are biologically more disposed than whites to crime). Instead, they suggest that if young blacks commit more crime than young whites, it is because young blacks are becoming part of an inner-city underclass, characterized by the absence of jobs, income, and housing. According to this argument, "black crime" is a consequence of appallingly harsh economic conditions.

C H A P T E R **3**

From Chicago to Birmingham and Beyond: The Development of Subcultural Theory in the United States and United Kingdom

INTRODUCTION

What makes adolescent deviance both distinctive and disturbing is its collective appearance. When adolescents behave badly, they often do so in public and in the company of others. Indeed, it is the group basis of much delinquency and deviance that originally attracted sociologists to the phenomena. In trying to understand why adolescents break both major and minor rules in cliques, groups, or (occasionally) gangs, sociologists have formulated what has become known as subcultural theory. The purpose of this chapter is to trace the development of the subcultural concept from its original application in American delinquency theory through to its more recent manifestation in British accounts of deviant youth cultural activity. I will also briefly consider some of the reasons why deviant and delinquent subcultures have historically been less prominent in Canada than in the United States and United Kingdom.

THE DELINQUENT TRADITION IN AMERICAN SOCIOLOGY

When juvenile delinquency emerged as a significant problem in the latter part of the last century, its causes were originally linked to biological factors. The progenitor of this approach is usually taken to be Cesare Lombroso, an Italian physician who, as a result of the autopsies that he performed on convicted adult offenders, believed that criminals and non-criminals were biologically different, and that the defects with which the former were born predisposed them to a life of crime.

Biological theories were gradually replaced by psychological ones, with a focus usually on the personality traits that preceded delinquency. Various problems associated with the emotional and moral upbringing of adolescents—poor relationships with parents, the failure to teach them right from wrong—rendered them maladjusted and thus prone to delinquency.

Although criticisms of these biological and psychological theories are legion, I will focus on only one. Whether the concern is with inborn, biological traits or psychodynamic factors, delinquents are depicted as abnormal individuals; however, as we saw in the last chapter, most adolescents have committed a delinquent act at some time or other. Some youthful rule-breakers may be biologically or psychologically aberrant, but most are fairly ordinary adolescents.

Indeed, it is the very normality of delinquent behaviour—normal in the sense that for some young people in some places it is a regular occurrence—that arouses sociological curiosity. Explanations of delinquency that revolve around the impulses and urges of individuals leave important questions unanswered. Why, for instance, are delinquency and deviancy a collective enterprise? Why do delinquents—particularly serious and repetitive ones—share common backgrounds and similar experiences?

Answering these questions has become the mandate of sociological approaches to delinquency. From the sociological perspective, "delinquency is not just a conglomeration of individual acts" (Hood and Sparks, 1970, p. 80), but an activity that draws much of its significance and meaning from being done collectively. Sociologists have therefore sought to understand delinquency as a social and cultural phenomenon that is often conducted in small groups referred to as subcultures.

The sociological study of delinquency in these terms really began at the University of Chicago in the 1920s. Among the many observations made by the sociologists of the Chicago School (as they became known) was that crime and delinquency tended to be concentrated in certain areas of the city. Similar conclusions had been reached by Charles Dickens in his novels about Victorian London and by the investigative journalism of Henry Mayhew, but it was left to the Chicago School to come up with an explanation for these patterns.

The task that two of them, Henry Shaw and Clifford McKay (1942), set for themselves was (literally) to map out the relationship between juvenile crime and geographical areas within Chicago. Using official court records, they plotted the residential locations of 55 998 known delinquents. They found that delinquency tended to be located in the core of the city, just beyond a central business district, and declined progressively as the inner-city area gave way to the suburbs. Moreover, they were able to show that high-crime areas had been that way for considerable periods of time, regardless of the shifting social and ethnic composition of those who lived there. In certain parts of Chicago, therefore, crime was sufficiently patterned for it to be described, at least by local standards, as normal.

How did Shaw and McKay explain the patterns of delinquency that they had uncovered? As they and other members of the Chicago School saw it, delinquency was a consequence of social disorganization. Those parts of the city that experienced the largest amount of crime and other social problems (mental illness, alcoholism, and so on) were characterized by a lack of social cohesion. Social controls had broken down, they argued, because the areas in question had attracted wave after wave of rural and foreign migrants unfamiliar with the mores of urban American life. These transients, moreover, had few social ties and exercised minimal parental control over the behaviour of their children.

Although he did not use the term, the concept of subculture developed from the work of another Chicago sociologist, Frederick Thrasher (Fine and Kleinman, 1979). Best remembered now for his massive tome on youth gangs (1937), Thrasher similarly argued that delinquency was a consequence of growing up in a city where, because of the massive social changes taking place, adult control of adolescent behaviour was in short supply. Thrasher viewed the phenomenon of youth gangs in his era as "one of the many symptoms of the more or less general disorganization" of inner-city street life. Confronted by disrupted family patterns and a limited physical and social environment, young males reacted by constructing "a world distinctively of their own—far removed from the humdrum existence of the average citizen." The result was a delinquent street culture, motivated not by frustration and deprivation as later theorists would have it, but by a desire for fun and excitement (Bordua, 1969).

More contentious was Thrasher's linking of autonomous street gang activity to the concept of social disorganization. Later research by William Whyte on slum boys in an Italian community in Boston noted that what looked like a disorganized world to outsiders was, in fact, a highly—albeit differently—organized one to those on the inside (Whyte, 1955). Other critics of the disorganization concept similarly like to point out that even unsophisticated criminal activity requires a modicum of organization for its successful execution.

Although the concept of social disorganization is a problematic, and perhaps misconstrued (Downes and Rock, 1995, p. 75), one, most of the insights into delinquent behaviour provided by the Chicago School have held up remarkably well.[1] For instance, the observation that delinquency is a defining feature of certain parts of large cities and is reproduced across the generations is fundamental to virtually all sociological approaches to delinquency; few contemporary sociologists would disagree with Shaw and McKay's pronouncement that "to a very great extent ... traditions of delinquency are preserved and transmitted through the medium of social contact with the unsupervised play group and the more highly organized delinquent and criminal gangs" (Shaw and McKay, 1942).

Just before the Second World War, Robert Merton (1938) developed a theory of criminal behaviour that connected the Chicago sociologists' insights regarding delinquent areas and traditions within cities to broader inequalities within American society. In doing so, he modified Emile Durkheim's concept of anomie to show how societies unintentionally exert pressure upon individuals to engage in rule-breaking behaviour. All societies, he says, are in the business of establishing culturally approved goals for their members, as well as prescribing socially approved means of achieving those goals.

However, the problem is that in some societies—such as the United States—more attention is paid to the goals of wealth, power, and prestige than to the proper way of reaching them. This uneven emphasis upon goals and means creates stress for lower-class individuals. They want, says Merton, what all Americans want—a nice house, a big car, a steady job—but lack the legitimate means (school and work opportunities) to achieve them. Rebuffed, they respond or adapt in a variety of deviant ways to a situation that they find stressful. One of the modes of adaptation—what Merton calls innovation—involves the use of criminal means to achieve economic success goals. Those who turn to property crime are described by him as innovators.

Merton did not intend his theory—the prototype for what has become generally known as "strain theory"—to explain the specifics of juvenile delinquency. He focuses upon why and how working-class individuals are under pressure to innovate, but does not explain why adolescents do so collectively. Nor does his argument account for the destructive character of some serious delinquent behaviour. Although his version of strain theory predicts involvement in property crime, he is unable to tell us why young criminals do not always, for example, steal cars in order to strip them down and sell (to "chop-shops," to use the contemporary parlance) the component parts and accessories. Some go joyriding instead and ultimately destroy and dump the cars. Why is so much juvenile delinquency non-utilitarian and apparently devoid of purpose? How is the content of much delinquent behaviour, in other words, to be explained?

Answering this question was left to Albert Cohen (1955). Writing within the strain paradigm pioneered by Merton, but focusing more explicitly on delinquent behaviour, Cohen developed a theory that would account for both the class-based origins of delinquency as well as its apparently senseless qualities. He saw the roots of delinquency in the limited opportunities available to working-class boys to achieve success in middle-class status terms. Their problems begin in high school, where they continually find themselves judged by what Cohen refers to as a "middle-class measuring rod." They are expected to show respect for teachers, to be dedicated students, to control aggressive impulses, and to forego immediate gratifications (such as watching television or reading comics) in exchange for future rewards (the educational qualifications that will secure them good jobs). Unfortunately, a working-class childhood does not prepare them very well for success in these terms. For instance, their parents do not teach them the value of deferring gratification or the link between school performance and occupational success. As a result, they experience schooling as a process of accumulating failure, increasing anxiety, and mounting frustration.

Moreover, their feelings and experiences are shared with others. Collectively they respond to this stressful situation by turning the middle-class measuring rod on its head, and giving status to the values and activities that are the very opposite of those sponsored by the educational system. A delinquent subculture is the outcome of this "reaction-formation" and is characterized by gang activities that are expressive (rather than instrumental), malicious, and negativistic—vandalism, assaults on people and property, and so on.

Although their aggressive and destructive behaviour might appear senseless to others, to the working-class boys who participate, it is a powerful way of hitting back at a system that has done them no favours. The delinquent subculture is therefore, a solution—an imperfect and short-term one perhaps, but a solution nevertheless—to the status problems confronting working-class youth.

The broad sweep of Cohen's formulation has made him an easy target for the critics. Two basic flaws have been identified. First, by explaining both the origins and content of delinquent subcultures as an inversion of prevailing middle-class goals and standards, Cohen glosses over the similarities between delinquency and ordinary working-class adult cultural patterns. Second, he exaggerates the differences between the values and behaviours of working-class gang members and non-delinquent adolescents.

The first of these defects was explored by W. B. Miller (1958). On the basis of his extensive field work with youth gangs in Boston, Miller concluded that much ostensibly delinquent behaviour is not noticeably different in spirit or kind from working-class adult cultural activities. He sees delinquency as being little more than an intensified version of focal concerns—toughness, excitement, fate, trouble, smartness—common to different age groups in working-class communities. According to this argument, merely conforming to value configurations and behavioural dictates shared with the parent generation is enough to bring working-class adolescents into conflict with law enforcement officers and other representatives of middle-class respectability, such as teachers and social workers. Where Cohen construes delinquency as a collective reaction against middle-class values and status concerns, Miller sees it as a youthful extension of established working-class adult cultural patterns.

However, in correcting the first design fault in Cohen's model, Miller ends up reinventing the second one. Whether group delinquency is a reaction to middle-class culture (Cohen) or a continuation of working-class adult cultural concerns (Miller), both approaches fail to explain the varied response of working-class adolescents to delinquency-inducing situations and conditions. As sociology's critics are fond of pointing out, not all working-class boys join delinquent gangs.

A third variant of strain theory, combining elements from both Merton and Cohen's conceptualizations, has tried to resolve this issue. Focusing less upon the high school than Cohen, Cloward and Ohlin (1960) argue that in addition to deviant motivations, working-class adolescents need access to deviant opportunities if they are to become successful participants in subcultural activities. They suggest that whereas all young working-class males may be under pressure to innovate, as Merton supposes, they do not share the same opportunity to do so. Those who have the chance to interact with, and learn from, adult thieves will involve themselves in property crime. In contrast, those denied access to the appropriate networks of criminal enterprise will join "fighting gangs"—but only if they have the proper entry requirements: toughness, combat skills, and so on. Those who lack qualifications for both conventional and criminal careers—the double failures in Cloward and Ohlin's terms—will gravitate toward drug-based subcultures (the "retreatists" in Merton's typology). Moreover, because deviant opportunities vary by neighbourhood, different working-class communities throw up distinctive sorts of subcultural gang activity based variously on thieving, fighting, or drug use.

But in focusing upon the relationship between delinquency and opportunity, Cloward and Ohlin pay (much) less attention to the question of conformity in high-crime areas. Why is it that a considerable number of adolescents who grow up in working-class neighbourhoods avoid serious subcultural involvements of any kind?

This issue has become something of an Achilles heel for subcultural approaches to delinquency. Because the various theories provide ample reasons why working-class adolescents should become delinquent, they encounter considerable difficulty in explaining why more of them do not do so. The theories end up, in other words, predicting more delinquency than actually occurs.

In countering what he saw as the determinism of subcultural theory, David Matza (1964) proposed a different formulation. He argues that most working-class adolescents—including those who engage in delinquency—are far from committed to deviant belief systems or oppositional activities. Their enduring sensitivity to conventional values is revealed, for instance, in expressions of guilt about wrongdoing, and in the highly episodic and selective nature of their delinquent acts; delinquency is not the full-time alternative career for working-class boys that theorists like Cohen suggest. In order to justify breaking the rules, they have to make use of what Matza refers to as "techniques of neutralization." For example, like other members of society, delinquents in principle condemn interpersonal violence—they would agree that hitting people is wrong—and defend their own racial attacks or assaults on homosexuals as self-defence against "outsiders" who have invaded their territory or space. According to Matza, delinquents are adolescents who have learned deviant justifications rather than deviant values or motivations. Rather than being forced into delinquency by social circumstance, they drift into it.

How then does Matza explain the indisputable fact that adolescents are more inclined to (certain kinds of) law-breaking than adults? His answer is that adolescents are preoccupied with fun, excitement, and risk-taking, and that leisure values underpin the style and spirit of much delinquent behaviour. Delinquency is thus the unintended outcome of a search for the sorts of hedonistic pleasures that have been expressed in contemporary terms, by the late Ian Dury, as "sex and drugs and rock and roll." As Matza puts it, "Adolescents in general and delinquents in particular [are] members of the last leisure class" (Matza and Sykes, 1961). Compared to adults, who know when and where to indulge their recreational values—New Year's Eve, summer vacations—and when to hold them in abeyance, adolescents are less discriminating and more single-minded in their pursuit of hedonistic risk-oriented leisure activities. Collectively, therefore, their crime is largely a matter of "bad timing" (Matza and Sykes, 1961, p. 716). Delinquency stands, not as a challenge to the social fabric of society, but as a "disturbing reflection or caricature of it" (p. 717).

Not only does Matza's work represent a partial break with traditional subcultural theory, it also makes clear that delinquency is often the result of an interaction between adolescents engaging in some behaviour and the reaction of others to that behaviour—the main theme of the opening chapter. In this sense, Matza's ideas might be seen as linking the behavioural and definitional concerns of American delinquency theory. It is the visible presence of adolescents on the streets and in shopping malls, their preference for risk-taking, and their interest in leisure that gets them noticed and provokes a response by the police, shopkeepers, ordinary citizens, and the mass media. The nature and quality of symbolic interactions between adolescents and the broader community is central to what has become known as "labelling theory."

The concerns of labelling theory closely parallel those of the constructionist approach to social problems outlined in the opening chapter and, as such, emphasize not the causes of delinquent behaviour but the consequences of defining that behaviour as deviant or delinquent. The assumption is that designating some behaviours or individuals as deviant increases the prospects for more of the same. This is the process described by Howard Becker as "deviancy amplification" (1963).

According to this argument, labelling a clique of males a "gang" because they are wearing skinhead garb (or backward-facing baseball caps) or routinely pulling over black drivers of expensive sports cars undermines respect for the police and the principles of law and order and makes serious deviant activity that much more likely. Regardless of the reasons clique members had for seeking out subcultural activities in the first place, these reasons will only be intensified by the critical attentions of the community. You will notice that it is this part of the labelling argument that inspired Stanley Cohen's study of the mods and rockers and underpins many of the discussions about youth and moral panics. Labelling theory has also had its part to play in the development of newer British approaches to the study of deviant youth cultures that have focused upon, for instance, the meaning of skinhead or punk styles. Ironically, in the case of the latter subcultural adaptation, the labelling perspective has influenced the interpretations that the more self-reflective punks have made of their own actions.

Labelling theory is, of course, not without its critics. First, research has not always supported its assumptions about the relationship between behaviours and labels (Gove, 1975; Hirschi, 1975). In particular, it has been found that the problematic behaviour of adolescents sometimes precedes the application of a deviant label and is therefore a cause of that label rather than a consequence of it. Second, there are undoubtedly some adolescents who, as a result of their contacts with police officers, are deterred from further wrongdoing. Rather than setting them on a course of more frequent and serious deviant activity, getting apprehended by, and a dressing-down from, police officers discourages them from future involvement in deviant activities. Third, labelling theory is predicated on a view of the deviant adolescent as the innocent recipient not only of a damaging label, but a passive one as well (Bordua, 1969). This depiction of the deviant as a passive victim does not always fit easily with either the image of the glamorous rebel found in subcultural theory or real life, where it is often the case that rebellious adolescents deliberately affect a style that invites a censorious response from the authorities.

However, if one part of Matza's legacy is a growing integration of the traditional subcultural concern with behaviour and labelling theory's emphasis on society's response, a second aspect of it is that his ideas have contributed to a decline—only recently reversed—of interest in subcultural theory and research in the United States during the 1960s and 1970s. His concern to show that delinquency is not obligatory, that even the most disadvantaged adolescents drift into it rather more often than they are driven into it, and that delinquency is an intermittent activity, rather than a constant one, complemented findings from other research that was at odds with the key precepts of the subcultural paradigm.

Subcultural theory has been nonetheless influential in inspiring both past and present research on collective deviance and delinquency. For example, several studies of motorcycle gangs have produced findings that are consistent with the ideas, variously, of W. B. Miller and Albert Cohen (Thompson, 1967; Montgomery, 1976, 1977; Watson, 1980). In fact, the most recent of these is a Canadian ethnographic investigation of an Edmonton-based motorcycle club, the Rebels, with whom researcher Daniel Wolf rode for a period of time (Wolf, 1991).

The Rebels are an outlaw motorcycle club. Outlaw motorcycle groups originated on the West Coast of the United States just after the Second World War. They are defined—officially—as outlaw clubs because they do not seek registration with either the American or the Canadian Motorcycle Association. Unregistered clubs—"the outlaws"—are viewed as the 1 percent deviant fringe responsible for the poor public image of bike gangs. Bikers have, in turn, usurped this deviant designation by, literally, wearing the 1 percent label as a badge—a badge of rebellion.

Media reaction helped create the image of the deviant bike gang.[2] On July 4, 1949, the world's first motorcycle riot took place in Hollister, California. The event—which lasted 36 hours and involved 2500 bikers affiliated with the official AMA and 500 non-affiliated bikers—was given national exposure in *Life* magazine. Another article, based on *Life*'s largely pictorial account of the incident, was published in *Harper's* magazine, where it was read by filmmaker Stanley Kramer. Kramer used it as the basis for his movie *The Wild One,* starring Marlon Brando and Lee Marvin (Wolf, 1991), and his cinematic rendition of the incident in Hollister has become the main, if not only, source of public information and imagery about bike gangs.[3]

Although the mass media was not responsible for the original event, its coverage ensured that a local event become a national, and later an international, one. More importantly it supplied the world with the enduring image of the motorcyclist as folk devil. Since *The Wild One* was first released, in 1953 (and banned in both Britain and New Zealand), the motorcycle and leather jacket (along with blue denim) have become essential ingredients of young, male, working-class rebellion everywhere. Indeed, this rebel style was basic to the stage persona of Rob Halford, lead singer of Judas Priest (a now-defunct heavy metal band) and one of the newer breed of folk devils. It is precisely the outlaw image of the motorcycle gang that, according to Wolf, makes it attractive to young working-class males. Becoming a biker is about a search for identity. Membership in a bike gang offers a meaningful lifestyle to working-class males who would otherwise find the world an inhospitable and alienating place, and who get no satisfaction from the unskilled labouring jobs available to them. As he puts it, "if the labourer is a young male in search of himself, he will find nothing in his self-image at work that will excite them; he had best look elsewhere. Men who are chained to their circumstances share a compelling desire to escape" (Wolf, 1991, p. 31).

The "escape hatch" for an individual in this predicament comes in his non-work time. It is in his leisure hours that he creates a more authentic identity for himself that revolves around motorcycles: more specifically, Harley-Davidson motorcycles.

Outlaw bike gangs are a form of subcultural solution because they serve the psychic needs of their members. At the same time, Wolf recognizes that, for all its distinctiveness, the bike gang is not very different from other types of street culture found in working-class neighbourhoods. They are all characterized by heavy drinking, risk-taking, and sexual exploitation. Membership in an outlaw bike gang is simply a more exotic version of the time-worn search for "independence, freedom, self-reliance, toughness, impulsiveness and masculinity, all of which will be embodied in a highly romanticized image of the anti-hero" (Wolf, 1991, p. 33).

Wolf, of course, was focusing upon a group that has been repeatedly and publicly defined as deviant, and is attractive to some alienated youth for that very reason. Researchers like Matza, however, would doubtless argue that the rebellious attitudes and behaviour displayed by bike gangs are not common, even among working-class male youth. Skepticism about the oppositional commitments of other delinquent subcultures in the 1960s was only reinforced by research projects that documented that the gap between what various theories predicted and what delinquent adolescents actually thought and did was frequently a large one.

For instance, interest in gangs began to dwindle when it was found that they were less well organized, less cohesive, and more fluid in their membership than subcultural theory implied (Yablonsky, 1962; Felson, 1998). Likewise, extensive research on Chicago street gangs by Short and Strodtbeck (1965) found little evidence of the delinquent specialization outlined by Cloward and Ohlin (1960). Instead, most gangs involved themselves in a range of criminal pursuits, rather than limiting themselves to just thieving, fighting, or drugs.

Similar findings were reported by Spergel (1964) in his examination of the nature of delinquency in three high-crime areas. Spergel found little evidence to suggest that different neighbourhoods were characterized by distinct types of subcultural activity. Instead, he found elements of each subculture represented in all the neighbourhoods. Nonetheless, despite the apparent failure to confirm the Cloward and Ohlin thesis, more recent research (to be examined in Chapter 5) has shown that the structural and cultural characteristics of different communities within proximate geographical areas does influence patterns of inner-city youth crime. Individual variation in criminality within delinquent areas remains, however, an uncomfortable fact for subcultural theory to explain.

More generally, it is the conceptualization of delinquent subcultures as an expression of collective opposition to dominant middle-class goals, values, and institutions that has been most seriously damaged by empirical research. Field researchers have been unable to confirm the idea that street gangs are unambiguously motivated by a collective need to reject middle-class goals and lifestyles, and quantitative researchers could not consistently document evidence of rebellious values in their surveys (Braithwaite, 1989).

Likewise, if subcultural activity is inspired by an opposition to middle-class belief systems, why is it that adult members of the working class are no more supportive of crime in their communities than are the residents of more prosperous ones? Furthermore, most working-class delinquents do not grow up to become adult criminals; on the contrary, delinquency declines with age—a fact not easily explained by theories driven by assumptions of enduring conflict with middle-class goals. Finally, findings from survey research seemingly disproved a notion that had been fundamental to the sociological approach to delinquency since the 1920s: namely, that regardless of whatever else it might be, delinquency was, in the final analysis, a class-based phenomenon.

In the 1960s self-report techniques were developed as an alternative means of collecting information about delinquent behaviour. The findings from self-report studies indicated that delinquency was more common among middle-class adolescents than was revealed by official police and court data. In the process of discovering hitherto hidden middle-class delinquents, survey researchers were seemingly denying the existence of an inverse relationship between class and delinquency. The fact that delinquency was apparently no longer the exclusive domain of deprived and disadvantaged working-class adolescents living in inner-city neighbourhoods, but also attracted middle-class kids from the suburbs, discouraged criminologists from pursuing the connections between class and criminality. Persuaded that delinquency had become a classless phenomenon, they abandoned the search for its causes in macro-structural and cultural factors and focused instead upon its more micro-social psychological antecedents (Sullivan, 1989).

The initial result was "control theory," which is an approach to delinquency causation that focuses upon the social and psychological ties that bind adolescents of all class and racial backgrounds to the dominant, normative order. Over the past thirty years it has become the vogue explanation in criminology. Although control theory has a long history and is associated with a number of theorists, its most prominent contemporary exponent is Travis Hirschi (1969). Hirschi argues that no special theory of delinquent motivation is required because a taste for deviant behaviour is something that human beings come by naturally: if allowed to follow our natural instincts, all of us would participate regularly in rule-breaking behaviour.

Of course, most of us, most of the time, are not inclined to break the rules, and the question is why. The answer given by control theory is that our deviant urges are more than tempered by the fact that most of us have developed bonds or ties to society and consequently are more regularly inclined to conformity than deviance. Those whose bonds to society are broken, or were never very strong in the first place, will commit more deviance. In the language of the control theorists, they are now free to deviate. But most of us are not in this situation since "we have loved ones we fear to hurt and physical possessions and social reputations we fear to lose" (Box, 1981, p. 122).

Hirschi argues that individuals are either encouraged to deviate or deterred from doing so on the basis of the strengths of various affective and emotional bonds that they have to society. He identifies four elements as making up the social bond: attachment, commitment, involvement, and belief. The stronger the bond that a person has to society, the less likely he or she is to become involved in deviant activities.

Attachment refers to the emotional contacts that we have developed with parents and friends whose opinions and evaluations of ourselves we value. *Commitment* concerns the investments—in time, money, and effort—that we have made with regard to conformist behaviour. Our investment in conformity is potentially jeopardized by excursions into deviant activity. *Involvement* is about participation in conventional pursuits: in school, for instance, it includes joining sports teams and the debating society rather than smoking behind the bicycle sheds, or attending the math class rather than visiting the shopping mall. *Belief* refers to the endorsement of pro-social values supported by parents, teachers, and friends.

Like virtually all noteworthy sociological theories of crime and deviancy, control theory was first developed in connection with adolescents. Hirschi tested out his ideas with black and white male high school students in Richmond, California. Confirmed and validated in the course of a number of replications, control theory enjoys a very solid reputation in the criminological community. There is little doubt that it provides a reliable and valid account of minor deviance, committed by ordinary adolescents. However, it is less useful when more serious, collectivistic deviancy is under the microscope.

The limitations of control theory stem from the assumption that deviant behaviour requires no special motivation—all that is needed is a weakening of the ties that bind individuals to the conventional normative order. This portrayal of adolescent deviance is plausible when the offences in question are trivial (and common), when pleasure-seeking and risk-taking are sufficient inducements to break the rules. But it is less credible when more serious gang delinquency, involving aggression and violence, is considered. Moreover, serious subcultural delinquency is inclined to be repetitive, whereas control theory is mainly concerned with occasional bouts of primary deviance that have not been responded to in the stigmatizing ways described by labelling theorists (Box, 1981, p. 121). Something more than unrestrained natural impulses or unchecked teenage exuberance is required to explain more serious and systematic patterns of deviant activity.

In particular, control theory fails to explain why it is that the ties that bind are so closely related to existing class and racial divisions in society—a pattern that suggests that bonding is rooted in common structural and cultural experiences as well as individual ones. Similarly, it ignores the collective nature and meaning of delinquency. It is worth reminding ourselves that what alarms ordinary people is not occasional acts of theft or vandalism, but those deviant activities that take the form of a "collective conspiracy" (Box, 1981, p. 131). In the British context in which Box was writing, this means the predatory behaviour of skinheads, football hooligans, and so forth. Substitute North American examples (youth gangs, rappers, swarming) for British ones and the argument remains much the same: these deviant group actions are not easily explained by the "situational" and "subjective" bonds that are the stock in trade of control theory.

For example, the young blacks who looted and robbed in Los Angeles after the police officers accused of brutalizing Rodney King were originally acquitted could be conceptualized as lacking commitment to the conventional normative order. Yet, this argument would ignore more fundamental questions, such as why the rioters felt they had so little stake in conformity in the first place or why they shared the same racial background and social experiences. As Box points out, prioritizing the immediate social ties of adolescents strips deviant activities of their cultural context. Instead of viewing the riots as a product of numerous weak ties, they could be seen as a collective reaction to shared problems of poverty, unemployment, and racial injustice.

In making this argument I am not suggesting that the participants in the riots are necessarily able or willing to fully articulate their motivation, nor am I proposing that their chosen solution was a good one or that innocent people were not hurt by their actions. What I am saying is that collective action of that sort is never going to be fully understood by explanatory concepts that fail to take full account of broader social and cultural influences on deviance.

Similarly, it is all very well to argue that because of weak social bonds kids spend their evening out on the street and their routine activities in bars and shopping malls get them into trouble. But again, this begs the question as to why they are not at home with, and under the control of, their parents more regularly. The routine activities of some adolescents undoubtedly contribute to delinquency, but this observation in and of itself does not explain why some youth develop or construct the sort of lifestyle that brings them, as either offenders or victims, into deviant environments and situations.

More recently, control theory has evolved into self-control theory. Working with Gottfredson, Hirschi now argues that the criminal ranks are overpopulated by people with low self-control; that is, people who have, variously, failed to study hard in school, are short-tempered, are easily tempted, and so forth. Hence, they get into all kinds of trouble, not all of it actually against the law. Those of us who become criminals are thus also more likely to be reckless drivers, destructive drinkers, and heavy smokers and to embroil ourselves in volatile social relationships. And all of this can be traced back to early childhood, when parents failed to teach us important lessons of self-control. The trait of low self-control is therefore the general cause of all crime and deviance (Gottfredson and Hirschi, 1990).

Now, these observations about the life-long importance of self-control do not strike me as unreasonable or even particularly remarkable. But, as with control theory, this approach fails to emphasize the structural factors responsible for the failed development of self-control, or to explain why the distribution of that trait seems to correspond so closely to the distribution of economic, social, and cultural capital in society. Poverty and unemployment, for instance, undoubtedly undermine the ability of parents to teach their children the virtue of self-control. Thus while a lack of self-control might be the immediate cause of any and all antisocial behaviour, this does not explain why this trait is more likely to be absent in some parts of the population than others.

These critical comments are not meant to imply that aspects of control and self-control theory cannot be incorporated into more structural accounts of delinquency. As will be seen in Chapter 5, sociologists have begun to explore the connections between school and family-related bonds and subsequent involvements in subcultural delinquency. These micro-structural variables emerge as significant intervening factors in the causal chain that links social class to serious subcultural delinquency.

What these attempts at integration (of types of theory and levels of explanation) have in common is a growing recognition that criminologists have to account for both the macro- and micro-determinants of delinquent behaviour. They have to explain, for example, why serious delinquency is more character-istic of some subgroups or populations than others and why one individual rather than another commits a delinquent act (Messner, Krohn, and Liska, 1989; Short, 1989).

In any event, it is unlikely that the sort of serious subcultural deviance exemplified by the Los Angeles riots has ever vanished from the urban American landscape. The fact that street gangs disappeared from view in the 1970s and 1980s probably says more about the spread of self-report surveys (the findings from which were a considerable driving force behind the development of control theory) than it does about the declining significance of such groups in American society. As was discussed in Chapter 2, self-report instruments are mainly used in school settings, where the most seriously alienated and recalcitrant youth are unlikely to be found. Self-report surveys therefore rarely reach seriously deviant youth populations. This limitation becomes more perti-nent when it is realized that changing economic conditions and patterns of work and employment are responsible for pockets of increasingly serious subcultural activity among contemporary youth. American sociologists are therefore turning, once again, to more structural accounts of criminality in order to make sense of the connections between youth crime and homelessness, economic decay and the development of an urban underclass. Once again, explanations for seriously antisocial behaviour are sought in the flawed characteristics of society rather than in the personal defects of its individual members (Messner and Rosenfeld, 1994, 14–15).

British Subcultural Theory: Style into Revolt?

Ironically, at just about the same time in the late 1960s that American criminologists were declaring subcultural theory dead and buried, it was enjoying something of a resurgence on the other side of the Atlantic.

Since the Second World War, Britain has produced a number of deviant—if not necessarily delinquent—youth subcultures. The most important of these, the mods, skinheads, and punks (as well as the more obviously violent and aggressive football hooligans) have received significant international media attention.

Beginning with the "Teddy boys" in the early 1950s, all of those subcultural groupings have been characterized—indeed, even defined—in terms of their distinctive clothing styles, haircuts, and musical preferences. For all the differences between them—differences that, in the mid-1960s led to pitched battles between the mods and rockers on English beaches—these deviant youth groups have in common a public display of style that has shocked, offended, and threatened many adult members of society.

Nonetheless, "American-style" crime and delinquency has rarely been the defining characteristic of these British working-class youth groups. Instead, leisure and distinctive leisure styles have been at the forefront of youth subcultures in the United Kingdom.

An early application of this focus was provided by David Downes (1966) in his ethnographic study of male working-class youth in the East End of London. Collective delinquency was the result not of frustrated occupational ambitions but, instead, of an inability to achieve more important (from the boys' perspective) leisure goals. Leisure was the site of their putative subcultural solution; when leisure ambitions were thwarted (because, for instance, they could ill-afford scooters, motorbikes, and records) they drifted (cf. Matza) into delinquency.

As was noted in the opening chapter, leisure—particularly commercial leisure—is commonly seen as a corrupter of youth and as such a potent cause of delinquency. In this approach, the focus is upon what leisure does to adolescents. However, it is possible to reverse this sequence and examine what young people do with their leisure and how this is related to school and work experiences. This reversal is central to a body of work that has focused on subcultural activity among working-class adolescents in the United Kingdom. What has become known as the Birmingham School (because it was located at the University of Birmingham's Centre for Contemporary Cultural Studies) argues that various aspects of youth leisure—in particular, music, clothes, and hairstyles—are used by disenfranchised working-class youth to contest or resist the class-based inequalities and injustices that confront them in everyday life. According to this argument, leisure becomes an important site for youthful revolt or "resistance."

In making sense of the expressive deviancy of working-class youth groups, the Birmingham School turned, in the first instance, to the classic American subcultural formulation of A. K. Cohen and, to a lesser degree, labelling theory. Their starting point, therefore, was the now familiar argument that the successive waves of Teddy boys, mods, rockers, skinheads, and punks were, by their behaviour and appearance, attempting to collectively solve problems encountered at school, at work, or on the streets.

However, ideas drawn from Marxism were also quickly incorporated into the basic American formula, particularly an emphasis upon class and class conflict. No longer were deprived and disadvantaged working-class adolescents just adapting to their social environment, they were challenging it in a fundamentally political way. In the words of Stanley Cohen, "the delinquent changed from 'frustrated social climber' to cultural innovator and critic" (1980, p. iv). Skinheads, mods, punks, and all the rest are depicted as resisting the dominant normative order and its major institutions—schools, police, employers. Leisure is the chosen site of resistance and style—the clothes, the haircuts, music that shocks and offends—its main weapon. Style, in other words, has become a form of revolt.

The British subcultural theorists are therefore primarily concerned with symbolic behaviour—understanding the meaning of green hair, shaved heads, swastika emblems, and other elements of style. Their emphasis is upon expressive, rather than economic (or "instrumental") deviance, and this emphasis influences how they view the problem-solving functions of youth subcultures.

Both American delinquency theory and British subcultural theory agree that problems facing working-class adolescents inspire the formation of, and recruitment to, deviant and delinquent subcultures. In Albert Cohen's version of strain theory, working-class youth collectively react against goals they cannot reach and standards they cannot achieve, and give status to those within their grasp. In British subcultural theory, deviant styles are not mere inversions of bourgeois values, they are self-conscious attempts to dramatize and resolve their marginalized status in class society. Thus, although listening to thrash metal or wearing Doc Marten boots is not going to solve any real problems (such as difficulties with teachers or finding a job), doing so might help young people to feel better about themselves and provide them with a more positive alternative identity.

SKINHEADS AND PUNKS

How has this argument been applied to specific youth groups? We will begin with skinheads, depicted by the Birmingham School as champions of traditional working-class interests, defenders of a cultural community threatened by unwanted social change. Their street style—work clothes and boots ("Bovver boots"), "half-mast" jeans (with suspenders), and short-cropped hair (hence their name)—is read as a self-conscious reflection of proletarian roots. Their dress code is also taken as disdainful rejection of that other highly visible youth subculture of the same era: the hippies. Skinheads, as value carriers of working-class Puritanism, were offended by the hippies' middle-class softness and effeminacy (signified by shoulder-length hair and kaftans), as well as their penchance for "underground" rock music (P. Cohen, 1972; Brake, 1985). The other main source of case study material for the Birmingham theorists are the punks. The punk subculture first emerged in the mid-1970s and was similarly understood as an expressively resistant class-based youth movement, born out of specific socioeconomic circumstances in Britain, particularly rising rates of youth unemployment.

Although all young people, and indeed many adults, are vulnerable to its ravages, unemployment cut deepest into the life conditions of the unskilled, unqualified, working-class young who largely were denied access to the material and non-material rewards of work. Punk is thus construed as a spontaneous response within this constituency to a situation of diminished life chances and, in particular, work opportunities.

What is especially interesting about punk and what certainly distinguishes it from earlier generations of skinhead and mod deviance is its degree of self-consciousness. Through fanzines (magazines for fans) like *Sniffin Glue,* the punk vanguard analyzed events more or less as they occurred. Moreover, their interpretation of what happened on the street closely paralleled the sociological viewpoint. Punk ideologists, like the sociologists, believed that their revolt was rooted in the dramatically changed nature of employment prospects for youth in England. This belief affected both how most punks saw themselves and their attitude toward the rest of society.

In essence, the punks were saying, If society deems us expendable and, by extension, worthless, then we shall make sure that we confirm every one of their worst fears; we shall make ourselves as unemployable and disreputable as possible; our ability to cause shock and outrage will be its own reward.

This ideology was central to the punk mandate. Its success as a deviant subculture was largely attributable to its ability to receive the kind of reaction—from politicians and the media—that its style and gesture provoked. Without an audience to define punk in the most morally pejorative terms possible, it would have been a nonstarter as a rebellious youth cult (Everett, 1986). Indeed, punk was born and performed with an audience in mind (Kanter, 1977, p. 215).

Punk's desire and capacity to offend did not escape the notice of its subcultural interpreters, who have offered a commentary on punk fashion that clearly owes much to traditional American subcultural theory, particularly Albert Cohen's theory of gang delinquency. The difference, however, is that the British subculturalists tend—as we have already noted—to interpret teenage defiance as political gesture. The punk dress code thus not only spurned conventional notions of fashion but also subverted them. It made objects such as garbage bags, razor blades, and safety pins symbols of revolt. The overapplication of make-up by young women undermined orthodox notions of femininity and hair dyed every conceivable colour does not conform to expectations of what the well-coifed head should look like. Sometimes the elements of revolt were made more explicit, as with the desecration of the school uniform. As Dick Hebdige put it, "The punks wore clothes that were the sartorial equivalent of swear words" (1979, p. 114).

Musically, punk has been read, on the one hand, as a return to the classic simplicity and amateurish enthusiasm of early rock and roll—an incisive reminder, with its jack-hammer beat, that the electric guitar is the modus operandi of rock music. On the other hand, punk music was different from its predecessors. First, it was sometimes overtly political, in that it dealt with issues germane to the young (e.g., the Clash's "Career Opportunities"). Second, and more importantly, it deliberately courted bad taste and notoriety via controversial themes, song titles, and group names. The Sex Pistols (under the astute management of their Svengali, Malcolm McLaren) were the ultimate practitioners of this art. Their first single, "God Save the Queen," released in Jubilee year, was banned by the BBC, which resulted in the record reaching the number two spot in the British "Top 20" chart. Similarly, it seems reasonable to suppose that the American punk band the Dead Kennedys was no less offensive to most adult Americans, particularly when it released a song with the title "Too Drunk to Fuck."

From the perspective of the new subcultural theorists, the fashions and music of youth culture are, in Dick Hebdige's phrase, "pregnant with significance." Given this starting point, it is not all surprising to find punk's revolting style and abrasive music interpreted as a "challenge to hegemony ... expressed obliquely" (Hebdige, 1979, p. 17). Distinctive music, clothing, and dance communicated a coded statement about growing up in a time and place that offered "no future."

YOUTH CULTURE AS RESISTANCE: A CRITIQUE

Punk, like all the deviant working-class youth cultures before it, is thus treated as a veiled expression of political deviance—class war by other means. However, the subculturalists who advance this argument do so recognizing its limitations. In particular, they acknowledge that both the defiance offered and the solutions sought and found are only partial and temporary.

First of all, the punk subculture was firmly and irrevocably rooted in style: revolt took place in leisure and consumption rather than at school or work. Collective problems were not directly confronted in those arenas where they were primarily encountered; they were dealt with symbolically in non-school/non-work time. This considerably muted the challenge offered to the dominant normative order that was only symbolically confronted. The subcultural solution was based in leisure rather than where the root of the problem lay—at school, at work, and in the unemployment line.

In the same way, other problems flowed from punk's basis in consumption, particularly commercial leisure activities. The most visible features of punk culture were bought and sold in the teenage marketplace; that is, they were available to all adolescents who could afford them, regardless of whether their personal life circumstances warranted involvement in a problem-solving youth culture. This created a quite specific and predictable shortcoming. Many of the punk artifacts, notably fashion and music, were consumed and enjoyed by non-deviant youth. It becomes difficult to interpret (in an unambiguous way) youth culture as symbolic resistance to schooling, work, and unemployment when the artifacts central to this culture are not, and cannot be, the monopoly of those individuals faced with the most formidable school and employment problems. Thus, the scope of revolt rooted in style is strictly limited because of the ability of the teenage entertainment industry to incorporate and emasculate oppositional symbols, to turn "revolt into style" (Melly, 1970).

Commercial reaction to youth culture "attempts to universalize, at a purely stylistic and consumptional level, the innovations made by distinctive 'youth cultures,' while simultaneously defining the oppositional potential of the exclusive lifestyles" (Clarke and Jefferson, 1976, p. 157).

This problem is particularly pronounced in Canada, where many of the distinctive youth cultural styles are imports—often from the United Kingdom. It is hard to read punk as a deviant working-class youth culture spawned by disadvantage when it is spotted in the affluent suburbs of Toronto.

Punk's legitimacy as a subcultural solution clearly rests upon the argument that its adherents have been drawn from the ranks of the working-class young—that section of the youth population most likely to be collectively facing problems at school or in the labour market. Informal observation suggests that these propositions are not well supported in Canada: punk seems to have been every bit as attractive to the middle-class young as it was to the working-class young. Doubt about the working-class basis of punk opens up the possibility that, rather than being part of a solidly proletarian youth tradition, punk might more usefully be interpreted as a "hard" form of bohemianism (cf. Matza, 1961), recruiting from the ranks of the culturally adventurous of both the working and the middle classes (Frith, 1978b). Punk, particularly in Canada, appears to have been a lifestyle chosen by its followers rather than one that they were forced into because of a lack of economic opportunities. This voluntary element weakens subcultural theorists' reading of punk as a working-class youth culture.

Punk can also be used to illustrate broader problems with British subcultural theory. The preoccupation with resistance causes theorists to concentrate on the most visible and spectacular aspects of youthful rule-breaking. Two problems ensue from this focus. First, it divides the adolescent population into deviants (the minority) and non-deviants (the majority) and assumes that those most involved in youth culture are most committed to deviant roles and careers. The fatal flaw in this conceptualization is that the elements of teenage style—the clothes, the music, the hair—might, as I have implied, be false indicators of deviance and resistance. Those adolescents who seem most committed to a deviant youth culture— as reflected in their willingness to embrace the symbolic accoutrements—are also the individuals displaying the greatest eagerness to jettison those artifacts and replace them with others when another trend appears on the horizon. What we are dealing with, then, are cycles of fashion rather than deviant lifestyles. The overwillingness to interpret style as cultural resistance neglects the purely faddish character of much teenage behaviour.

Adolescent lives are not as firmly anchored in these styles as the subcultural theorists would have us believe. Involvement in different groups does not necessarily betoken any underlying commitment to them. Membership is fairly transitory and, over the course of time, many adolescents take on and discard the cultural trappings of many different youth cultures (Frith, 1978a). This process seems to be accelerating with more recent youth cultures, such as "rave." Both Thornton (1995) and Weber (1999) emphasize that by age twenty-five most "ravers" have abandoned their commitment to the scene and have moved on to more "adult" pursuits. Second, the concern with high-profile youth culture style overlooks the fact that is not of this attention-grabbing type. As was documented in Chapter 2, the bulk of youthful deviance involves relatively minor property crimes.

Ironically, for all their concerns about media coverage of youth, the Birmingham School has shown a marked tendency to use the same media sources for their own theoretical interpretations. Thus they are able to present skinheads and punks as resistant youth groups because media accounts emphasize the same threatening qualities in their appearance and behaviour. At the same time as media stories give voice to fears about violent youth crime, they also overstate the amount of rebellion by the youth groups in question. The targeting of spectacular deviance has the effect of exaggerating the scope, strength, and significance of the threat posed and resistance offered by members of deviant youth cultures (Frith, 1985).

Moreover, considering that most working-class adolescents do not enter the most spectacular peer cultures, we might have expected the British subcultural theorists to devote more of their energies to explaining the pattern of differential involvement in youth culture. The problem is a quite simple one and was earlier faced by American theorists of gang delinquency: Why do some adolescents become gang members or punks when others, whose lives are dominated by much the same kind of experiences and institutions, do not? The fact is that attendance at roughly similar types of schools and entry into the same labour market produces different responses from young people, not all of which are deviant, let alone coded forms of political rebellion. Subcultural theorists provide few clues as to what the factors determining the pattern of differential involvement might be.

These difficulties arise because of the strategy of first identifying deviant youth groups and then working backward to uncover group members' class roots and experiences in school and in and out of work. The chosen style is then declared to be a "solution," albeit tentative, partial, and imaginary, to the subordinate position in society of working-class adolescents. However, if the process is reversed—if class location and school and work situation are taken as a starting point—then a much wider spectrum of leisure styles and activities is discovered, and a much looser fit between class base and the symbols of youthful resistance is revealed (Murdock and McCron, 1976).

This problem is then compounded because the signs and symbols of expressive youth deviance require interpretation. Whereas the meaning of much economic crime or instrumental delinquency is (relatively) straightforward—it is reasonable to assume that street kids steal because they are hungry and homeless—it is considerably more difficult to interpret patterns of deviance that rely on symbolic expression or style. Just how should green hair be interpreted? What is the significance of Doc Marten work boots, suspenders, and close-cropped hair for skinheads? Take the use of the swastika in the punk ensemble as an example. How should this be understood? There are, in fact, a number of possible interpretations:

1. Its popularity with the punks could signify that punks are fascists, and that it is therefore used by them as a celebration of fascism.

2. It could be that punks are anti-fascists who display the swastika in order to shock and offend the bourgeoisie; it is worn, in other words, for its ironic effect.

3. Punks may simply be conforming to peer group norms about what is currently fashionable and have no interest in politics whatsoever (Cohen, 1980; Leong, 1992).

As you might have guessed, subcultural theorists tend toward the second option. It is the only one consistent with their prior *theoretical* assumptions about punk. However, they provide no *empirical* justification for choosing this interpretation over the other two. This, of course, leaves them open to the accusation that they have projected their own political convictions onto punk culture—they want to believe that punks are political rebels—and read into it motivations that the participants do not intend or perhaps even recognize (unless, of course, they have taken a course in deviancy or "cultural studies" at the local university [Frith, 1985]). Resistance theorists want to believe that punks are engaging in a symbolic form of class politics.

Nowhere is this tendency more apparent than in the treatment of violent criminal activity. For British subcultural theorists, it is axiomatic that, as far as the young are concerned, the main division in capitalist society is between the dominant class interests (of school, employers, the police, the juvenile court) and youthful working-class resisters. According to this argument, it could be anticipated that most skirmishes in which working-class youth are involved would be between themselves and the adult representatives of middle-class authority. However, the available evidence suggests that adolescents primarily victimize other adolescents (see Chapter 2). Thus, a shared class location has not precluded rockers and mods attacking each other (Cohen, 1980) or rockers attacking skinheads or skinheads attacking punks (Baron, 1989b).

The willingness to construe subcultural activity in terms of class politics, as opposition and resistance, has other effects as well, notably a tendency to romanticize violence and aggression; for example, the way in which skinhead behaviour has been interpreted. There has been a pronounced tendency to argue that appearances are deceiving and that skinhead attacks on Asians in Britain cannot just be understood in racial terms. Geoffrey Pearson (1976), for instance, prefers to explain "Paki-bashing" as a "primitive form of political and economic struggle," an example of "resistance from below": that is "really" a response to unemployment and economic decline that, regrettably, manifests itself in assaults on Asian minorities. Even more imaginatively, Dick Hebdige has argued that because white skinheads enjoy black (West Indian) music and sense of style, Paki-bashing can therefore be interpreted "as a displacement manoeuvre whereby the fear and anxiety produced by limited identification with one black group was transformed into aggression and directed against another black community" (Hebdige, 1979, p. 58).

The argument that class factors are more important than racial ones in explaining skinhead violence—never very compelling to begin with—has become even less persuasive as the skinhead subculture has become international in scope, and racial attacks have expanded to include blacks in the United States, Turks and Arabs in Western Europe, and Jews everywhere. The role that skinheads occasionally play in right-wing racial politics demonstrates just how romantic (not to mention deluded and misguided) some of the early conceptions of skinhead ideology and behaviour really were. The gap between what subcultural theory posits (resistance and class struggle) and what actually takes place (the oppression of racial minorities—"hate crime" as it has become known) is attributable to the theorists' willingness to project their own political beliefs onto working-class youth, combined with a reluctance to do the necessary field or survey research that would disprove some of the more far-fetched and fanciful interpretations of subcultural symbolism.

In the opening chapter it was noted that moral panics involving adolescents have their origins in adults' anxieties about social change that they project onto youthful behaviour. However, the same process can happen in reverse when resistance theorists start projecting their own political hopes and ambitions onto patterns of youth deviance.

A different set of problems with resistive formulations of "youth culture" has recently been raised by Sarah Thornton (1995). In contrast to the Birmingham School's thesis that newspaper coverage erodes resistant youth culture of its bite and authenticity, she insists that the opposite is the case: media attention is instrumentally vital in building rebel cultural identity. Her counterargument is, in effect, "no media coverage, no youth culture." It is public labelling by the media that establishes a group both in its own eyes and in the eyes of others. She uses rave subculture to illustrate her point. Although the mainspring tabloid press in Britain presents ravers as deviant "folk devils," much of the alternative, youth-oriented media use those same negative depictions as a "badge of rebellion" (1995, p. 120). She also argues that public hostility toward, and moral panics about, disreputable leisure activity (such as raves) have been used as a marketing ploy by those in the business of selling their services to young people.

Her argument, in other words, is that, rather than weakening deviant youth groups, media condemnation often strengthens subcultural bonds and boundaries. Young people do not always want public approval of their lifestyles and cultural tastes. In Britain the state-run BBC is seen as typifying the mainstream cultural status quo, particularly with regard to pop music. Hence, the banishment of a song from the radio or television play lists stands as testimony to, and an authentication of, a musical genres' rebel sensibilities. This also leads, ironically, to the oxymoronic phenomenon of the "underground hit." In the U.K., there is a relatively long list of songs banned by the BBC because of references to sex and drugs (and politics) that have gone on to become big hits. A partial listing would include, in addition to the Sex Pistols' "God Save the Queen," "Relax," by Frankie Goes to Hollywood and the Shamen's "Ebeneezer Goode" (Thornton, 1995, 129–30).

Finally, according to some commentators, youth culture has now entered a postmodern phase in which young peoples' leisure interests and consumptive patterns have become increasingly disconnected from both resistance and class. As part of the new "risk society" era, involvement in different sorts of youth culture has become a matter of individual preference—people choosing to become ravers or rappers regardless of social background or prior experiences. Ironically, this postmodernistic view of pluralistic youth cultures only loosely tied to class describes much existing modernistic North American youth culture, where—apart from bike gangs and recently emerging forms of black youth culture such as hip-hop—adolescent subcultures have never been as visible or easily identifiable as in Europe. It is to this issue we now turn.

SUBCULTURAL DELINQUENCY AND YOUTH CULTURE IN CANADA

Although there is little or nothing in either American or British subcultural theory that makes their accounts of deviant youth specific to their respective societies, the fact remains that Canada has not followed a similar path of subcultural formation. Despite being an English-speaking, liberal democracy, Canada has not historically produced the delinquent groups that populate American inner cities or the flamboyant youth cultures that periodically capture attention in the United Kingdom. As a result, the tradition of subcultural research is less well developed here. There is a large body of literature on crime and Canadian society (see, for example, Silverman, Teevan, and Sacco, 1991; Sacco and Kennedy, 1998) but little of it has focused upon the sort of subcultural deviance that elsewhere provokes moral panic and invites sociological research. What factors have limited the emergence of deviant youth groups in Canadian society?

One person who has tried to solve this conundrum is Mike Brake in his comparative analysis of youth culture in the United States, Great Britain, and Canada (1985). Although he has little to say directly about American and Canadian differences, he does argue that the muted appearance of deviant youth culture in Canada is attributable to a cultural emphasis upon individualism and an attendant belief in the possibilities of upward mobility (Marchak, 1981). Such beliefs blunt the hard edge of class divisions that, particularly in Britain, are the mainspring of visible and collective patterns of delinquency and deviance.

One of the functions of youth culture is to compensate for restricted mobility opportunities. Optimistic projections about future adult roles and identities might, therefore, be expected to reduce adolescent dependency upon, or need for, youth culture. Simon Frith has suggested as much in his comparison of American and British adolescents. He observes that "American teenagers seem to believe in the possibility of changing their lives (if only by moving across the country) for much longer than British teenagers who ... have a greater need to dramatize their duller local identify" (Frith, 1985, p. 376). The same observation might apply equally to young Canadians. An ability to hold onto what might be seen objectively as an impossible dream discourages Canadian adolescents from involvement in the sort of subcultural activity that could jeopardize those aspirations.

The idea that getting ahead is desirable and, more importantly, possible is connected instrumentally to education. For many young Canadians, personal mobility is contingent upon the acquisition of skills and qualifications. As a result, more students in both Canada (Ashton, 1988) and the United States (Frith, 1985) stay in school beyond the minimum legally permissible leaving age than in Great Britain. Canadian youth culture therefore lacks the street focus that, in Britain, makes it both visible and threatening.

Two further factors mentioned by Brake limit the scope of deviant youth culture in Canada. First, Canada is a nation of immigrants, populated by people whose forebears were anxious to trade the closed, class-bound society of the Old World for the apparently meritocratic and open society of the new one. In so far as these beliefs have been successfully passed on from generation to generation, young people in Canada may be unwilling to embroil themselves in subcultural activities that openly challenge them.

Second, Brake suggests that the sheer physical size of the country, the linguistic division between French and English, and regional differences and ethnic diversities inhibit the development of an indigenous Canadian youth culture. Instead, Canada's recalcitrant youth have to rely on styles developed elsewhere—usually in the United Kingdom, though more recently, black American styles have also become more evident. Thus, Brake claims, much of the youth culture that actually does occur here is derivative and, by implication, lacking authenticity.

I have already mentioned that many of the symbolic trappings of subcultural membership are commodities acquired—with money—without reference to their buyers' values and beliefs and, although older versions of British subcultural theory have always assumed that resistant style is underpinned by resistant attitudes and behaviour, this is not necessarily the case. This is particularly so in Canada, when the individuals who attach themselves to a particular style are so far removed—in both time and place—from the context that originally produced it. Doc Marten boots, for example, at one time (in the 1960s), symbolized British skinheads' resistance to social change that threatened working-class values and a working-class lifestyle. In Canada in the 1990s, they have become a very fashionable (and expensive) fashion statement for a broad cross-section of the nation's teenagers. In the process of travelling from the United Kingdom to Canada, many of these one-time symbols of resistance have lost their teeth and been transformed into articles of teenage conformity rather than indicators of deviance. The Canadian experience with British subcultural imports thus provides a further illustration of one of the broader truths about seemingly deviant youth groups: what starts out as "revolt" ends up as "style" (Melly, 1970).

However, there is little doubt that the most important youth cultural development in Canada over the past decade or so has American, not British, roots. I am referring to rap or hip-hop— now a global phenomenon but originally a subcultural adaptation formulated by young, working-class blacks in America's inner cities. To round out my discussion of deviant youth culture in Canada, I want to consider the nature of this subculture, inter-pretations that have been made of it, and the difficulties posed for these interpretations by its worldwide diffusion.

As a recognizable and distinctive subculture, hip-hop has been around since the mid 1970s; it was born out of the conditions experienced by young African-Americans and Hispanics growing up in inner-city neighborhoods subjected to profound economic and social change: the elimination of stable blue-collar jobs in manufacturing and their replacement by "non-standard" (that is, low-wage, short-term, and temporary) jobs in the expanding service sector; an increasing shortage of affordable housing; and federal government cutbacks that shrank the size of local social safety nets (welfare and so on); and, of course, systemic racism.

It has found expression in graffiti art, break dancing, distinc-tive styles of dress—baggy pants, Nike shoes, reversed baseball caps—and, most importantly, rap music. Hip-hop and rap—more or less interchangeable terms—have diverse roots in Jamaican reggae, street poetry (Dezzins or "spoken song"), religious call and response, and improvisational jazz.[4] Lyrically, the music is con-cerned with self-identity, women, sex, violence, and gangs. It is the last two themes, of course, that make hip-hop a threat, par-ticularly in its "gangsta rap" (antiestablishment) version. Reflecting the influence of the Birmingham School and its reading of urban youth cultures, the street style of hip-hop is taken as a statement about being black and disenfranchised in a white society. As one of its chroniclers has put it: "'B-boys' [mem-bers of black urban hip-hop subcultures] ... combine the explosive elements of poverty, street-knowledge and unfocused political anger" (George, 1992).

But how well does this interpretation hold up? First of all, we now take notice of hip-hop precisely because of its general popularity: its appeal is no longer confined, if it ever was, to inner-city minority youth in the United States. It is relatively easy to view hip-hop culture as a resistive street culture when based on racial disadvantage in rundown urban settings, but considerably more difficult to do so when its patrons also include young inhabitants of "white" suburbs. Second, particularly when the focus is upon the music, there is a tendency to view participation in hip-hop as incompatible with involvement in other youth cultures. Although this may be the case for black youth, there is reason to believe that white hip-hoppers listen to rap at the same time as they also listen to other more obviously "white" musical styles (Oasis, Red Hot Chili Peppers) and, moreover, do so without giving any consideration to the political rhetoric associated with hip-hop culture: they are consumers of a taste culture rather than active participants in an oppositional youth culture. (A recent Hollywood movie, *Black and White,* offers its version of this phenomenon, positing the idea that the preference for rap among white adolescents is merely a transitional phase in the passage through high school, in contrast to black youth whose involvement is both more substantial and longer term.) In a similar vein, research on Japanese adolescents shows that rap is used as a cultural marker whereby those who want to distinguish themselves from the teenage mainstream do so by declaring an affinity with black American youth culture.

Third, despite the rhetoric of resistance, rap songs do not always challenge the dominant social order. Although some rap music does offer antiestablishment themes, even a casual viewing of rap videos reveals an overweening concern with material wealth, "brand" consciousness, an unhealthy preoccupation with guns and violent imagery, and, of course, rampant sexism.

On the other hand, there is evidence indicating that, even when far removed from the original American milieu of racial disadvantage, rap does serve the political, as well as pleasurable, needs of young people. In Germany, research suggests that members of ethnic and racial minorities draw on rap music as a means of psychologically combatting their everyday experiences of discrimination. Likewise anti-racist youth in Denmark gravitate toward rap because of its message of resistance. And in England, white, working-class adolescents in Newcastle have appropriated and reworked rap and the black American experience to help them make sense of their own experiences of growing up poor and disadvantaged (Bennett, 1999).

But the doubts still persist: as rap/hip-hop moves from the margins to the mainstream, from downtown to the suburbs, do its signs and symbols become a less reliable guide to oppositional attitudes and behaviour? Is the wearing of a Malcolm X cap a political statement or a fashion statement? Are rap songs that include extracts from the speeches of Malcolm X and Dr. Martin Luther King junior exercises in political education or are they just good to dance to? Are we, in other words, talking about resistance or style?

CONCLUSION

This chapter has traced the development of the subcultural theory in deviancy and delinquency from its American origins in the Chicago School to its more recent application in British studies of deviant youth culture.

In documenting the career of the subcultural concept several points have become evident. First, whereas American thinking about subcultures in the 1950s and 1960s reflected the broader structural functionalist perspective in sociology of which it was part, and is liberal in its political agenda, the newer British theory is more explicitly influenced by Marxism and its emphasis upon class conflict. Nonetheless, in both perspectives, subcultural activity is functional for adolescents; subcultures are micro-structural problem-solving institutions.

Second, when it began, subcultural theory was concerned more or less exclusively with the causes of troublesome adolescent behaviour. However, as it has evolved and made the journey from Chicago to Birmingham, it has gradually incorporated elements from labelling theory into its agenda. In particular, subcultural theory, both old and new, relies on the idea that how the broader community responds to troublesome behaviour affects the personal and collective identities of those defined as deviant or delinquent. Finally, I gave some thought as to why delinquent and deviant adolescent subcultures of the sort found in the United States and United Kingdom have not hitherto been very prevalent in Canadian society.

Although I have had occasion to make reference to various empirical studies, the focus of this chapter has been very much on the theory of subcultural formation and development. In the next two chapters I switch the emphasis to concentrate upon how the different approaches to, and components of, subcultural theory have been used to explain delinquency and deviancy in the two principal domains in which they occur: the school and the street.

NOTES

1. There is, as several different writers have suggested (Pearson, 1983; Bernard, 1992; Sullivan, 1989; Messner and Rosenfeld, 1994), a cyclical quality to much thinking about juvenile delinquency. And while the concept of social disorganization at one time fell out of favour, it has recently made a reappearance in theories and research trying to explain the causes and consequences of inner-city decay in the United States. See, for example, Anderson (1994).

2. Bike groups have also provided a large amount of the illustrative material for discussions of moral panic, as we saw in the last chapter. Hunter S. Thompson, the pioneer of "Gonzo journalism," recognized the traumatic effect that the Hell's Angels had upon respectable citizens in the United States in the early 1960s. Motorcycle outlaws were

   > as uniquely American as jazz. Nothing like them had ever existed. In some ways they appeared to be a kind of half-breed anachronism, a human hangover from the era of the Wild West. Yet in other ways they were as new as television. There was absolutely no precedent, in the years after the Second World War, for large gangs of hoodlums on motorcycles, reveling in violence, worshipping mobility and thinking nothing of riding five hundred miles on a weekend ... to whoop it up with other gangs of cyclists in some country hamlet entirely unprepared to handle even a dozen peaceful tourists. Many picturesque outback villages got their first taste of tourism not from families driving Fords or Chevrolets, but from clusters of boozing "City boys" on motorcycles. (Thompson, 1967, p. 75)

   And, of course, the British mods (who rode scooters) and the rockers (who rode motorbikes) that Stanley Cohen analyzed are recognizable in similar terms.

3. It has to be admitted that both the bike gang and the Harley-Davidson are, or are in the process of becoming, dubious symbols of youth subcultural activity. First, bikers are often adult males (in their thirties and forties) whose deviant pursuits—the manufacturing and distribution of synthetic drugs—are closer to organized crime than juvenile delinquency (I am indebted to Steve Baron for this observation). Second, recent newspaper articles have suggested that Harley-Davidson motorcycles have become popular with prosperous, respectable, middle-aged citizens. Yesterday's symbol of youth rebellion has become today's adult status symbol.

4. For this account of the hip-hop subculture, I rely on the work of Asbridge (1995) and Falkenstein (2000).

Schools, Delinquency, and Youth Culture: Questions of Conformity, Deviance, and Resistance

INTRODUCTION

Much of the early sociological work on delinquency centred on the street activities of largely working-class male youth. Beginning in the 1950s, however, researchers directed their attention away from the street and toward the high school as part of a broader search for the causes of delinquency. The popular culture of the day shared this concern, as evidenced by movies such as *Blackboard Jungle,* which dealt with the growing problem of delinquency in New York high schools.

Research on the relationship between high schools and delinquency was inspired by various strands of strain and subcultural theory, particularly the work of Merton and Cohen, whose ideas were introduced in the last chapter. The focus was on the pressure to succeed in the competitive arena of high school, and how failure to do so induces deviant responses. In particular, there was and is a recognition that the ways in which schools organize teaching and learning and the nature of the interaction between teachers and students contribute to delinquent outcomes.

Schools are obviously not institutions completely separated from the wider society, but they can and do have an influence on delinquency that is not simply reducible to the background characteristics of their students or to the environmental qualities of the catchment areas in which they are located. Several studies have demonstrated that schools have an effect upon patterns of adolescent deviance independent of other factors.

In England, Power et al. (1972) reported large differences in delinquency rates among twenty similar secondary modern schools in Tower Hamlets (part of London's East End) that could not be explained by the delinquency rates of the schools' intake areas. Although critics have suggested that the high delinquency schools in Power et al.'s survey recruited a higher proportion of problem boys than low delinquency schools (thereby intimating that prior anti-school orientations and conduct norms, rather than school characteristics, were responsible for delinquency rates), another British study has substantiated the findings of the earlier research. Rutter et al. (1979) studied pupils over time from twelve London secondary schools located in an inner-city area disadvantaged in several ways. They found significant differences in the delinquency rates for boys, but not for girls, among the schools after controlling at intake for variations in the children's verbal reasoning skills and parental occupational status. Rutter et al. felt able to conclude that characteristics of the schools themselves, rather than of the individual students, appeared to explain differences in school delinquency rates. There appears to be something about some schools that affects the volume of deviancy and delinquency committed by their students.

HIGH SCHOOL AS A CAUSE OF DELINQUENCY

What these factors might be has been identified in other research that, directly influenced by Albert Cohen, has explored the strains experienced by students in high school and how the manner in which academic learning is organized adds to those strains.

Indeed, much of the research on schools and delinquency in Canada and the United States has proceeded as a debate about the relationship between class, schooling, and delinquency. In this regard, I want to begin with an important study conducted by Arthur Stinchcombe (1964).

You will recall that Albert Cohen argues that working-class boys respond to failure in school by involving themselves in subcultural delinquency. Stinchombe agrees that school failure is the important stimulus for delinquency, but argues that the delinquent adaptation is by no means limited to working-class school failures: if middle-class kids are failing in school, then they too will become alienated and rebellious and turn to delinquency. Stated in its most basic form, Stinchcombe's thesis is that an adolescent's "status prospects" (that is, where he or she is apparently headed in the social class hierarchy) are a more important determinant of delinquency than his or her "status origins" (that is, the characteristics of his or her class background). Rebellious delinquency will be most prevalent and intense among those young people facing the poorest jobs in the adult labour market. In other words, Stinchcombe postulates a causal connection between a prospective working-class future (defined occupationally as a manual job) and delinquency.

This conclusion is arrived at as a result of his own investigation of rebellion in a California high school. He shows that rebellious delinquency is least evident among those youths—regardless of their class origins—who are high academic achievers and/or intend to go on to college (university). Delinquency is better predicted by various measures of current school status than by class background.

Stinchcombe has not, however, strayed that far from the basic outlines of strain theory and its emphasis on status frustration; nor, no less importantly, does he conclude that class origins are irrelevant to the generation of delinquency. Indeed, he emphasizes the fact that the high school is precisely where individuals are most explicitly exposed to "universal goals" and where the economic and cultural advantages of middle-class youth that enable them to achieve those goals are most manifest:

> The school system, particularly the secondary school, is one of the main institutions in the society where universal standards of success are applied over the whole range of the class system. Students are placed under great pressure to force a decision on the degree of success they expect, and the (symbolic) means of success, especially grades, are deliberately and systematically allocated differently. Further, the ritual idiom of the school, by defining only middle-class choices positively, allows but a very limited redefinition of the meaning of "occupational success." (Stinchcombe, 1964, p. 135)

However, it is at this point that Stinchcombe amends the basic strain formula. He argues, first of all, that those adolescents under most pressure to do well in school will be the most rebellious and that, second, because middle-class students are under more pressure than their working-class peers to succeed, those who are unsuccessful will be most rebellious. By and large, this pattern is confirmed by his findings. A lack of scholastic achievement is related to rebellion and the most rebellious students of all are male middle-class failures.

Stinchcombe's study has prompted a number of similar reformulations of basic strain theory. For instance, Kenneth Polk has examined the relationship between class, strain, and delinquency among male adolescents in the Pacific Northwest of the United States (1972). He found, like Stinchcombe, that there is a strong and significant relationship between status prospects and rebellious delinquency: those who had low grades or who were not in college-bound programs in high school were more involved in delinquency than their academically successful peers. Similarly, these rebellious outcomes are unconnected to humble class origins. However, Polk could not replicate Stinchcombe's finding that middle-class failures are more rebellious than working-class failures. Partly because middle-class students respond no differently to school failure than working-class ones, Polk argues that in emphasizing the importance of future job prospects as a motivation for delinquency among young males facing working-class futures, Stinchcombe has perhaps neglected the importance of more immediate factors related to the experience of schooling itself.

Polk is referring to what might be called a culture of failure: low grades, the labelling and stigmatization of inadequate students by teachers, the imposition of what is perceived as unfair and arbitrary punishment, and so on. He suggests that the ways in which high school responds to poor academic performers is a more important source of hostility and alienation and, hence, delinquency than more distant and abstract concerns about future working-class occupational status.

Prominent among the more immediate stimulants to delinquency is the manner in which academic learning in high school is organized. Virtually all American, Canadian, and British secondary schools are structured around the practice of streaming or tracking of students and, despite the rhetoric and pretence of school authorities, different tracks or streams are not viewed equally by teachers or students. Streaming thus has a substantial bearing upon the sort of identity—deviant or conformist—that high school students are able to construct for themselves.

A number of studies have shown how streaming has either caused or contributed to delinquent outcomes. One early examination of the connection between streaming and delinquency conducted by Schafer, Olexa, and Polk (1972) compared students in two high schools in the American Midwest who had been consigned to either a "college prep" track or a "non-college prep" track. They found that, using official delinquency counts (juvenile court records) as their measure, those not being groomed for university were significantly more delinquent than those who were being prepared for university entrance. Of course, it is possible that those in the non-college track were delinquent in advance of the track allocation—that it was the behaviour that determined the track allocation rather than the other way around. The researchers dealt with this possibility by restricting their analysis to students who did not have a record of official delinquency prior to high school. This procedure did not, however, alter the track-based variations in delinquency. Similarly, and not surprisingly, track position is also related to misconduct in schools. Non-college prep students were likely to have worse discipline records and more likely to be suspended in the course of the school year than college prep students. Again, it seems probable that assignment to a non-college prep track weakens students' commitment to school and, correspondingly, increases the prospects for rebellion in the future.

Why might streaming have this effect upon delinquency? Some clues have been provided by David Hargreaves in his ethnographic study of an English secondary modern school in which he taught and observed (1967). At Lumley School, the boys were placed in one of five hierarchically ranked streams on the basis of examination performances at the age of eleven (the "11 plus" examination). The status disparity between the different streams was broadly recognized by both teachers and students, and boys in the different streams had very little contact with each other in either formal or informal settings. They neither took lessons together nor interacted much socially in friendship groupings outside the classroom.

The main contribution, then, that streaming makes to delinquency is that it polarizes student populations into pro- and anti-school subcultures. As Hargreaves put it:

> Although the aims and efforts of the teachers are directed towards deleting such tendencies, the organization of the school and its influence on subcultural development unintentionally foster delinquent values ... For low-stream boys ... school simultaneously exposes them to these values and deprives them of status in these terms. It is at this point they may begin to reject the values because they cannot succeed in them. More than this the school provides a mechanism through the streaming system whereby their failure is effected and institutionalized, and also provides a situation in which they can congregate together in low streams. (Hargreaves, 1967, p. 173)

One of the principal reasons that streaming leads to delinquency, according to Hargreaves, is that it makes low-stream boys—the unchosen, if you will—casualties of a self-fulfilling prophecy with regard to their interactions with teachers. The latter expected, and received, more academically from high-stream boys. Conversely, little was expected of those in the D stream—and that is exactly what the boys delivered. Moreover, the very fact that teachers were dealing with D-stream boys generated imputations about their deviant proclivities. They were labelled as troublemakers and treated as such:

> In a streamed school the teacher categorizes the pupils not only in terms of the inferences he makes of the child's classroom behaviour but also from the child's stream level. It is for this reason that the teacher can rebuke an A stream boy for being like a D stream boy. The teacher has learned to expect certain kinds of behaviour from members of different streams ...
>
> It would be hardly surprising if "good" pupils thus became "better" and the "bad" pupils become "worse." It is, in short, an example of a self-fulfilling prophecy. The negative expectations of the teacher reinforce the negative behavioural tendencies. (Hargreaves, 1967, pp. 105–6)

Assignment to a low-status stream can have a stigmatizing effect upon those placed there. It has this corrosive effect upon a student's sense of self because the various programs that make up the secondary school curriculum do not carry equal amounts of prestige. In a North American context, this means that, in the eyes of students and teachers, alike, non-matriculation programs in high school are not only different from matriculation, or university-bound, programs, they are inferior as well. How this message is conveyed to students is nicely described by Stinchcombe: "The school puts all those who can do algebra into a class in algebra, but those who can do automobile mechanics are put into that class only if they cannot do algebra. Thus the school defines talent at algebra as success, talent at auto mechanics as failure" (Stinchcombe, 1964, pp. 7–8).

Not surprisingly, therefore, allocation to a matriculation, or university-bound stream is associated with success, while placement in a non-matriculation program, particularly a vocational program, constitutes failure. This arrangement, research suggests, polarizes the study body into pro- and anti-school factions and generates a delinquent response among the latter. Furthermore, this outcome is made that much more likely because, once assigned to a low stream, students are rarely promoted to a higher stream (Lawrence, 1998).

For an account of just how streaming might (unintentionally) facilitate anti-school peer cultures, we again turn to David Hargreaves. Taking his cue from Albert Cohen, Hargreaves proposes that upon assignment to the D stream, boys are provided with a thorough informal socialization in anti-school attitudes and behaviours: they learn that belligerent words and deeds are rewarded and that doing the opposite of what the school prescribes (a process sometimes referred to as "reverse psychology") garners them prestige among their classmates.

This culture of dissent contrasts with what is happening in the A stream, where the favoured ones absorb the value configurations of teachers, fulfil official expectations of academic performance, and enjoy the rewards that their privileged status bestows on them. In the upper streams, therefore, there is a fairly close symmetry between the formal "academic" culture of the school and the concerns of the informal peer group. Meanwhile, back in the D stream, that culture is being turned on its head.

Barriers between the streams, once created, are hard to break down and, indeed, are even reinforced by the scheduling of the curriculum and classes. Insidious stereotyping grew because the organization of learning allowed few opportunities for boys from different streams to interact. As they progressed through their school careers, boys in the same age cohort lived in increasingly differentiated and polarized subcultural worlds:

> The informal pressures within the low streams tend to work directly against the assumption of the teachers that boys will regard promotion into a higher stream as a desirable goal. The boys from the low streams were very reluctant to ascend to higher streams because their stereotypes of "A" and "B" stream boys were defined in terms of values alien to their own and because promotion would involve rejection by their low-stream friends. The teachers were not fully aware that this unwillingness to be promoted to a higher stream led high informal status boys to depress their performance in examinations. This fear of promotion adds to our list of factors leading to the formation of anti-academic attitudes among low stream boys. (Hargeaves, 1967, pp. 77–78)

Other research, in the United States, Britain, and Canada has similarly explored how high school, by itself and in conjunction with "prior" social class and/or family influences, affects the formation of delinquent and deviant subcultures. One strand of this research has focused upon the question of which is the more important source of delinquency and rebellious youth culture—a lower class background (as Albert Cohen infers) or factors indigenous to high school (as Stinchcombe and others have proposed). Here we can draw on some Canadian data to illuminate what has become quite a lively and complex debate. Reduced to its basic form, the relationship between class, schooling, and delinquency can be understood in terms of two competing perspectives.

Advocates of what has become known as the class background model, drawing their inspiration from Cohen's theory, propose that social class is directly related to such in-school factors as academic achievement and commitment to school: the higher the class background, the stronger the academic performance and commitment to school. In turn, these same school-based variables will be inversely related to delinquency. On this argument, high school experiences intervene between class origins and delinquent outcomes.

On the other hand, proponents of what has become known as the school status model discount the salience of social class for either school-based experiences or delinquency. The crucial variables for them are all autonomous to high school: scholastic performance, school commitment, and track allocation are the main determinants of rebellion and delinquency.

In 1976, Tim Hartnagel and I explored the competing claims of these two perspectives with information collected from 733 students in three junior and two senior high schools in Edmonton, Alberta (Hartnagel and Tanner, 1982).

What did we find? In terms of the competing perspectives, we found more support for the school status than class background model of delinquency. Among junior high school students, our basic school status measure, commitment to school, was the only significant predictor, where commitment was weak, of involvement in theft and violence; it was also the prime determinant of school rebellion. In senior high school, the predictive scope of school commitment broadened: a low commitment to school was associated with theft, vandalism, and school rebellion. Although school commitment was not related to the more violent forms of delinquency, academic program—another school status variable—was: those in non-matriculation programs reported more violent behaviour than their university-bound peers.[1] By contrast, class background only predicted underage drinking among junior high school students: students from modest backgrounds reported higher levels of alcohol consumption than their more privileged peers.

It is entirely possible, of course, that, particularly at the senior high school, the most serious delinquents were not in school on the days when we administered our questionnaires, and their absence might explain the weak predictive effects of class background. Similarly, like most self-report instruments (see Chapter 2), the one that we employed did not include questions about the sorts of really aggressive and violent delinquencies that are more likely to be class linked. Nonetheless, with these limitations borne firmly in mind, our findings suggest that in the search for determinants of delinquency, schooling produces relatively independent effects—a finding repeated in later studies, as we will see.

But before we finish with streaming and its effects, we need to add a caveat. According to the research that has been reviewed here, schools contribute to delinquency because they categorize and label students in negative ways. However, not all investigations of tracking have uncovered the effects that I document, namely, an intensification of delinquent outcomes, deviant identities, and antisocial behaviour.

An interesting counter-example is provided by a longitudinal study conducted in the United States of high school students who were interviewed four times in the course of their school careers. Wiatrowski et al. (1982) found little indication that delinquent behaviour in either the final year of high school or in the first year out of high school were related to tracking.

It appears that research that finds a relationship between tracking and delinquency explains the connection in terms of stigmatization: students resent being negatively labelled and react against the school's definition of them as educationally substandard. According to this argument, however, for tracking to carry a sting, to produce the deviance-inducing effects that I have outlined, students need to feel that the principle and process of streaming is illegitimate, unjust, and unfair. It is precisely this feeling of injustice that is absent from the attitudes of the respondents in Wiatrowski's study: some 87 percent reported that they were satisfied with their track allocation. A reasonable conclusion might be that a sense of fairness about appropriate track allocations reduces delinquency. Clearly one of the important tasks facing schools that practise streaming is to persuade their students that allocation to a particular course or program of study is in their own best interests.

PATTERNS OF DISENGAGEMENT FROM SCHOOL

The research that I have looked at so far implicates schooling as a potential cause of delinquency. Other research in the subcultural tradition has focused upon the oppositional expressionism and out-of-school experiences of anti-school students: how do rebellious youth articulate their disengagement from or opposition to schooling? What symbolic resources do they draw on and what activities do they participate in? How do they construct a counter-school style? These questions have been addressed in research that modifies Albert Cohen's formulation of delinquent subcultures and focuses upon the relationship between deviant youth culture and the high school.

In the 1960s, Barry Sugarman explored the inclination of school-rejecting male adolescents in London to participate in an expressive youth culture, the standards of which—in line with Cohen's thinking—were considered right simply because they were wrong by the standards of the school (Sugarman, 1967). In

Sugarman's study, anti-school students wore teenage fashions, listened to pop music radio stations, went out with girls, and smoked cigarettes.

On this side of the Atlantic, during roughly the same period, researchers in Oregon discovered a similar phenomenon: anti-school students were involved in their own informal anti-school culture. Polk and Pink (1971) found that recalcitrant students, both male and female, were involved in a youth culture in which they smoked cigarettes, dated, and went "cruising," an activity that is possibly most familiar from the movie *American Graffiti* that Polk and Pink define as the "ritualistic driving of cars up and down designated streets." Thus, Sugarman and Polk and Pink depicted the secondary school as harbouring two groups of students: pro-school students and anti-school students who, in the process of reacting against school culture, created their own, informal, alternative youth culture.

However, two other British investigators later argued that this formulation oversimplifies the very complex relationship between conformity and peer group deviance in high school. Murdock and Phelps (1973) suggest that there are, in fact, two central patterns of out-of-school leisure use by which anti-school students may articulate their disengagement from school. They label these two cultural constellations "street culture" and "pop media culture" and, although the two occasionally overlap, they generally represent separate patterns of roles, activities, and symbols, and tend to attract different categories of school disaffiliates.

Strongly reminiscent of the lower-class culture identified by W. B. Miller (1958), discussed in Chapter 3, street culture emphasizes informal male leisure activities undertaken within the confines of the urban working-class community—hanging around street corners or playing pickup football, for instance. Pop music, on the other hand, particularly pop records, is the basis of pop media culture that Murdock and Phelps (1973, p. 479) define as the activities, values, and roles "… sponsored by those sectors of the mass media which are produced primarily for adolescent consumption." Although music is the main pop medium, the style and themes recur and spill over into other facets of pop media culture such as fashion, magazines, television, and movies.

On the basis of a nationwide survey in Britain, Murdock and Phelps conclude that adolescents with a low commitment to school gravitate toward one or the other of these two sets of leisure activity: working-class pupils, particularly males, with a low commitment to school will orient themselves toward street culture because it is the best developed and most easily accessible source of oppositional activity available to them. Middle-class pupils, particularly girls, on the other hand, not having access to a situationally based street culture, will tend to gravitate toward pop media culture for activities and symbols counterposed to the world of school. Thus, the argument underpinning differential involvement in the two forms of youth culture is that, denied access to a class- and sex-based "neighbourhood culture," the pop media become an important source of anti-school symbols and activities for particular groups of adolescents.

Some years ago, I wanted to find out whether a similar pattern of deviant youth cultural involvement existed among Canadian high school students. Were young Canadians with a low tolerance of schooling inclined to involve themselves in street and pop media cultures? Are school-rejecting boys more likely than school-rejecting girls to be involved in street culture? Conversely, are anti-school girls more likely than anti-school boys to participate in pop media culture? Finally and most importantly, do sex and class interact in such a way that it is male working-class school rejecters who are most deeply involved in street culture, while pop media culture becomes the principal means of expressing disaffiliation for middle-class females?

What did I find? First, that while students with a low school commitment did disproportionately involve themselves in both a delinquent street culture (approximated in my study by five self-reported delinquency items) and a pop media culture (measured by questions about record buying, attendance at rock concerts, and self-identification as a rock fan), it was sex (or gender) that was a more important source of variation in youth cultural activities than social class. Among students with a low school commitment, boys, particularly working-class boys, were most heavily involved in self-reported delinquency. Girls with a weak commitment to school less regularly participated in delinquent activity, though working-class girls were significantly more delinquent than their middle-class counterparts.

More surprisingly, the students most supportive of pop media culture were boys with a low commitment to school—regardless of their class origin. By contrast, girls with a low commitment to school exhibited no significant involvement in pop media; again, social class did not modify this pattern. For school-rejecting boys, therefore, a delinquent street culture and pop media culture are not mutually exclusive youth anti-school adaptations. Those males who do not like school draw on the contemporary media culture as well as traditional, and more obviously, delinquent street activities when constructing their oppositional identities and routines.

And what of the girls? Their lack of involvement in delinquency, even among those with a low commitment to school, is perhaps not that surprising. Many studies before and after my Edmonton study have revealed girls to be less delinquent than boys, even when they are exposed to the same deviant stimulants. But I had anticipated a significant involvement in pop media among school-rejecting females, and I did not find this. What makes girls' lack of involvement especially puzzling is that female respondents in the study had as much disposable income as the boys: they were not, therefore, denied acccess to pop media culture because of limited finances.

I suspect, in retrospect, that those teenage girls who most reject school express their distaste for their experiences, not by buying records or going to concerts, but by displaying the sort of precious femininity—lavish makeup, sexually provocative clothing—most likely to upset adults. My study was conducted years before the arrival of Madonna, but I suspect that she became a role model for rebellious females because of her exuberant display of "trash style." I will have more to say about this topic in Chapter 6.

Finally, I want to say something about the connection between delinquent adaptations to school and students' interactions with pop music. One of the revelations of my Edmonton study was that adolescents do not share the same tastes in popular music. In particular, students differ according to whether their preferences were more or less conformist. A basic division in my study was between the majority of students who favoured mainstream "Top 40" artists as their favourite performers (Donny Osmond and Debbie Boone were prominent contemporary examples), and the smaller number of respondents who preferred heavy metal, which in 1974 meant bands like Black Sabbath, Deep Purple, and Alice Cooper.

Those who nominated safe, adult-approved mainstream music tended to be female and had a relatively positive commitment to school. As you might have predicted, students (both male and female) with the weakest attachment to schooling and the most extensive involvements in delinquency were the principal champions of the heavy metal bands (Tanner, 1981).

I want to make it quite clear that I am not positing a causal connection between heavy metal and delinquency. There is no evidence to suggest that listening to heavy metal (or punk or rap or any other form of popular music) results in delinquency or any other deviant behaviour. Nor am I insisting that a prior involvement in aggressive and violent delinquency necessarily predisposes some adolescents towards heavy metal (or any other form of antisocial music) in any deterministic process. But what I am proposing is that already established anti-school activities and orientations help to make heavy metal rock the music of choice among rebellious youth. For the more deviant peer groups in high school, heavy metal exists as a repository of oppositional styles and values. In a symbolic sense, heavy metal reflects and affirms many of the central preoccupations of the delinquent subculture. I am suggesting, therefore, that there is a correspondence—a homology—between metal and a subcultural solution rooted in action, physicality, and collective solidarity. Heavy metal is drawn on as a symbolic means of contesting school-sponsored values and activities.[2] Ethnographic research conducted in England at roughly the same time has reported similar findings. Paul Willis (1976), in his exploration of the culture of motorbike boys, noted that their preference for the music of early rock and roll dovetailed with their masculine self-image.

Subsequent research conducted in Sweden has revealed a similar sort of pattern, with punk rock joining heavy metal as a musical preference of rebellious teenagers. (Roe, 1983, 1987). In the mid-1980s, Roe was exploring the media usage of Swedish high school students. He notes, first of all, that much of the previous research in this area has concentrated on the impact of television, rather than pop music, on adolescents. However, his respondents were not particularly interested in television; it confirmed "no extraordinary identity or status"; nor was television consumption significantly linked to school achievement.

Popular music, by contrast, was important to students, particularly to anti-school students who gravitated toward punk rock. As Roe puts it, "the real conflict between school and the mass media is not that between school and television, but that between school and hard rock, school and punk or, we hypothesize, between school and any socially disapproved media form (such as viewing violent video films)" (1983, p. 207).

In this regard, the anti-school subculture is of considerable importance: it mediates the relationship between school experiences and mass media consumption. Roe is able to trace a pattern over time whereby low school achievement leads to more intense peer orientations (that develop at the expense of parental orientations) and preferences for punk and other hard forms of pop music. (Although it is not specified, they presumably do not include a taste for ABBA.)

It is important to note that home background—a variable that closely approximates social class—has little bearing on the oppositional pop tastes of the males in Roe's sample. It is low school achievement, not family class, that determines peer-group activity and pop media preferences. Among the girls the pattern is slightly different. Home background predicts school achievement, parent–peer orientations, and media choices. In particular, working-class girls who underperform in school are more involved in punk than academically successful middle-class girls.

Finally, the nature of his longitudinal panel data allows Roe to "unequivocally" conclude that school achievement determines musical preferences, and not the other way around. For both boys and girls of all home backgrounds, high academic achievement early in their school careers predicts a preference for classical music three years later. Similarly, at mid-school career, low academic achievement anticipates a preference for punk two years hence.

In sum, punk rock was the music of choice for Swedish high school students with a low commitment to schooling. However, patterns of deviant and conformist pop taste are shaped less by class background (particularly for males) than by factors related to the experience of schooling. Punk may therefore be a form of rebel rock that is principally attractive to bored and alienated high school students, but it is by no means the exclusive voice of working-class underachievers.

RESISTANCE THEORY AND SCHOOL DEVIANCE IN CANADA

In the previous chapter, I noted that there have been two main phases of subcultural theory. The first was of American origin and centred on the formulations of gang delinquency produced by Albert Cohen, Cloward and Ohlin, and W. B. Miller. It peaked in the late 1960s. The second phase began in the United Kingdom in the early 1970s.

There are many similarities between the two traditions, as Stanley Cohen (1980) has emphasized. Both are concerned with class-based inequalities as a cause of collective deviance, both rely on ethnographic studies for their supporting evidence, and both focus on male youth to the exclusion of females. However, there are also differences between them, especially in how subcultural deviance is interpreted. As I pointed out, the Birmingham School reads spectacular youth deviance as a coded form of class conflict: disadvantaged and exploited youth are, in this new wave of subcultural theory, construed as "resisters." And of course, one of the important sites where resistance takes place is high school, which brings us to the research on school resistance that has started to proliferate in Canada and the United States.

The inspiration for this body of research is Paul Willis (1977). His ethnographic study, *Learning to Labour,* has become something of a classic, and is frequently quoted as the exemplary guide to how working-class deviance might be better understood as working-class resistance. In his formulation, anti-school peer groups—or school countercultures as he prefers to call them—are actively engaged in class-based resistance to middle-class schooling.

Willis's ethnography is an exploration of the process whereby working-class boys in a secondary school in the English Midlands end up in working-class jobs. He tries to answer the question of why working-class adolescents tend to end up in doing the same sort of menial manual work that their parents do, despite participation in an educational system that affords opportunities for them to escape that fate.

The answer that he proposes centres upon the activities of the anti-school subculture—the school counterculture. There is nothing very original about this argument, you may say—it is a fairly straightforward application of American subcultural theory, highlighting negative school experiences as the catalyst for school rebellion. However, Willis sees the school counterculture created by the "lads" as the cause of low school achievement and early leaving and not (as subcultural theorists from Albert Cohen on have proposed), a consequence of those in-school experiences.[3]

Based on values and prior expectations derived from and shared with the broader working-class community, the school counterculture exists as a stark alternative to the culture of the school: its participants deride book learning and are contemptuously dismissive of white-collar jobs, preferring instead the unambiguously masculine world of manual labour.

Their active participation in the school counterculture prepares the lads for the sorts of low-paying unskilled jobs that they enter upon leaving school. But—and, this is the crucial theoretical theme in Willis's analysis—this preparation is experienced not as oppression, but as freedom, autonomy, and independence. The lads' counterculture creates opportunities for, and rewards, "cheeking" (talking back to) teachers, refusing to do school work, "bunking off" (skipping), smoking, drinking—activities that are eminently enjoyable but that guarantee working-class destinations for them in the post-school labour market.

Working-class boys end up with working-class jobs not as a result of a grand conspiracy to rob them of equality of opportunity or because they have been labelled by middle-class teachers who are biased against them. Instead, they acquire working-class jobs because of their participation in a resistant subculture that they themselves have created. Resistance to school begins when the boys start to realize that there is no payoff for their compliance with the school's authority structure. Armed with this insight, they turn to a familiar set of activities: truancy, smoking, drinking, theft, vandalism, and refusing to comply with the school's dress code.

However, it is important to remind ourselves that Willis's *Learning to Labour* is not just another account of how working-class boys become delinquent. The anti-school peer culture created by these boys is more than a repository for delinquent acts, it is the spark for an essentially political challenge to school authority. Willis and those who have followed him (for example, Corrigan, 1979) have, in other words, politicized youthful deviance (Davies, 1994b, p. 424). Those students who misbehave in class, are rude to teachers, refuse to do their homework, and leave school at the earliest possible opportunity are now in the business of opposing capitalist schooling.

That rebellious youth in Canada might similarly be seen as class rebels is evident in Randy Nelsen's account of school disaffiliation in Thunder Bay, Ontario:

> It is these youth [the vandals, the school skippers, and the early school leavers] who, in questioning the authority of the school to command their time and attention, are acting both responsibly and rationally. For it is they who are squarely facing both the reality of school boredom and the clear evidence that there is not much compelling opportunity beyond school. By skipping and leaving school at an early age they are "voting with their feet" to give up the frivolous fantasy of school life. (Nelsen, 1987, p. 126)

Nelsen's research is one of a number of American and Canadian studies, usually ethnographies, that now have a resistance theme. So in addition to Willis's lads, we now have the "hallway hangers" (MacLeod, 1987), "cool guys" (McLaren, 1986), and the "burnouts" (Eckert, 1989). In each of these reports, groups of pro-school students are compared and contrasted with groups of resisters. Hence in Eckert's study of a suburban Detroit high school, the "jocks" and the burnouts are juxtaposed:

> In the early 1980s, the stereotypic Belton High Burnout came from a working class home, enroled primarily in general and vocational courses, smoked tobacco and pot, took chemicals, drank beer and hard liquor, skipped classes, and may have had occasional run-ins with the police; the Jock was middle class and college bound, played sports for the school, participated in school activities, got respectable grades and drank beer on weekends. The Jock had a cooperative, the Burnout an adversarial, relationship with the school. (Eckert, 1989, p. 3)

The popularity and spread of resistance theory to North America invites questions about other candidates for designation as school resisters. In particular, might high school dropouts be added to this pantheon? This is a pertinent query, since the problem that Willis was speaking to—the notoriously low levels of educational participation and achievement by working-class kids in Britain—parallels the North American concern with dropouts. Given the similarity of the issues involved, resistance theory becomes an attractive resource for researchers wanting to make sense of deviant activities in and outside of high school in Canada and the United States.

Much of the public debate about the dropout problem focuses upon the "costs"—economic and social—incurred when large numbers of young people fail to complete their secondary education. But there are other, less obvious, factors involved in the emergence of an identified dropout problem.

Public education in North America emphasizes mass participation. Young people are expected to stay in school and compete for elite positions in society. However, the fact that large numbers of adolescents abandon their studies and become dropouts suggests a significant degree of rejection of this normative expectation. Dropouts are therefore a visible reminder of the failings of an allegedly meritocratic educational system. Particularly when dropouts share similar class or racial characteristics, it is hard to maintain the fiction that success and failure in school is determined only by individual talent and effort; instead, dropping out looks like an expression of the sort of collective, cultural resistance to schooling emphasized by Willis.

To explore the possibility that dropouts from Canadian high schools can be considered school resisters, I will turn to several recent studies that have focused on this issue. The first of these is a study of dropouts in Edmonton, Alberta, in which I was involved with Harvey Krahn and Tim Hartnagel (Tanner et al., 1995). In the early 1980s, we interviewed a non-random quota sample of 168 young people who had left high school in the Edmonton public school system without completing their grade 12 education. Our respondents were both male and female, employed and unemployed, living at home and out on their own, in contact with social service agencies and independent of them. We tried, in other words, to interview a broad range of dropouts in a variety of different settings.

In the first part of the study the motivations for leaving school early were examined. It was found that factors associated with schooling were the most important reasons for quitting. These included objections to particular teachers, teachers in general, specific subjects, or the curriculum as a whole; a smaller number reported poor grades or learning difficulties; and some had even been expelled (sometimes for hitting teachers). Moreover, dislike of school often went hand in hand with a desire for paid work. The anticipated attractions of work (adult status and adult wages) coupled with the known drudgery of the classroom made the decision to leave an easier one. On the face of it, this looks very much like the oppositional culture described by Willis.

Nonetheless, although some of our respondents became dropouts because they repudiated the culture of schooling, the majority were far more tentative and circumspect about their motivations for leaving. Indeed, what struck us most about our respondents was not the magnitude of their opposition to school but the very opposite; given that dropouts, virtually by definition, are the Canadian educational system's most estranged clients, it was surprising to find how favourably that system was perceived and how qualified and muted many of their criticisms really are. Let me elaborate.

Dropping out of school had been a fundamentally ambiguous experience for most respondents. They saw it has having both good and bad aspects. On the one hand, it was a rational short-term solution to the various problems that they encountered in school; indeed, some saw it as the only option available to them, given the circumstances of their lives. On the other hand, these immediate benefits were more than offset by an awareness that their early departure from high school would pose more acute problems in the not-too-distant future. Short-term gains, in other words, were tempered by the prospect of long-term pain. Many respondents had come to realize that without a grade 12 diploma, they faced a future dominated by unemployment and ghettoization in a narrow range of low-paying, menial, and often part-time jobs. Moreover, the most important source of their information about dead-end jobs and how to avoid them came from their own post-school experiences. Although it would be an exaggeration to say that they had been converted to the inherent attractions of schooling, they had come to recognize the importance of educational qualifications as a means of improving their life chances. Indeed, some 70 percent of them said that they would like to get more education.

Matching their instrumental commitment to education were their aspirations for the future. Occupational ambitions centred, for both males and females, on professional positions and the skilled trades. While their aspirations are probably unrealistic and unlikely to be realized, they are important in that they indicate that even dropouts have not abandoned the hope for personal mobility. They were not interested in menial labour nor were they prepared to accept a working life of unskilled labour.

Our findings are different in this, and virtually every other, respect from those reported by Willis, Corrigan, and other exponents of resistance theory. Edmonton dropouts do not condemn book learning, reject white-collar jobs, or anticipate and celebrate the masculine culture of manual labour. They had not liked school very much, but their complaints and criticisms did not culminate in an inversion of school culture. By my reckoning, the accommodations that they had made did not count as "resistance," at least not in the way that term has been used in British subcultural theory. Similarly, these findings also suggest that dropouts may be less deviant than commonly supposed. Although there are differences between dropouts and graduates (in addition to achieving less educationally, dropouts report more criminal activity, an issue that will be revisited in the next chapter), there are also similarities between the two that are concealed by the dropout label.

Dropouts and non-dropouts are both primarily interested in getting good jobs and see qualifications as the main avenue of opportunity. Dropouts, however, do not always feel that high school helps them in this regard and are therefore less tolerant of that institution than other students. But their intolerance of schooling should not be confused with a complete rejection of it.

A similar conclusion has been reached by Scott Davies in a more recent, and much larger, study of dropouts in Ontario. In contrast to other researchers, who have sought and found resistance with ethnographic methods, Davies's analysis is based on survey data collected for a provincewide investigation of the dropout problem in Ontario (Davies, 1994a). He operationalizes resistance as overt behavioural and attitudinal opposition to schooling. In behavioural terms, it refers to patterns of dropping out that are accompanied by rebellious acts, such as (self-reported) disruptive classroom behaviour, low levels of effort at academic work, and having dropout friends. Attitudinally, resistance is measured by a perception that schooling is irrelevant to future life goals and an alternative less attractive than employment. Finally, resistance involves some critique of education and schooling, as inferred by dissatisfaction with streaming, teaching, the curriculum, teacher biases, and so forth.

Couched in these terms, Davies certainly finds evidence of resistance among his sample of dropouts. However, it is only weakly correlated with class background. Placement in a non-matriculation stream and self-reported difficulty with school are significantly better predictors of resistance. Moreover, the weak connection between social class and resistance makes it unlikely that the latter is a prior cause of underachievement in school. More likely, contrary to what Willis argues, resistance is a consequence of—or a reaction to—disagreeable school experiences.

As Davies is well aware, his findings are essentially the same as those reported on previously by Stinchcombe and Hartnagel and Tanner in studies described earlier in this chapter. That is, regardless of whether it is called rebellion or resistance, anti-school behaviour has its origins in factors and experiences located inside the schoolyard gates rather than in the wider world.

Much the same pattern is repeated when Davies explores resistance among in-school students attending Ontario high schools (Davies, 1994b). Resistance in this survey was measured by the use of alcohol and other drugs, involvement in a network of delinquent friends, disrespectful attitudes to the police and the principles of law and order, anti-school attitudes, dislike of teachers, and so on.

As with the dropout survey, Davies has no difficulty in uncovering resistant attitudes and behaviour among these students, but again finds it largely unrelated to class background. Resistance is not, therefore, a prior expression of working-class cultural estrangement from school, but a more generalized response to unsatisfying school experiences. He concludes by suggesting that the high school system in Canada appears to be a relatively autonomous source of deviance and resistance for both high school graduates and high school dropouts.

However, greater evidence of the culture conflict described by Willis and other subcultural theorists is uncovered when attention is turned from class to race. Although most investigations of resistance in school focus upon class, a few studies have begun to incorporate race into the basic argument. One of these is Solomon's ethnographic study of black male students in a Toronto high school, which he calls Lumberville (1992). Focusing upon the conflictual relationship between the youths' subcultural practices and the school's predominately white authority structure, he argues that race-based resistance is a consequence of a culture clash between the backgrounds and experiences of the boys and the assumptions and demands of the school.

The subcultural group that Solomon concentrates upon is called "the jocks," who—as the name implies—are avid sports enthusiasts. Indeed, sport—along with language and communication patterns, dress code, and demeanour—supplies the jocks with their basic stock of oppositional symbols and activities. All recent immigrants from the West Indies, the jocks speak a patois among themselves that both marks them as an identifiable group and is incomprehensible to most teachers. And while some teachers are inclined to view the use of patois as a sign of low academic ability, most see it for what it is: an oppositional resource that is often directed against them in conflictual situations. The jock's use of patois is therefore an essential accompaniment to their subcultural activities. Other items of subcultural expression include name-calling and horseplay, which Solomon construes as being "symbolic of the solidarity and cultural comradeship that the jocks project within the Lumberville school community."

Roots music (reggae) fulfils a similar function: most white adult authority figures don't understand its often salacious, and occasionally defiant, messages: their ignorance of its origins and meanings and an association with Rastafarianism only adds to the appeal that it has for black youth. As with other quasi-deviant youth groups, the jocks of Lumberville developed their own distinctive dress style—some elements evolving from then contemporary teenage fads (the sequined glove worn on one hand à la Michael Jackson, for instance), while others are, more literally, of a homemade variety: applying what they had learned in the school's sewing program, the youths modified the dress pants that they wore in school.

The jocks also had contact with other boys, Rastafarians, whose style and demeanour were more explicitly confrontational. Among the jocks, the Rasta look was, therefore, also in evidence in the form of dreadlocks and berets. Needless to say, those elements of Rastafarian style were prohibited by school authorities, so the persistent exhibiting of them became both a further source of conflict and a symbol of resistance.

Given that Solomon is focusing upon the jocks as part of a black youth resistance movement, it is not surprising to find that all breaking of school rules—in the classroom, corridors, cafeteria, and so on—is construed in terms of resistance. Thus, talking in class, swearing, not sitting in seats, line-up jumping in the school cafeteria at lunch time, and slam-dunking empty milk cartons into garbage cans are all used as evidence for the existence of a racially based school counterculture.

Resistant behaviour reaches its apotheosis in the gym and the playground. The jocks are disrespectful spectators at intramural games at lunch time; they do not sit quietly in their seats while watching the girls' teams in action, but instead offer rude advice to their female peers on how the game of basketball should be played.

When it becomes their turn to play, they are abusive of both their opponents and their teammates and constantly dispute the referee's decisions. All of this is done to the accompaniment—particularly in inter-school sport competitions—of ghetto blasters, (boom boxes) and singing and dancing to dub reggae music (1992, p. 44). As Solomon puts it, "for the jocks and their acquaintances, the gymnasium and the playing field have become sanctuaries for activities that seriously undermine the behaviour norms of the school" (1992, p. 45).

A particularly intriguing aspect of Solomon's analysis is the examination of the role that sport plays in the lives of the jocks. On the one hand, the jocks are anti-school students—although their deviant (or "resistant") behaviour is not as accentuated as that of other groups within the school, such as the Rastas. On the other hand, sport—particularly sport conducted in high school, as part of the curriculum, part of intra-school competition—can be associated with pro-social attitudes.

These contradictory usages of sport provide Solomon with a key question. Are sports used as a strategy of resistance or, conversely, is organized sport a controlling and curbing device used by the school to moderate the anti-school behaviours of otherwise recalcitrant youth? There is little doubt that sport consumes much of the jocks' time. They played sports or worked out before school, at lunch time, and after school; they did this all year round! So preoccupied with sports are they that the jocks sometimes refuse promotion to a more "academic" high school because competitive sports are not part of the program. Conversely, some jocks want out of Lumberville because of the inadequacy of its sports program. Not surprisingly, some jocks aspire to careers as professional athletes—primarily in basketball.

The answer that Solomon provides to his own question suggests that sport is both an avenue of resistance (of sorts) and, more importantly, a controlling technique for the school authorities. For black youth culture, sport provides a racially based identity and a sense of machismo. Moreover, it encourages the idea that blacks, in terms of temperament, physical characteristics, and attitudes are scripted for athletic superiority. Involvement in sport also offers a degree of esteem to boys largely confined to the lower level academic programs in the school—an argument that Solomon takes from Willis, who asserts that in the British context, involvement in sport for black males "preserved a degree of machismo from the real and imputed degradation of their conditions" (Willis, 1976, p. 153). In sum, sport—like other cultural activities—becomes a means by which marginalized black youth momentarily retrieve what has been denied to them in other domains of their lives.

But, on the other side of the ledger, the involvement of otherwise churlish youth in sport is functional for school authorities. Participation in sports teams is made contingent upon acceptable standards of behaviour in the classroom: inadequate scholastic effort or excessive absenteeism or lateness results in exclusion from sports teams. Thus, whatever opposition the boys' in-school behaviour implies, it can be neutralized by the school's hold on sporting participation. As Solomon puts it, Lumberville provides "athletic opportunities in exchange for student acquiescence to official authority. Those at odds with the rules and regulations of the school are forced into an ambiguous and compromising relationship with the authority structure. Overt resistance is replaced by caged resentment and covert acts of defiance" (1992, p. 77).

Ultimately, Solomon ends up arguing that the involvement of young blacks in curricular sports contributes to the reproduction of their marginality. It does so in a number of ways. First, the time and effort that they put into sport deflects from commitment to more conventional academic subjects that provide qualifications for the post-school labour market. Second, their aspirations for careers in professional sport are unlikely to be fulfilled: there are very few opportunities to become a professional athlete. Young blacks, therefore, pursue sport at the expense of subjects that have a more promising long-term pay off. Their pursuance of sport, combined with other acts of resistance, increases their prospects for assuming low-paying, insecure jobs when they leave school.

There has always been a tendency in subcultural studies of adolescents and school to depict the high school community as being divided into factions of pro- and anti-school students. Resistance theory is not solely responsible for this polarized view of school life. However, this dichotomized image has reached new heights with resistance theory, largely because of the ideological significance now attached to anti-school peer culture. Students who have seen through the fraudulent claims of the capitalist educational system have become "primitive rebels" (Hobsbawm, 1963); as such, they are compared favourably to the majority of their peers, both working-class and middle-class, who have been successfully duped by the system and accept its (false) claims regarding effort and success.

What this polarized account misses is that most working-class adolescents (not to mention middle-class ones) are not engaged in permanent guerrilla warfare in the classroom. Critics have suggested that no more than 10 percent of the male working-class youth in the United Kingdom can be categorized as "resisters" in Willis's use of the term (Ashton, 1988; Blackledge and Hunt, 1985; Brown, 1987). They and other commentators contend that many pupils are involved in relationships with school that are more complicated than allowed for by depiction of dichotomized pro- and anti-school subcultures. Many high school students accept some aspects of education (such as the value of qualifications), while rejecting others (arbitrary discipline, paternalistic teachers). They are, therefore, neither completely conformist nor totally rebellious but a mix of the two—including those who have made the decision to drop out of school.

Moreover, crude dichotomizations mean that conformist students are presented as slavish supporters of school authority while every rule infraction by the lads (or their North American counterparts) is celebrated as resistance. As a result, alongside plausible accounts of arson and vandalism as resistant acts are found more questionable interpretations of reluctance to answer teachers' questions as constituting passive resistance, as well as antisocial behaviour that is, in fact, directed not against teachers or the "system" but other students (Blackledge and Hunt, 1985). What Willis and those who have followed him insufficiently recognize is that student responses to school are more pluralistic than allowed for by polarized images of lads and ear-oles (translation: ravers and bookworms), and jocks and burnouts.

One final point about the politics of school resistance. The Birmingham School, although aware that participation in recalcitrant activity in school ultimately provides very little positive payoff, does regard all challenge to school authority as a progressive force, as a rudimentary attempt to redress injustice and inequality. However, recent research from Germany suggests that if there is any self-conscious political content to delinquent behaviour at all, it as likely to take on a right-wing as a left-wing form (Boehnke et al., 1998; see note 1, page 129), and that both vandalism and violence while in school and racist activity later on have common cause in, among other factors, streaming.

At the same time, though, they contend that the general drift to violent and aggressive delinquency among otherwise anomic youth in post unification Germany is arrested in some family and, especially, school settings. They find that the aggressive delinquency and right-wing sentiments of youths from East Berlin, in particular, are moderated by the pro-social influences of controlling parents and schools in which students feel that they have an investment (Hagan, Merkins, and Boehnke, 1995). The next chapter takes a further look at the roots of youthful right-wing radicalism in Germany.

VIOLENCE IN SCHOOLS

Most, if not all, of the research reviewed so far has dealt with student behaviour that is directed against the formal school culture or, as embodiments of it, teachers. Of late, though, research, has begun to consider the hurts that students inflict upon their fellow students, focusing on violence, as well school crime more generally, where students are both offenders and victims. Obviously, Columbine has highlighted and exemplified these concerns; schools are as readily spoken of now as crime scenes as they are as institutions of learning, and have become places where safety and security issues have become as prominent as educational ones.

Given the amount of time that young people spend at school (thirty hours a week or more for nine months of the year), and getting there and coming home every day, it is reasonable to anticipate that the high school and its environs will be a significant site of both offending and victimization. Certainly, American research provides some support for this proposition: neighbourhoods, businesses, and shopping malls located near high schools experience more crime than their more isolated counterparts (Felson, 1998)

However, what this research also shows is that it is the journey to and (particularly) from school that provides more opportunities for, and fewer constraints against, crime, than the schools themselves. Several American studies show that adolescents are at greater risk from criminal victimization when travelling home from school than they are during school hours. Likewise, by Felson's calculations, adolescents who attend school events outside of the regular school day are more vulnerable to victimization on school premises than they are from routine school attendance (Felson, 1998; Lab and Clark, 1997)

Other research tells a similar story. Schools are not the principal place where violence by or against adolescents occurs. American research (Elliott et al., 1998) indicates that such incidents are more likely in or near the victim's home or on the streets of her or his neighbourhood. (Similar findings from Canadian police sources were briefly reported on in Chapter 2.) And even though there has been a reported increase in violent incidents in American schools in recent years, it has been a smaller increase than in those other locales (Elliott et al., 1998). In other words, high schools are still, in comparison to other environments, relatively safe places for most young people.

Needless to say, this is not how schools are currently viewed by young people. A national Gallup poll, conducted throughout the United States in 1995, revealed that the teenage respondents felt most safe at home, least safe at school, and somewhere in between in their local neighbourhood (Elliott et al., 1998). Columbine and, in Canada, the shootings in Taber, Alberta, and in the environs of a Toronto high school, as well as the knifing at an Ottawa-area high school, will only have intensified the feeling that schools are no longer safe places for adolescents.

Understandable fears about student safety in schools have prompted two main questions. First, to what extent is violence in school, and school crime more generally, a distinctive phenomenon generated by school-related factors? And second, is there anything that can be done to reduce or prevent the violence and aggression that does occur in schools? We will deal with each of these issues in turn.

It has to be acknowledged, first of all, that much less is known about the dynamics of school violence than is known about the violence that takes place in the family or neighbourhood (Laub and Lauritson, 1998, p. 127). But more importantly, we have to consider the possibility that although school may be a place where violent crime might manifest itself, it is not necessarily the cause of that violence. Although it is undoubtedly true, as we emphasized in the first part of this chapter, that there are school factors that contribute to both delinquency and victimization— one neglected factor is school size (Felson, 1998), with larger schools and larger classes more likely to promote violent behaviour (Lawrence, 1998)—it is also naive to believe that what happens inside high school is unaffected by what is going on outside the school in the broader community.

If a school is located in a community where the population is highly transient, poverty and unemployment are endemic, and rates of criminal offending and victimization are already high, it is likely to have more problems with its students than a school without those neighbourhood characteristics (Gottfredson and Gottfredson, 1985; Hawkins, Farrington, and Catalano, 1998; Lawrence, 1998). In other words, much of the criminal activity inside the high school might simply be a reflection of familial and neighbourhood problems imported into the school setting. Likewise, the sort of crime that takes place in school is not very different from the youth crime that takes place outside of school—with petty theft, property damage, and minor assault occurring more regularly than acts of serious violence (Lawrence, 1998, p. 29).

Moreover, the violence that does occur in school likely has its roots in experiences that chronologically predate school entry. Profiles of violent youth indicate that anti-social traits are learned early in life, often in the context of a an unsatisfactory family environment. Childhood experiences of punitive and coercive parenting are important reasons why young people leave home and why some are inclined toward violent solutions to daily problems (Hagan and McCarthy, 1997). Children and youth who are abused or violated at home have been found to be twice as likely as non-abused children to direct their own anger and aggression toward others as they grow up. And what they have learnt from the punishment inflicted upon them by parents—that violence is, at least sometimes, an acceptable form of conflict resolution (Goldstein, 1986)—is then brought into the school setting.

Substantiating this importation argument is (American) research indicating that the minority of students who take guns and other weapons to school have different prior experiences and pursue different lifestyles and everyday routines than the bulk of the student population. A study conducted in rural Texas reveals that a history of prior victimization and a willingness to persistently enter "dangerous situations," use crack-cocaine, and be unaware of conflict avoidance strategies were all predictive of students' carrying weapons (Kingery et al., 1996).

American research also indicates that the prime motivation for carrying weapons is self-protection, though few weapons carriers are without prior involvements with delinquency and knowledge of, or acquaintanceship with, others who have been victims. This is a pattern that also suggests, of course, that students who bring guns and knives into school are *not* otherwise law-abiding members of the community (Elliott et al., 1998). Likewise, the same sources show that the guns used in fatal school shootings have often been stolen (or "borrowed"), rather than bought. The nature of American gun laws are such that many people, including teenagers, have little difficulty acquiring firearms legally. However, the opportunity to steal guns is more likely restricted to those who have the right sort of (wrong) connections, which suggests that students who bring weapons to school already have links to an existing gun culture. Other studies (Sheley and Wright, 1993) of gun-possessing high school students indicate that they find it easy to acquire guns from family members and friends—again, a measure of the extent to which preexisting networks offer a pipeline to lethal weaponry, if not a motivation to use them.

But even if schools are merely the unwilling recipients of problems that originate beyond the schoolyard gates, can they make a difference in reducing and preventing the amount of violent and aggressive behaviour that takes place within their confines? The answer seems to be a qualified "yes."

Generally speaking, the features that distinguish good or successful schools from bad or unsuccessful ones are the same features that serve to prevent school-based youth violence. Thus, schools that are able to elicit the inclusive support and commitment of the student body as a whole (and not just the academically talented) are less likely to become sites of crime than schools that fail in this regard. For instance, schools that minimize the sense of failure among students and encourage a love of learning are also decreasing the risk that some students will turn against the school or their peers in violent fashion. Conversely, deviance of all sorts is encouraged in the absence of clear rules about appropriate behaviour in school or when agreed-upon school rules and policies are inadequately or inconsistently enforced.

Other interventive measures have, however, been more specific, and comprise a mix of "tough" punitive strategies and more "tender" preventive and rehabilitative programs. Examples of the former include "zero tolerance" policies (suspension and expulsion of the persistently unruly), metal detectors, and random locker searches. Counselling sessions, peer mediation, and conflict resolution courses are examples of the latter. Although some of these initiatives "show promise" (Hawkins et al., 1998), most are new and await proper evaluation. But there is already evidence suggesting that application of other measures may be counterproductive—at least from an educational perspective. And this brings us back to Columbine.

In the aftermath of the events at Columbine, concerns about safety and security issues have intensified in schools all across North America. Many (most?) schools have introduced measures designed to reduce violent conflict among the student population. However, I want to consider the possibility that some of these preventive measures may not only be ineffective, but may actually make things worse. For example, there is already evidence that, since Columbine, teachers are reevaluating the meaning and significance of verbal abuse from students. One story reported in *Psychology Today* (Easterbrook, 1999) tells of a male student, disgruntled with his grade on an assignment, casually remarking to his teacher that he was "mad enough to kill." She and the school responded by having him suspended from school for a considerable period of time.

Likewise, the same author reports of cases in which students have been similarly sanctioned for revealing, in class assignments, what are assumed to be violent tendencies: when, for instance, they have written about guns in school in creative writing classes. Teachers have been encouraged to interpret violent incidents described in essays and poems as predictive of real-life events because of the knowledge that one of the Columbine killers relayed his violent intentions over the Internet in advance of the act. Needless to say, experts on adolescent violence report no evidence supporting the idea that the violent imagery employed by young writers anticipates their own imminent violent behaviour.

Other commentators have raised further questions about the consequences for learning and achievement of introducing the more obviously intrusive security measure into the schools— emergency alert systems, spiked fences, closed-circuit video cameras, ID tags, and so forth. Some experts have questioned the wisdom of turning schools into institutions that in design and atmosphere resemble prisons. Is this the best environment in which students should be pursuing their education?

It has also been speculated that when guns and violence become frequent topics of conversation among adolescents it may increase their fascination with lethal weapons and encourage, rather than reduce, disrespect for authority. And finally, when zero-tolerance policies translate into police officers patrolling the hallways, when educational priorities become subordinate to issues of social control, and when the criminal justice system makes fewer and fewer concessions to young offenders, there is a real possibility that the more punitive response to school violence will only increase the number of more or less officially designated wrongdoers in the community.

Psychological profiling is another strategy deployed in some American high schools (described as "mental detectors" in one newspaper report). It is used to identify those members of the student body most likely to cause violence in schools. Already employed to track serious adult serial killers, advocates of this technique contend that it will make schools safer and more secure institutions.

Critics claim otherwise, however, pointing out that any benefits that accrue will come at too high a cost. They argue that psychological profiling is not an exact science and that its predictive capacity is much reduced because of the rarity of school shootings: many more students will fit the right "at risk" profile than will ever commit violent acts, meaning that most of those profiled will be inappropriately labelled in their schools and communities, treated with distrust and suspicion. As one expert, Laurence Steinberg, has put it, "it is virtually impossible to identify which kids are going to commit violent acts without mistakenly pointing to kids who won't" (*National Post,* January 17, 2000). And one can easily imagine, in terms of anticipating violent behaviour, what the social and educational consequences for students might be a school circulating among teachers and counsellors a list of "predisposing factors" that they should look out for in the classroom. Likewise, what might occur if schools set up hotlines so that staff members, parents, and people in the community can phone in their concerns about those young people whom they believe are trouble waiting to happen?

So with heightened fears about violence in schools and increasing reports of guns and knives in classrooms, we are back to a view of high school as a breeding ground of problematic behaviour that would not have looked out of place in the 1950s, when the *Blackboard Jungle* image of high school first became popular. That movie, despite a story line that was sympathetic to inner-city youth, alarmed adults and, through its use of "Rock Around the Clock" as theme music, cemented the association between rock and roll and delinquency (Murdock and Phelps, 1973, p. 93). Acland (1995, p. 115) suggests that contemporary movies—*Do the Right Thing, Boyz 'n the Hood, New Jack City,* and (I might add) *Higher Learning*—inspire similar fears about youth and violence. Not coincidentally, these are all films about black youth.

CONCLUSION

During the course of the previous century, the high school became an indelible part of adolescents' lives. Young people spent—and still do spend—a considerable amount of time going to school day after day, week after week, year after year. They attend an institution that provides them with countless formative experiences, both good and bad. In this chapter I have focused upon the bad experiences, concentrating upon the motivations and opportunities that high school affords for youthful deviance.

One of the first sociologists to assign schooling a pivotal role in producing delinquent subcultures was Albert Cohen, whose theory of gang delinquency formulation was first discussed in Chapter 3.

Cohen's ideas have proven to be very influential. In particular, he has inspired a body of delinquency research focusing upon the high school domain. One part of this tradition, beginning with Arthur Stinchcombe, has addressed the comparative import of class background and school experiences as determinants of delinquent outcomes.

Others have explored the different subcultural activities of anti-school students. In addition to the local environment of the street and the community, I examined how school-rejecting youth make use of the mass media—pop music and other aspects of commercial leisure activity aimed at young people.

The school has also been an important research domain for subcultural theorists interested in the notion of resistance. For cultural Marxists associated with or inspired by the Birmingham School, the high school has become a crucial site of class-based resistance to capitalist domination.

The resistance paradigm has been applied to Canadian high school dropouts, but the results have only partially supported its major contentions. In particular, it appears that dropouts reject school to a lesser degree than resistance theory predicts they should. Moreover, opposition to school and dropout behaviour relate more closely to immediate experiences in school than the continuing influence of class background. The findings from both the earliest Albert Cohen–inspired research and the more recent resistance approach therefore suggest that the high school is a relatively autonomous source of involvement in deviant and delinquent subcultures.

The last part of the chapter has addressed the issue of school violence. In large measure, school is the place where growing concerns about youth victimization have crystallized. I noted that although some students undoubtedly feel unsafe in school, most research indicates that adolescents are at less risk there than elsewhere. Finally, we raise the strong possibility that much so-called youth crime is a reflected manifestation of broader societal problems that have been imported into the school setting and that—particularly in the aftermath of Columbine—some attempts at curbing violence in schools may be counterproductive.

NOTES

1. More recent research conducted in Germany has also demonstrated broader societal effects of streaming/tracking. Boehnke, Hagan, and Hefler (1998) found that, more than any other variable, including social class background, an educational career spent in low-status tracks is the best predictor of subsequent, post-school, racist attitudes and behaviour.

2. The heavy metal subculture has been a popular form of deviant expression in Canada and the United States for over thirty years. During this time its core cultural elements—long hair, jeans, denim, and leather jackets—have changed very little. Its durability speaks to its authenticity as an outlet for rebellious white youth in North America, for whom heavy metal rock is the music of choice.

   In her excellent analysis of heavy metal, Deena Weinstein has referred to it as "the Beast that refuses to die" (1991). She also notes that the almost universal disdain for heavy metal—as articulated by both predictable sources (parents, teachers, politicians, church ministers) and less predictable ones (rock critics)—has solidified the metal subculture and given its members an important identity as "proud pariahs."

3. There is, however, more than a hint of W. B. Miller's conceptualization of "lower-class culture" as a generating milieu for deviancy in Willis's account (1976). Values and themes that are normative in working-class life are imported into the classroom where they clash with the middle-class prescriptions for a successful school career.

Out on the Streets: Subcultural Activity among the Young and Marginal

INTRODUCTION

There is, as I have mentioned, a recurrent character to much thinking about juvenile delinquency. The Chicago School in the 1920s, grappling with the theoretical and practical consequences of expanding and overcrowded cities, made the street and the community the principal setting for the study of delinquency. The street was where largely white, second generation European adolescents came of age, the place where the collective experience of dislocation manifested itself in delinquent networks that, at the same time, helped the youthful misfits adjust to their host society (Finestone, 1976, p. xiv). However, as more kids stayed longer in school, the high school gradually emerged in the years following the Second World War as an equally important milieu for adolescent deviance. Increasingly, delinquency was linked to adjustment problems in the school rather than on the city streets. Hence, as we saw in the previous chapter, a considerable amount of research has focused upon the causes and consequences of problems in high school.

The study of subcultural delinquency, however, has subsequently moved back to the streets. This is largely because young people are, once again, facing a range of dislocating social experiences—joblessness, homelessness—that have their origins in economic changes. It is to these changes, and their consequences for patterns of youthful conformity and deviance, that we now turn.

YOUTH UNEMPLOYMENT AND ITS CONSEQUENCES

Young people in advanced capitalist societies have been affected disproportionately by a series of far-reaching economic changes that have occurred over the past decade or so. Evidence of a fundamental restructuring of the economy can be found in the growing dominance of transnational corporations: deindustrialization, which has led to the permanent loss of traditional factory jobs; the large-scale flight of capital to hitherto undeveloped economic areas; the rise of new technologies; and the growth of the service sector, which contains more "bad" jobs than "good" ones.[1]

One of the more obvious and visible consequences of these changes is growing evidence of structural unemployment: a situation in which rates of unemployment remain persistently and perhaps permanently high because too many people are chasing too few jobs. More to the point, it is suggested that one of the attendant features of structural unemployment is the creation of an underclass, composed of unemployed and underemployed individuals excluded from participation in productive labour market activity, whose lives are increasingly defined by impoverishment and homelessness.

Labour force data reveal a significant long-term increase in unemployment in all capitalist societies. Box (1987) reports that between 1965 and 1987, unemployment in Britain rose by a factor of ten, meaning that roughly one person in seven did not have a paid job. Over the same period, the number of people unemployed in the United States tripled from 3 to 4 million to nearly 11 million, a rate of one in ten. A similar trend is evident in Canada. In 1965 the unemployment rate was 3.9 percent; by 1993 it stood at 11.2 percent.

Not only are the numbers of unemployed and rates of unemployment on the rise, there is also evidence that the duration of unemployment is increasing. Box (1987) calculates that of those unemployed in Britain in 1965, one-quarter found work within two weeks, while another quarter were gainfully employed within a couple of months. By 1985, 40 percent of the jobless had been without work for more than a year, and a further 20 percent had been jobless for between six and twelve months. Again, Canadian and American data similarly point to increasingly lengthy periods of unemployment: being without work has become a dominant feature of many people's lives.

What is also apparent from the labour force statistics is that young people are bearing the brunt of the economic changes that have resulted in high rates of unemployment. Study after study shows that it is the young (those aged between 15 and 24) who are most susceptible to unemployment—particularly those with the fewest educational credentials. Box has estimated that in 1987 one in four British males and one in five females aged between 18 and 24 were without work; this is also the age group from which the long-term unemployed are increasingly drawn. A similar picture is evident in the United States, where the unemployment rate for white males aged between 16 and 19 was double that of white males aged 20 to 24 and triple that of older white males. Among blacks, Hispanics, and other visible minority groups, the concentration of joblessness is even higher. (Not surprisingly, debates about an emerging underclass in the United States have centred upon these groups.) And in Canada, there has been a dramatic upsurge of youth unemployment from the 1970s, when it stood at 9.7 percent, to 1993, when it reached 20.2 percent. Although the rate for young adults between 20 and 24 has subsequently declined (in 1996, it was down to 13.6 percent), it was still at over 20 percent for 15- to 19-year-olds that same year.

One of the important consequences of global youth unemployment is that it has broadened the range of available public images of young people (Frith, 1985). To the traditional fears of delinquency and occasional outbursts of envy has been added an element of compassion: youth are recognized as the principal victims of economic transformation. Political and media commentators regularly draw attention to the creation of a "lost generation," make references to "Generation X," and talk about wasted human resources (see Chapter 1). Similarly, academic pundits ruminate on "the risk society" (Beck, 1992), and ponder its affect on young people. These declarations are recognition of the importance of a paid job for young people making the transition to adult life. For young people trying to establish their footing in the world, a (paid) job is vital for both economic reasons (money) and psychological ones (work is an important source of personal identity) (Jahoda, 1982).

Nonetheless, genuine expressions of sympathy are tempered by echoes of the older concerns. More specifically, the same media and political outlets are fearful of the collective consequences of an unresolved youth unemployment problem. Will those confronted by limited job prospects seek out delinquent, or even worse, political solutions?

The denial of both an income and a work-based identity is expressed by some claims-makers in particularly alarmist terms: unemployed youth may pose a major threat to public order. Two decades ago, the prime minister of the day, Pierre Trudeau, commented that high unemployment "is creating social discontent and many other uncertainties in the minds of young people"

(*Globe and Mail*, September 24, 1983). Trudeau's newly appointed youth minister echoed the concern with his assertion that "if we don't tackle the problem globally—by all of the partners in society—a generation will be sacrificed or a generation will revolt" (*Globe and Mail*, January 30, 1984). Events in Britain at that time provided the background for these fears. The director of Central Toronto youth services, referring to street riots involving gangs of unemployed youth in the United Kingdom, admitted that he was reluctant to become a "harbinger of doom but [his] prediction is there will be a lot of social unrest in a few years' time" (*Globe and Mail*, March 7, 1984).

Although none of these worst-case scenarios have ever materialized, similar fears have been repeated periodically and have a particular resonance in regions of the country where unemployment is a chronically serious problem. An example in this regard is Newfoundland, where economic crises in general, and unemployment in particular, have been linked to apparent increases in violent and aggressive criminal behaviour. Front and centre among these concerns—freely expressed in the local media, as well as by business groups, clergy, and the police—have been unemployed male youth, whose vengeful conduct, it is feared, will be directed against society. How the frustration and disadvantages of the unemployed might lead to violent crime was expressed by one witness to the Newfoundland Royal Commission on Unemployment:

> I see the young people in our community getting very upset and possibly there could very well be a sudden rage of the people towards the Government, and maybe in our community, towards whatever groups of people they see as being in authority, which are seemingly not doing anything to help. It's like a time bomb which is very soon, I should think, ready to explode ... The correlation between crime and unemployment is a reality. Many individuals find themselves in a rut. As long as the present unemployment situation continues, the crime rate will continue to rise due to the poverty cycle and the social and psychological effect that this cycle has upon the individual. (Clark, 1986, pp. 1, 2)

Testing the validity of these assumptions has been the focus of research conducted by Bill O'Grady (1991). He begins by noting that those who make such claims buttress their case with a liberal use of available crime statistics. Examining their data sources—Statistics Canada Uniform Crime Rates for Newfoundland and annual reports of the Royal Newfoundland Constabulary—O'Grady finds evidence to suggest that a disproportionately large number of convicted and incarcerated thieves in Newfoundland had substantial experience of unemployment. On the face of it, this would seem to confirm the causal connection between unemployment and crime. However, O'Grady remains skeptical because of the manner in which the statistics have been compiled and put to use.

Examining a study of violent retail crime conducted by the St. John's Board of Trade, he found that it reported a 26 percent increase in robberies between 1978 and 1983. However, if other comparison points had been used, either 1978 and 1982 or 1979 and 1983, a decrease in the number of robberies would have been observed. He concludes that, rather than increasing steadily on a yearly basis, the number of retail robberies, in fact, fluctuated: some years they were up, some years they were down. Second, the study did not take account of the fact that the City of St. John's had expanded to include a new suburb of 60 000 people. In the report, robberies were discussed in terms of reported incidents rather than rates standardized for size of population. O'Grady argues that had this computation been done, the study would have failed to find any substantial increase in retail robbery in St. John's.

An examination of other local crime statistics tells a similar story, and O'Grady concludes that there is no compelling reason to believe that any real rise in retail robbery in St. John's has occurred. How, then, does he explain the fact that conviction for violent crimes in Newfoundland is linked to increases in the number and length of custodial sentences? The argument advanced draws on labelling theory (see Chapters 1 and 3). In the minds of many people, including members of the judiciary, young unemployed males are a threat to law and order. Moreover, judges are in a position to actually do something about these anxieties. The result is a growing judicial recourse to punitive prison sentences designed to incapacitate and deter problem populations such as young, unemployed males.

A similar line of argument was developed earlier by Box and Hale, who have shown that in the United Kingdom members of the judiciary share conventional assumptions about the criminogenic conditions of unemployment and act punitively to restrict their effects. They argue that as unemployment has grown, so too has the prison population, and at a rate that cannot be explained by the number of crimes actually committed. Similarly, they found that as unemployment rates began to climb, the sentencing patterns of judges became harsher (Box and Hale, 1982).

O'Grady makes a similar case for what has happened in Newfoundland. He is able to show that more and longer sentences are being handed down by judges, even though statistical evidence supporting arguments about increasing numbers of violent incidents is not strong. He concedes that what constitutes a measured level of response to an unsettling condition or set of incidences is often debatable: at what point with, say, violent crime, does a justifiable level of concern become an overreaction (Waddington, 1986, p. 246)? Nevertheless, O'Grady is able to show that armed robberies are still only a small part of Newfoundland's crime problem and have not substantially increased in numbers in recent years. The fact that the response of both police and media in St. John's is out of proportion with the scope of the problem obliges him to conclude that this situation has all the hallmarks of a moral panic.

There is little reason to believe that the same conclusion does not apply more generally. Only rarely have responses to high rates of unemployment included street riots and other manifestations of collective dissent most feared by politicians and the media. However, the fact that youth unemployment fails to produce the dramatic effects often attributed to it does not mean that chronic joblessness has no bearing upon youthful deviance. Sociologists have been quick to criticize media-sponsored panics about unemployment and public disorder, but they do not reject the possibility of a real behavioural connection between youth unemployment and youth deviance, although the dynamics of that relationship are not always easy to discern. Indeed, one of the factors leading to the decline of American subcultural theory in the 1960s and 1970s was evidence from large quantitative studies showing that, at an individual level, the relationship between unemployment and crime was not always very evident. Some criminologists of the day therefore concluded that poor economic conditions are not significantly responsible for increases in criminal activity. However, these studies—based on aggregate-level data collected with self-report methods—do not always capture the local or community-based processes that steer inner-city adolescents toward deviant activity. The fact of the matter is that field workers using ethnographic techniques find it easier to identify the environmental pressures that turn some working-class communities into high-crime areas than do other researchers who rely on quantitative methods.

Ethnographic inquiries have taken two general directions. First, there has been a resurgence, particularly in the United States, of "gang studies" (for example, Huff, 1990, 1996). Here the concern is with what is happening to youth subcultures in the most disadvantaged segments of American society. Second, there has been a proliferation of research about street youth and how experience with unemployment, poverty, and homelessness might be related to crime and deviance.

CRIMINALITY AMONG AN UNDERCLASS

Turning to the first of these concerns, we find that the recent investigation of serious subcultural delinquency in the United States has focused not simply—as in the past—upon working-class youth, but upon minority youth: Chicanos, blacks, Puerto Ricans. A common thread that runs through these studies is that adolescents in racial and ethnic communities are increasingly part of a dispossessed, disenfranchised, urban underclass caught up in an ever-spiraling cycle of poverty and degradation that is very hard to break. Faced with few job prospects and limited non-criminal opportunities, they turn to both instrumental and expressive forms of gang delinquency as a means of relieving the pressures upon them and retaining their dignity. Subcultural membership is therefore an important source of income and identity in an urban wasteland.

Los Angeles has been the centre of the most persistent and intractable forms of street-gang activity in the United States (as evidenced by news reports and television documentaries about the "Bloods" and "Crips"). Although white gangs are not unheard of in L.A., they are outnumbered by those from visible racial and ethnic minorities. Blacks, Vietnamese, and—most notably—Chicanos (as we saw in Chapter 1) have been a frequent target of American fears about deviant youth (Vigil, 1990).

Barrio (neighbourhood) gangs have existed in southern California for over fifty years. During this time, successive waves of poor Mexicans have gravitated to L.A., where they have joined existing gangs or formed new ones. Historically, barrio gangs were not gangs at all—at least not in the sense of any systematic involvement in illegal activity. They originated as a focus for young males trapped in low-skilled jobs who sought relief in peer-group activities involving sports and entertainment. It was not until the 1940s that Mexican corner-boy culture began to be viewed as a problem by Anglo society, culminating in the famous Zoot Suit Riots (see Chapter 1).

During the 1950s, following repeated experiences of prejudice and discrimination at school, in the job market, and at the hands of the justice system, the informal street culture of barrio youth developed into more explicitly criminal activity. The barrio has become a fertile recruiting ground for Chicano gangs in L.A. They exist and have persisted over time because they speak to the problems facing the poor and the marginalized. In particular, barrio gangs offer a sense of identity and community for Mexican youth caught between the conflicting demands of the Mexican traditions of their parents and the American culture in which they are struggling to grow up. Needless to say, those who are most involved in barrio gangs are the individuals who are least involved in school, have the least contact with adult-sponsored youth activities, and whose parents, due to the immediacy of their own problems (unemployment, poverty, inadequate housing), have little time for them.

The cultural axioms and preferences of barrio youth are familiar to us from other studies of deviant adolescent subcultures: partying (including the liberal use of alcohol and other drugs), petty crime, and occasional bouts of fighting. Loyalty to family, friends, and neighbours is an important value, as is machismo. On the other hand, and predictably enough, scholastic achievement and regular employment is rejected—principally because good jobs are not available to barrio youth.

In terms of their subcultural style, the adaptation made by Chicano youth involves the "selection and re-shaping" (Vigil, 1990, p. 60) of various elements from Mexican-American and Anglo-American culture and, to a lesser degree, black culture. The resulting configuration is satisfying to subcultural participants but threatening to police and the mainstream community.

Most commentators agree that the subcultural activities of Chicano youth have escalated in recent years. The explanation is found in economic changes that have resulted in fewer job opportunities for those without skills or educational qualifications. This situation is further aggravated by the fact that in the Mexican communities in L.A. rents have increased while housing construction has declined. Barrio youth thus face two worsening problems: finding work and escaping from overcrowded conditions in the parental home.

These deteriorating conditions mean that young people remain gang members longer—they find it increasingly difficult to grow out of crime. Moreover, they become deviant role models for younger members of their community. Although most barrio youth make the transition to more conventional adult lifestyles, a small number establish households in which illicit activities (drugs in particular) are common. Not surprisingly, this provides a milieu in which the next generation learns deviant values and criminal techniques, and so the cycle continues.

That declining economic opportunities make it difficult for juvenile offenders to break criminal conventions is also evident from Hagedorn's study of youth gangs in Milwaukee (1988). Milwaukee had a gang problem in the 1950s that eventually disappeared when gang members—the children of visible minority immigrants—reached adulthood and found stable, albeit largely unskilled, jobs in Milwaukee's manufacturing industry. However, the collapse of these traditional industrial jobs in the 1970s and 1980s has resulted in a revival of gang activity among a newer generation of blacks and Puerto Ricans unable to find work in a depressed economy.

As Hagedorn tells it, contemporary youth gangs in Milwaukee began life as loose friendship groupings of neighbourhood children with shared leisure interests, most notably breakdancing. These developed into gangs after fights at local dance contests. Other gangs grew out of traditional corner-boy groupings already in existence. Violent incidents between different groups became more common, and increasingly their members defined themselves in gang terms. Both the police and the mass media started paying more attention to them, strengthening the burgeoning gang identity.

In contrast to the gangs of an earlier era, which were largely temporary adolescent adaptations to problems facing new immigrants to the United States, contemporary subcultures in Milwaukee are depicted by Hagedorn as being both more durable and less exclusively adolescent. This is so because jobs of the sort held by the parental generation are no longer available. Economic restructuring has eliminated the traditional working-class jobs that, in the 1950s in Milwaukee, represented an exit for minority adolescents from their delinquent careers. Whereas subcultural delinquency was once a transitory phenomenon that faded with entry into full-time employment, it has because an increasingly permanent condition involving young adults who, because of few work opportunities, are unable to break their ties to deviant activities and networks.

YOUTH CRIME AND THE INNER CITY

The work of Vigil and of Hagedorn and of others (for example, Horowitz, 1990; Anderson, 1994) is mainly concerned with the development and hardening of subcultural traditions in ethnic communities hard hit by economic decline; it is only tangentially interested in the broader phenomenon of youth crime. This, however, has been the focus of other studies of rundown inner-city areas in both the United States and Canada, where the work of Gordon West (carried out in Toronto in the late 1960s) clearly anticipated much of the subsequent ethnographic renaissance on the North American continent.

In an inner-city neighbourhood of Toronto, West observed (and interviewed) forty young thieves who came from the sort of background and had the sort of experiences regularly described as "disadvantaged." Their schooling had been poor, they were often dropouts or graduates of non-matriculation programs in high school, and significant portions of their post-school life had been spent unemployed. They were involved in a wide range of theft-related activities: they variously shoplifted, burgled houses, stole and stripped cars, "clouted" (stole goods in transit), and broke into and stole from factories and warehouses (West, 1978, 1979).

At the same time, West acknowledged that there were working-class adolescents in the same community who did not become thieves. Those who did so had access to the sort of adult criminal networks described by Cloward and Ohlin (1960). Experienced adults taught their young charges the few rudimentary skills necessary for the thieving game. Despite this deviant occupational socialization, the career of serious thieves is, according to West, very short. Various factors—low economic rewards, arrest and imprisonment, development of conventional liaisons (wives and girlfriends)—undermine commitment to a deviant career. Many leave the "profession" within two or three years.

It is probable that West was conducting his research at a time (and place) when illegal drug transactions were less prevalent than they are now. Exploring the connection between youth crime and the drug trade has been the objective of Felix Padilla's more recent observational study of a Chicago-based Latino gang (1992).

The Diamonds, as he calls them, are involved with instrumental or economic crime, and are depicted by the author as rationalists who have made a calculated decision to traffic drugs because, as minority males with few skills or qualifications, more legitimate business prospects are not available to them. Throughout his ethnography, Padilla consistently draws a parallel between the Diamonds' illegal activities and legitimate business practices—a similarity that is captured in the title of his book, *The Gang as an American Enterprise*. Like more conventional work organizations, gangs provide their members (or employees) with the skills and training for successful transactions, as well as offering them a degree of security. New members are recruited and deals are made with potential rivals over services and territory—just as in the legitimate business world. Moreover, they share the same motivation for their behaviour—making money.

Padilla links the resurgence of gang activity in America to the increasingly lucrative profits to be made from the drug trade. Youth gangs have replaced organized family-based crime syndicates as the principal suppliers of cocaine and crack, as Uzi and AK 47 automatic guns have superseded fists, knives, and other "low-tech" weapons as the stock in trade of gang conflicts.

"Rational choice" arguments have also filtered into the two other recent studies of American gangs. Jankowski similarly explains involvement in gangs as a calculated decision, motivated by the realization that they provide more opportunities—for money, girls, good times—than an equivalent commitment to conventional activities. Gangs therefore provide an avenue of advancement for ambitious but disadvantaged "minority" adolescents (1991).

As we saw in Chapter 3, one of the recurring problems with subcultural theory, American and British, is that it fails to explain why not all adolescents born into conditions of disadvantage grow up to become delinquent. Subcultural theorists do not find it easy to explain why delinquent motivations do not always lead to delinquent outcomes. Mercer Sullivan is a researcher working in the subcultural tradition who is sensitive to this problem and he has tried to overcome it (1989).

Sullivan's focus is upon sources of variation in criminal activity among members of youth cliques drawn from three different communities in the Brooklyn area of New York City. Although there are individual variations in group members' criminal experiences, more important basic similarities in patterns of involvement could be found within each neighbourhood group. The neighbourhoods in question were a black public housing project (Projectville), a Hispanic area (La Barriada), and a traditional white working-class neighbourhood (Hamilton Park).

Youth crime was less of a problem in Hamilton Park than in the other two communities. Factory jobs were still available to school leavers who had the appropriate personal contacts and networks. Family life was relatively secure and parents were able to impose non-coercive controls upon their children.

By contrast, La Barriada and Projectville youth fared much worse in the labour market and were much more involved in street crime. Particularly during the mid-teenage years, clique members from the two minority neighbourhoods were involved in what Sullivan calls "high risk, low-return theft" as their main source of income. This pattern is then explained in terms of the greater poverty of the households in the two communities, the absence of legitimate employment opportunities, and the weakened system of local social control.

Although youths in all three neighbourhoods participated in group acts of exploratory theft in early adolescence, those from Hamilton Park tended not to progress to regular acts of burglary, larceny, or robbery as they grew older: their relatively greater access to legitimate jobs meant that they did not have to resort to economic crime.

In making this point, Sullivan is emphasizing that deprivation and lack of opportunity were not the motivating forces underlying initial youthful excursions into criminal activity. Like the delinquents who have been studied since the days of

Thrasher and the Chicago School, the youths in Sullivan's study originally became involved in crime, not because of rational decision-making, but through play. Over time they became increasingly immersed in crime as they began to calculate the relative merits of committing themselves to school, work, and illicit enterprises in light of their access to those domains.

The decision to choose criminal rather than conventional options is prompted by other experiences as well. Probably the most important of these were early encounters with the criminal justice system. The Hamilton Park youths had resources for coping with the attentions of police and courts that were not available to their counterparts in the other neighbourhoods. Money and personal connections allowed them to manipulate the system to their own advantage. They—or more accurately, their parents—had sufficient money to make bail or hire defence lawyers if they were arrested for their crimes. Lacking these resources, the minority youth of La Barriada and Projectville had to depend upon (poor quality) public defenders, were more likely to plead guilty to charges, and therefore were more likely to end up in prison.

As a result, youths in both of the minority neighbourhoods became more and more embedded in criminal activity, travelling farther away from their home turf to commit increasingly serious economic crimes, which netted them progressively heavier punishment. The various drug deals and break-and-enters in which they participated were income-generating activities, but the gains were only short-term ones because these activities further estranged and isolated the youths from the legitimate labour market and schooling. The working-class white youths were able to take advantage of parental contacts to get jobs and were buffered from the stigmatizing effects of encounters with police and courts, but the minority youth were becoming more embroiled in illicit activities.

Two other factors served to strengthen the burgeoning criminal careers of the Hispanic and black youth: in La Barriada there was an open market for illegal goods and services, while in Projectville factories and warehouses were physically isolated and therefore easy to break into and enter.

This brings us to the title of Sullivan's book: *Getting Paid*. The phrase comes from the street argot of the ghettos. It is not meant literally: street youth are not unaware of the conventional moral distinction between "crime" and "work." They do not, however, accord much significance to the differences between these two ways of making money. Indeed, they use the term as a derisive comment on the money-making enterprise. As Sullivan puts it, "they are inverting mainstream values with conscious, albeit savage, irony" (Sullivan, 1989, p. 245).

The analysis of youth crime proffered by Sullivan has clearly been influenced by the work of the British subcultural theorists, particularly Paul Willis. There is a similar emphasis upon subcultural adaptations, nominally freely entered into, that make the present more tolerable but whose long-term effects reproduce the status quo. Like Willis' "lads," Sullivan's youths have "chosen" unemployment over low-grade jobs, crime over the conventional labour market, the streets over school. In doing so they challenge—partially, temporarily—the dominant culture, by rejecting goals that are beyond them. Echoing Willis, Sullivan argues that his sample members have ideologically penetrated the structural constraints that encumber their lives. However, those youthful insights carry a heavy price—a lifetime of economic marginality and endless confrontations with the various agents of social control. Once again, it is a case of short-term gains being cancelled out over the long haul of the life cycle. With the passage of time, their insights become a liability, binding them into unwelcome, low-skilled, unstable jobs as adults. And these are the more fortunate ones, as Sullivan concludes: "Alternatively, some will die: others will spend much of their lives in prison or mental hospitals. Few will graduate to lucrative criminal careers, and few will continue in the patterns of street crime of their youth" (Sullivan, 1989, p. 250).

These largely ethnographic accounts leave little doubt that serious subcultural delinquency is still with us. Indeed, the economic changes that we discussed at the beginning of this chapter suggest that in the United States, at least, rather than fading away, adolescent street gangs have become increasingly entrenched or "institutionalized" (to use Hagedorn's phrase). Unemployment and its attendant hardships have made it increasingly difficult for working-class adolescents to find work and abandon fledgling deviant careers that they might otherwise have grown out of. In this respect, contemporary American gangs are different from those originally investigated by Thrasher and Shaw and McKay.

The youth gangs studied by the Chicago School were, at least in retrospect, a transitory phenomenon. They helped white European immigrants adjust to a new and very alien society. As working-class adolescents started to learn the language and acquire the culture, they began to assimilate; they eventually found jobs, secured housing, and began the process of settling down. The subcultural solution was therefore a "single generation" adolescent adaptation to the rigours and uncertainties of slum life. This is no longer the case: growing problems of poverty and unemployment have made gang life a more stable and permanent feature of the urban underclass in the United States.

SKINHEADS AND THE POLITICS OF RACE

Lest the impression be conveyed that serious delinquent activity in the United States is now the exclusive preserve of a minority underclass, I need to say something about a predominately white youth group that is growing in prominence. I am referring to skinheads, a group motivated more by racial ideology than economic hardship, but whose activities, nonetheless, have at least partially been fueled by recession and unemployment.

In the theoretical discussion of deviant subcultures in Chapter 3, I argued that in the British literature skinheads were originally presented as working-class traditionalists who defiantly oppose encroachments upon existing economic and cultural patterns. According to this formulation, unemployment—in the guise of economic restructuring and redevelopment—was one of the principal factors responsible for the emergence of skinheads in the United Kingdom. The Birmingham School sees skinheads as a class-based youth movement motivated by resistance to capitalism. I also mentioned that since their first appearance in England in the mid-1960s, skinheads have become something of an international phenomenon, and are now a highly visible presence on the streets of most major North American and European cities.

The skinhead subculture is also, and more importantly, unambiguously associated with racism—although this aspect of skinhead behaviour was not given much emphasis by British subcultural theorists. As skinheads have become internationally prominent, and as their racist behaviour has become more inescapable, greater sociological attention has been paid to them on this side of the Atlantic.

In his book *American Skinheads* (1993), Mark Hamm's starting point is the growing prevalence of racist attacks on non-white minorities by skinhead groups in the United States. He then goes on to note that there are at least two important differences between neo-Nazi skinheads and the traditional sort of street gangs studied by American criminologists. First of all, American skinheads organize their recruitment policies, ideology, and day-to-day practices around the principle of racism: skinheads are white, while nonwhites (along with Jews and homosexuals) are targets for their violence. Second, violence characterizes their activities more comprehensively than is the case with any other deviant youth subculture; so much so, in fact, that Hamm refers to skinheads as a "terrorist youth subculture."

How do we make sense of American skinheads? To answer this question Hamm initially observed and subsequently interviewed a small number of skinheads in different parts of the United States. These structured interviews were supplemented by further contacts and additional interviews with members of various skinhead organizations. In total, he interviewed thirty-six skinheads on topics familiar to all strands of subcultural research: backgrounds, goals, politics, style, music, and criminal involvement. His reading of the skinhead movement in the United States follows.

Hamm argues that, in the first place, they are products of (white) working-class families. They grow up conforming to the dominant achievement ethic and set for themselves realistic occupational goals that they are easily capable of reaching. Successful in high school and set to enter university, they nonetheless also harbour traditional working-class aspirations for manual employment. Leaving high school, they abandon the more abstract and esoteric middle-class goals and orient themselves toward traditional blue-collar manual jobs in local factories and on construction sites. In their preference for a "good" working-class job, putative skinheads are no different from countless other working-class youth growing up in the industrial heartland of the United States.

What diverts these youth toward a skinhead ideology, according to Hamm, is their exposure to white power, heavy metal music. It is worth quoting at length the process whereby Hamm believes that ordinary working-class youth become converted to the neo-Nazi cause and develop their intense hatred of racial minorities and gays:

> White power rock exposes these youths to the raw and vitriolic language of racial and ethnic hatred. It does so by presenting an elaborate fantasy wherein minorities and Jews are portrayed as agents in a conspiracy to threaten the well-being of the average blue-collar worker.
>
> And it will do so with such powerful emotion that youths will begin to link musical messages to their focal concerns about employment. Through almost daily exposure to songs such as "Nigger, Nigger," and "Race and Nation," these youths are transformed into adherents of a bizarre form of Nazism.
>
> This transformation process occurs at a metaphysical level through a sort of seat-of-the-pants shamanism. That is, players in white power bands transform themselves from ordinary musicians to extraordinary ones through the expression of highly forbidden messages and symbols that are part of a larger and widely known consciousness.

Listeners of this music, in turn, seek to transform themselves from their ordinary realities to something wider, something that enlarges them as people. They become skinheads. (Hamm, 1993, p. 211)

Paralleling this development is an increasing fascination with and exposure to firearms, and "they select the Smith and Wesson .357 magnum revolver as their subcultural symbol" (1993, p. 212). Finally, there is the crucial element that drives the whole subculture: "those youths then mix in the most powerful elixir contained within this theory of terrorist subcultures—beer. And it is beer, and only beer, that triggers a terrorist act against individuals perceived as threats to the skinhead way of thinking" (1993, p. 212).

Although it strains credibility to believe that a "terrorist" subculture can be created by excessive amounts of beer and the right (wrong?) sort of heavy metal music, Hamm argues more plausibly that economic changes in the United States heralded by the Reagan presidency made it much more likely that racist messages would receive a favourable hearing from a minority of largely white working-class males. He suggests that the economic prosperity of the Reagan era was based on defence buildups coupled with massive cuts in domestic programs (1993, p. 213); easy opportunity was promised at the same time that an impoverished and homeless urban underclass was emerging:

Reaganomics created the decade of greed in which tens of millions of American white youth became so culturally, intellectually, and spiritually vacant that their main way of defining themselves and achieving self-respect was to "go to the mall." The value of profit-grabbing and the full-scale publicity fraud of the savings and loan debacle left behind a plethora of charmless and hugely blunt architectural designs in American shopping malls that are, in the words of [Paul] Fussell, "Hitler-resonant: brutal and despotic." (1993, p. 32)

This is, as Hamm sees it, the moral vacuum in which the skinhead subculture in the United States has been allowed to flourish. He recognizes that after the replacement of Reagan by Bush, a new ingredient was added to this dynamic; the prosperity and confidence of the white American working class has been further eroded by recession and unemployment, a development that has done nothing to diminish the appeal of skinhead culture to (relatively) small numbers of other working-class young males.

As we have just seen, Hamm depicts skinheads as ordinary working-class males brought up in ordinary, functional working-class families whose frustrations drive them toward racist ideologies and political movements. He and other American researchers report little evidence suggesting that young skinhead males who embrace racist violence are drawn from particularly disadvantaged or unstable family backgrounds.

More recent Canadian research disputes this characterization of skinhead culture. Steve Baron examined the behaviour and political consciousness of a skinhead subgroup in his larger Edmonton sample of street youth (1997). He found that this subsample came from seriously and multiply disadvantaged families where violence and parental abuse were rife, the deleterious effects of which were only reinforced by negative school experiences and, later, homelessness. They had grown up as highly aggressive individuals who were not averse to attacking racial and sexual minorities. However, their violent behaviour was unorganized and unfocused and totally lacked any kind of political understanding or coherence. Baron is disinclined to view skinheads as primarily political actors.

SKINHEADS AND THE POLITICS OF IDENTITY

A second Canadian study has also questioned the commitment of skinheads to explicit racist ideology. Nonetheless, Kevin Young and Linda Curry (1997) do find that race is integral to the meaning of being a skinhead in Canada. They begin with the familiar commentary that the concern about skinheads in Canada, as elsewhere, stems from their now global reputation as xenophobes, responsible for attacks upon racial minorities and gays. Similarly, they note that skinheads have adopted Nazi ideals and goals, periodically desecrating Jewish cemeteries and synagogues, for instance.

However, Young and Curry also insist that there is no unequivocal relationship between skinhead style and racist behaviour. First of all, not all racist attacks, in either Europe or North America, are instigated by those wearing what in effect has become the skinhead uniform; many self-styled "white supremacists" dress and look like ordinary young citizens. Second, some of those who adopt the skinhead style and appearance and proudly identify themselves as skinheads deliberately distance themselves from the racist public image. Using participant observation methodology, Young and Curry observed a group of non-racist skinheads in western Canada (Calgary?). The skinheads were "OI skinheads," a variant of the more commonly self-styled "SHARP" subculture—the acronym for skinheads against racial prejudice.

These investigators found, as is typically the case with skinheads worldwide, that a skinhead identity is indelibly linked with a working-class identity.[2] This does not mean that all, or even most, skinheads come from working class backgrounds. But it is the working class with whom participants identify: a working class that is defined, literally, as those who work for a living—a nomenclature that allows them to morally distance themselves from hippies and punks, who are seen as preferring a welfare-based lifestyle to a work-based lifestyle.

Attitudes to race and ethnicity were complex and ambiguous. Although explicitly anti-racist and, by their own reckoning, "non-political," the Calgary skinheads share an enthusiasm for aggressive, racially chauvinistic white power music and a distaste for rap and hip-hop with other, more obviously xenophobic members of the skinhead community.

The Calgary skinheads also saw themselves as patriots, with a deep commitment to Canada and the Canadian way of life. But part and parcel of their love of country is a rejection of government-sponsored multiculturalism and the suggestion that Canada is, or should be, a multiracial society. And in that belief, they are probably not very different from some supporters of the Canadian Alliance (formerly the Reform) party or members of the armed forces, who in style and appearance they very much resemble.

In socially situating skinheads, Young and Curry end up, like others before them, under the influence of Paul Willis, arguing that while participation in the subculture helps the membership with their sense of well-being, it also hinders them with regard to personal social mobility. For instance, their anti-intellectualism and repeated paeans to the (moral) superiority of manual over mental labour cuts them off from many of the better jobs in the labour market.

Nor—and I don't think that this will come as much of a surprise—are these OI skinheads sensitive, New Age men as far as gender relations are concerned. As unreconstructed male traditionalists, they oppose homosexuality and accommodate females only insofar as the small number of female skinheads ("Chelseas") are able and willing to play the same sorts of minor (and sexualized) roles reported on in other studies of deviant youth culture.

In many respects, the beliefs and trademark concerns of these Canadian skinheads are not far removed from those held by ordinary Canadian adults. Although staunchly opposed to nakedly racist exercises and episodes, their critical views on cultural diversity are shared with many respectable, politically conservative Canadians. Skinheads are not the only group in Canadian society suspicious of nonwhite immigration, resentful of "special-interest groups," anxious for an end to "welfare dependency," and so on. So once again, we find that a deviant appearance notwithstanding, and despite their own posturing, skinheads have much in common with conventional adult society.

RACIAL POLITICS AND GERMAN YOUTH CULTURE

The image of the politicized skinhead, defender of the white race and Aryan nation, found in Hamm's account of American skinheads and challenged by the two Canadian studies we have just looked at is derived, in some measure, from events in Germany, where, since unification, there have been several high-profile incidents involving skinheads and racial minorities, usually Turks. Although not focusing specifically upon skinheads, John Hagan and his colleagues have, in a series of reports, addressed the nature and dynamics of right-wing extremism among young people in the newly unified German Republic (Hagan, Hefler, Classen, Boehnke, and Merkens, 1998; Boehnke, Hagan, and Hefler, 1998; Hagan, Rippl, Boehnke, and Merkens, 2000).

Their analysis revolves around the relationship between rapid social change and xenophobic attitudes and behaviour directed against ethnic and racial outsiders. It is an analysis that draws on theories and ideas previously encountered in this book, particularly strain explanations of subcultural delinquency and the notion of subterranean values.

In a little over ten years, German society has been transformed. The collapse of communism has seen the former East Germany's centrally planned economy replaced by market values, and its institutions integrated with those of the former West Germany. Change of this magnitude has demanded massive adjustment from all Germans—but particularly young Germans, who also have to contend with the normal problems of growing up.

Social change generates moral panics about young people, as we have already seen. It does so in some measure because it loosens constraints on normative behaviour, thereby making social control more problematic. Likewise, it permits beliefs and attitudes that are publicly disapproved of but not entirely rejected—in other words, subterranean values—to surface and become more prominent and explicit. Racial prejudice is the subterranean value of interest in this study, along with a particularly virulent and mean-spirited capitalist ethos.

They also draw on psychodynamic theories that contend that adolescents can improve their own feelings of well-being by identifying outsider groups upon whom they can confer a lower status. Again, the willingness to do this is very much enhanced in times of turbulent social change. In the German case, feelings of insecurity kindled by the rapid ascendance and diffusion of often ruthless market rules are frequently resolved, particularly among young people, by the expression of xenophobic sentiments.

Hagan et al. thus argue that the subcultural delinquents—the individuals most inclined to support racist attacks and other versions of extreme political deviance—are individuals most committed to what the authors refer to as "hierarchic self-interest." This is perhaps best understood as an especially competitive form of individualism that also discourages empathy for the poor and marginal. These individuals have experienced blocked aspirations and are not restrained from targeting racial minorities by familial, school, or labour market controls or constraints.

The data (largely) supporting this argument come from samples of high school–age students drawn from communities in both the former East and West Germanys surveyed, in some cases, at different times. However, not all of the authors' hypotheses were supported. In particular, they could find no evidence that low self-esteem was associated with xenophobia. In fact, they found the opposite: those with the most self-confidence were the most enthusiastic xenophobes! No less significantly, they also found that factors and experiences not central to the thrust of their thesis were important independent sources of subcultural xenophobia. The most important of these related to school. As we have noted in a previous chapter, an important immediate or situational cause of delinquent racism was tracking: those not in university-bound programs were, independent of all other factors, more inclined to xenophobic delinquency than other students were.

ECONOMIC DECLINE AND THE RISE OF DEVIANT YOUTH GROUPS IN CANADA

Times have changed since the boom years of the 1950s, 1960s, and 1970s, and the material and ideological factors that in the post-war years may have retarded the development of oppositional youth culture in Canada may be less effective. Certainly Mike Brake, writing in 1985, entertained that possibility: he postulated that a period of economic decline could lead to an increase in deviant youth activity in Canada. Similarly, McLaren (1986) has drawn parallels between the large cities in Canada and their equivalents in the United States and Britain with regard to growing problems of unemployment and poverty; these are precisely the sorts of conditions in which deviant subcultures might be expected to thrive.

Simon Frith (1985) has pointed out that youth unemployment widens the gap between media images of youth (supplied in Canada, for instance by MuchMusic and programs like *Melrose Place* and *Dawson's Creek*), which emphasize freedom, mobility, and discretionary income and the everyday experiences of constraint at school, home, and work. The implications of this contradiction were recognized some time ago by David Downes (1966) and discussed briefly in Chapter 3. He argues that for (British) working-class youth, denied much opportunity for satisfaction in school and work, leisure time takes on a huge cultural significance. Leisure becomes the one arena where they have an opportunity for meaningful action and constructive identity. This was the vacuum, aided and abetted by commercial interests, that "teenage culture" filled. However, as Downes emphasizes, there has always been a segment of working-class youth that did not have money to indulge in "teenage culture." Lacking the economic and cultural resources to achieve in school or work terms, they now find themselves denied access to leisure opportunities. At this point they resort to delinquency as a solution to a lack of meaning in everyday life. According to this formulation it is easy to see how youth unemployment might lead to increased delinquent activity: frustrated leisure ambitions would encourage the drift to delinquency (cf. Matza, again).

This argument is also found, though rarely made explicit, in media accounts of deviant youth activity. Some newspaper reports see a growing presence of youth subcultures on city streets and in shopping malls as a response to joblessness. Likewise, swarming, the popular (but non-legal) term for group attacks by adolescents on individuals in public places, has been construed as the behaviour of financially desperate teenagers who are unable to secure coveted consumer goods—expensive leather jackets and shoes—by more legitimate means.

THE RAVE SUBCULTURE: A BOHEMIAN RHAPSODY?

There was a time when the same depressed labour market conditions were used to explain the flowering of the less predatory rave culture. What gave this thesis some credibility was that this youth cult began life in the economically depressed traditional manufacturing cities of Northern England—Manchester in particular—where the original sites of rave activity (primarily all-night dances) were deserted warehouses and disused factories, potent symbols of industrial decline.

However, as rave culture has globalized, it has increasingly become a commercial proposition; serious raving now costs serious money—thereby making it a pursuit well beyond the reach of most unemployed youth. Thus, while rave participants and (particularly) ideologues see their subculture as an outlet for marginalized and disaffected youth, it is hard to construe the rave "scene" as a product of unemployment and impoverishment.

Until recently, much of what is known about rave has come to us from mainstream newspaper and television reports and, from a different perspective, underground fanzines. The former sources tell us (repeatedly) that it is a drug-centred culture driven by use of the drug ecstasy (a name easier to remember, pronounce, and spell than its scientific designation of methylenedioxymethamphetamine) that seems to fulfil the same sensory heightening function that amphetamines—"speed"—did for an earlier generation of mods. At the same time, rave culture apparently does not require full-time involvement; it is largely a Saturday night phenomenon, where, we are told, participants shed their ordinary weekday identities and concerns and indulge themselves in a night of escapist fantasy, frenzied dancing, and bizarre clothing.

Those best connected to the culture—promoters, journalists, and their key informants—all emphasize its problem-solving qualities. According to one participant quoted in the *Globe and Mail,* the rave "vibe" helps to "reassure each other that there is hope and love out there" (October 9, 1993). Another says in the same article: "There's no work. Kids are depressed. With the rave scene, they can go out and have a good time and forget about their problems." As with other subcultural solutions, there is an emphasis upon the search for community. "That sense of family is there for people who lack it. I think they get a lot of love and affection in the rave scene."

To what extent is this not entirely disinterested view of rave culture corroborated by more rigorous social scientific field research? Some answers have been provided in a recent study conducted by Tim Weber (1999). His research team interviewed some seventy-five rave participants and observed the action at a number of rave venues in Toronto. His findings are a mix of the expected and surprising. Confirming my own suspicions that it is the more bohemian members of Generation X (a term coined by Canadian novelist Douglas Coupland in 1991) who are attracted to the culture, he found that most were from middle-class backgrounds and over a third were students. But contrary to received wisdom, marijuana was the drug of choice, not ecstasy.

Rave has been a focus of concern for adult guardians of morality because of media stories of ecstasy-related deaths. However, Weber reports that up to 1997 there had been no such deaths in Canada. This is not to suggest that taking "E" has no consequences. After all, it is a drug and, like all drugs, it has an impact on the human body. But most of its negative effects are indirect. Medical evidence from the United Kingdom suggests that deaths associated with its use derive less from its toxicity and more from the fact that it induces sweating and increases the heart rate. The fatalities that do occur are a result of heat stroke—a condition brought on by a failure to drink enough water. And, at least according to some reports, ravers consume too little water because it is not freely available to them, promoters preferring instead that their customers buy expensive beverages, including bottled water, provided on-site. Weber also suggests that drug entrepreneurs have begun to contribute to a worsening drug problem because the ecstasy sold is increasingly laced with other more lethal substances such as PCP and even Drāno.

But to a very important degree the media focus upon and (subsequent) public anxiety about drugs are a distraction: drugs are an accompaniment to, not a focus of, the rave scene. For the participants themselves, raves are about what adolescent subcultures have always (arguably) been about—a short-lived escape from families and everyday realities, a search for community among friends.

In this regard, Weber suggests that the rave subculture performs a particularly important role for those who have been forced to consider themselves outsiders in high school—the bookworms and nerds of popular mythology. The hitherto marginal find raves to be an essentially non-judgmental environment, as do gays, lesbians, and women, who report favourably on the absence of predatory sexual behaviour at such events. Indeed, the traditional pickup or "meat market" role of bars and dances is rejected—and those who attempt to reproduce this behavior risk censorship from serious ravers, for whom the music is the thing.

Likewise, there are norms about drug use; those who attend raves just to do drugs are subject to censorious comments. For all but the deviant (by the standards of the subculture) few, drugs are a background mood enhancer rather than the focus of the night's entertainment. Commenting on those who break these conduct norms, one of Weber's respondents says of them, "all they care to do is go there and get drugs and look at women all night. They're not really there for the music. They're not there for partying, not there for the vibe. They are not there for anything."

Some writers have identified important differences between North American and British rave cultures—the former more middle-class than the latter (Singh 2000). On the other hand, although some British commentators note the heavy working-class presence at raves (Reynolds, 1999), others have remarked upon the relatively classless nature of its appeal and that, unlike earlier generations of mods, rockers, skinheads, and so on, the rave subculture has a significant middle-class representation (Merchant and MacDonald, 1994). Consequently, they argue that rave cannot be understood as a subcultural response to inequality and disadvantage. If the subculture can be linked to a politics of resistance at all, the link stems from opposition by participants to legislative attempts to criminalize their leisure time activities. Instead, rave—and club culture more generally—is better understood as largely individual efforts to assert cultural distinctiveness and superiority by favouring certain musical forms over mainstream "chart pop disco" culture.

What rave *does* have in common with earlier youth cultures, of course, is the ability to arouse adult fears. The highly publicized case of a recent ecstasy-related death in Toronto, for instance, led to a coroner's inquiry that heard recommendations (from the police and some civic politicians) that raves be outlawed. So far, these suppressive efforts have been unsuccessful, largely because of the lobbying efforts of pro-rave interest groups (largely the participants themselves).

For fairly obvious reasons (the overrepresentation of the middle class and well educated, the relative absence of violence and aggression, the interest in mood-enhancing drugs) rave subculture has drawn comparisons with the hippies of an earlier era. (In this regard, it would be interesting to know to what extent today's ravers are the sons and daughters of yesterday's hippies.) Certainly, I would regard both as examples of the bohemian strand of subterranean youth tradition originally identified by Matza and discussed in Chapter 1.

DOWN AND OUT IN CANADA

The emerging interest in raves notwithstanding, most research on youth deviance in Canada has been concerned with crime and delinquency. The research on skinheads discussed in this chapter is a component of this tradition, as is earlier research on the street culture of punks in Victoria (Baron, 1989a; 1989b). Increasingly, the focus has been on the relationship between economic and social marginality and subcultural activity on the streets of Canadian cities.

HOMELESSNESS AND CRIME

I want to begin with Hagan and McCarthy's exploration of the connections between inner-city street life and criminality among homeless youth in Toronto. According to the two authors, the downtown core of Toronto has one of the largest concentrations of street youth of any city in North America. Being the country's largest urban centre, Toronto attracts disaffiliated youth from all over Canada. Hagan and McCarthy calculate that in 1988, when they began their research, for every twenty youths in school there was one on the streets. Moreover, they reckon that this is a "conservative estimate." The best calculations put the street youth population of Toronto at between ten thousand and twenty thousand. The purpose of Hagan and McCarthy's research was to explore if and how street life, and its attendant problems of homelessness and hunger, led to delinquency (McCarthy and Hagan, 1992; Hagan and McCarthy, 1992; McCarthy and Hagan, 1991; Hagan and McCarthy, 1997).

Although it might seem intuitively obvious that being without food and shelter is more than adequate motivation for theft and other economic crimes, criminologists have not always prioritized these immediate causes of criminal behaviour. McCarthy and Hagan maintain that whereas sociological criminology once emphasized harsh material conditions (poverty and unemployment, for example) as determinants of delinquency, this focus upon situational pressures has given way to a growing emphasis upon offenders' social origins and environmental factors that retard conventional progressions into adult life.

For instance, strain theorists—such as Merton, Cohen, and Cloward and Ohlin—view delinquency as a function of blocked opportunities. Control theorists are fixated on the social bonds that delinquents fail to develop at home or in high school. Theorists of differential association address the social networks of adolescents. None of these theoretical perspectives is much concerned with the immediate pressures or the exigencies of current class location (as opposed to the class position of parents) as causes of delinquency. The effect of these omissions is reinforced by the growing dependence on self-report instruments as the means of gathering data on, and testing theories of, delinquency. Self-report studies rarely inquire about the situational precursors of delinquency, nor do they pay much attention to youthful respondents' own class position. Finally, as I have mentioned before, street youth have been underrepresented in previous research because, by definition, they are not in school—and therefore are unavailable for filling out questionnaires regarding their delinquent behaviour. Their absence from the classroom has similarly served to weaken linkages between class and subcultural delinquency—again, because those from the most disadvantaged and therefore most seriously delinquent backgrounds are not in attendance.

McCarthy and Hagan set themselves the task of rectifying the omissions of previous research. They focus on the situational pressures—the immediate problems of hunger and shelter—that might generate a criminal response. They acknowledge that prior events and life experiences affect delinquent motivation and therefore have a bearing upon which adolescents are likely to become street kids. But they also hypothesize that street life creates its own independent inducements to delinquency.

To test these ideas, the authors surveyed both street kids and adolescents living at home and attending high school in the Toronto area in 1987 and 1988. Respondents from both samples were questioned about stealing (food, in the case of street youth), serious theft (money, tape decks, and other items from cars), shoplifting, breaking and entering, drug use, and prostitution.

There were differences in their background characteristics. Street youth were older than the high school students and more likely to be male. They also came from poorer class backgrounds—"surplus population" families, as McCarthy and Hagan call them—and had grown up in homes with at least one biological parent absent. They had also been exposed to more coercive forms of parental control. Street youth had also responded less favourably to school than those still at home. They were less likely to have done their homework, acknowledged more conflictual relationships with teachers, and had lower occupational ambitions. When they had lived at home, street kids were more delinquent than the high school students and were more likely to have friends who had been arrested.

Hagan and McCarthy infer that disputes with parents and teachers preceded and indeed, precipitated, an early exit from home. However, their main objective is finding out what happens to these individuals after they hit the streets. They conclude that several adverse conditions created by street life lead to delinquency. The problem of hunger is alleviated by the theft of food. Hunger is also—along with homelessness—responsible for property crime. Finally, among female street youth, unemployment and lack of shelter are a prelude to prostitution.

Hagan and McCarthy conclude their study by suggesting that street life is a significant and neglected source of delinquency. Although only a small number of adolescents become street youth, those who do, commit a disproportionately large amount of delinquency, particularly serious delinquency. The omission of street youth from studies of delinquency, therefore, results in an underestimation of the amount of serious theft by adolescents, neglects the role of street life in generating delinquency, and precludes any discussion as to why and how some adolescents become street kids in the first place.

A few years after they conducted the initial Toronto study, Hagan and McCarthy embarked on a second, similar one. This time they collected data in two cities—Toronto and Vancouver (1997). Among other purposes, their aim was to find out if civic policies toward homeless youth have an effect on the quantity and quality of street crime produced by this population.

At the time of their research, Toronto and Vancouver had very different strategies for dealing with street youth. Vancouver adopted a harsher, more punitive view of youth homelessness, viewing it as a law-and-order problem requiring control by arrest, punishment, and deterrence. By contrast, Toronto has, historically, preferred to view homelessness among young people as a problem of social welfare best resolved by the provision of better shelter accommodation and more generous benefits.

These differing approaches have resulted in different patterns of street youth crime in the two cities—particularly with regard to common, minor property crime. Because Vancouver is less willing to support shelters and daily drop-in centres, homeless youth in that city spend more time on the streets, thereby availing themselves of the opportunity (as well as the need) to commit money-making economic crime. At the same time, police officers in that city are more inclined to arrest and charge the street youth whom they encounter. Toronto's historically more enlightened orientation to the young homeless has, on Hagan and McCarthy's evidence, resulted in a lower youth crime rate in that city than in Vancouver. However, recent political developments in Toronto do not augur well for the continuance of this trend. The city is moving away from liberal social welfare policies and replacing them with more authoritarian crime-control strategies.

The model in this regard is New York, where Mayor Rudi Giuliani has enthusiastically applied zero-tolerance policies to public order issues. The intellectual stimulus for these policies is a tract that has become known as the "broken windows" philosophy that began life as an article in *Atlantic Monthly* magazine (Wilson and Kelling, 1982), and was subsequently turned into a book (Kelling and Coles, 1997). Its thesis is that the best strategy for reducing crime in the community is an early and vigorous response to small and seemingly minor transgressions of prevailing standards.

The price that communities pay, so the argument goes, for not fixing broken windows, removing abandoned cars, countering rude and insolent teenagers, or cleaning graffiti from walls is that disgruntled citizens either relocate to other neighbourhoods or, if they stay, invest in expensive private security systems—thereby making crime a private problem rather than a public issue. It also signifies to disreputable and possibly malevolent outsiders that the community is open for criminal business.

Although there is little in the broken windows manifesto that requires the police to sweep the streets clean of homeless youth, this is how it has been interpreted (following the New York example) by civic leaders in Toronto. However the best available information—Hagan and McCarthy's comparison of ameliorative policies in Toronto and Vancouver—suggests that the transition from social welfare to crime-control responses will likely lead to an increase in non-violent criminal activity among street youth. And, as you might have suspected, it is squeegee kids who have attracted the most negative amounts of attention in this regard from civic politicians

SQUEEGEE KIDS: CRIMINALS OR ENTREPRENEURS?

Anybody visiting the downtown core of any of Canada's largest cities will be familiar with the phenomenon of small groups of unconventionally clad young people who wash car windshields at major intersections for small change. They are the successors to the Victorian street urchin. A hundred years ago, similar children and youth would have been selling matches or newspapers for a living.

It would be an understatement to say that not everybody approves of this means of making money. Indeed, squeegee kids have very quickly become seen as a significant social problem in urban areas. Motorists are not always given a choice as to whether their windshield gets cleaned. (I'm sure I'm not the only person who has had his or her car washed twice within the time it takes to get from downtown to home.) Squeegee cleaners are also not necessarily very polite when their services are spurned or when drivers refuse to pay for a service they may not have wanted in the first place.

Nor are squeegee kids welcomed by civic politicians, who see them as a blight on the urban landscape, tarnishing the city's image and making the downtown area unattractive to tourists. Squeegee kids are also held responsible for violent incidents— some generated by competition among different cliques of squeegeers for the best work location, but more frequently because they invite an aggressive response from reluctant clients and the police.

So for these sorts of reasons, squeegee kids are deemed to be a problem in need of a solution. First, and predictably, various get-tough policies have been proposed. Influenced by the success of New York's broken windows approach to inner-city problems, the aim has been to legislate youth off the street with new anti-squeegee legis-lation and increased police surveillance. (This has already been done in Toronto with the passage of the Safe Streets Act.)

Second, others have advised policy makers against these punitive measures and in their place proposed strategies for channeling—via job-training programs—squeegee workers into more legitimate forms of (largely self-) employment: bicycle repair work, for instance, and street vendorships (selling T-shirts or offering shoeshines).

How successful either or both of these anti-squeegee strategies may turn out to be is, at the moment, a moot point. For now, though, I want to focus on a more basic issue: what impact does squeegee work have upon those who participate in it? In particular, does it influence levels of criminal activity and mental health? In terms of these criteria, are squeegee kids more or less of a problem than other street youth?

To answer these questions, we can turn to a small-scale study conducted in downtown Toronto by Bill O'Grady and his colleagues (1998). Their goal was to compare the lives and lifestyles of two groups of homeless youth—those who earned money as squeegee workers and those who did not (and who, instead, resorted to begging and panhandling to survive). The two samples—matched in all background characteristics (age, sex, time on the street, family origins)—were compared with regard to their criminality, housing situations, and psychological well-being.

What did O'Grady et al. find? First, that although squeegee youth are by no means unfamiliar with criminal activity, they are less involved with both violent and property crime than are non-squeegee youth. As far as drug and alcohol use is concerned, both groups consume similar amounts of illegal substances. However, squeegee youth drink less alcohol than their unemployed counterparts. These findings suggest that the ongoing campaign against squeegee kids is misplaced if the motivation for doing so is to rid the streets of the most criminogenic youth

The two groups also reported different living arrangements. To their surprise, the researchers found that quite large numbers of both groups reported that they had a place of their own. What this usually meant was that they had short-term accommodation—usually on a week-to-week basis in a rooming house. Even so, it was the squeegee workers who were most likely to report an arrangement that was seen as much more advantageous than the shelter living that the non-squeegee youth were more likely to be reliant upon. Finally, the squeegee kids enjoyed better mental health than their non-working peers: they were happier, less distressed, and experienced fewer bouts of depression.

It would be tempting to conclude from this small study that it is squeegee work that makes the difference. But such a conclusion may be premature. After all, it is possible that some street youth become squeegee workers because they are less inclined to criminality, are more moderate drinkers, and enjoy better mental health than other youth out on the streets. Rather than being a consequence of squeegee work, their more robust, less antisocial lifestyle may facilitate entry into work-centred street activity.

Although this question of cause and effect cannot be answered definitively with the cross-sectional design of their study, O'Grady et al. report that the young people they interviewed felt that the quality of their lives had been improved by their decision to do squeegee work—by their own reckoning, keeping them out of jail and curbing their dependence on alcohol. However, those involved in it did not regard squeegee work as a panacea for their problems.

Squeegeeing is an adaptive response to otherwise unpromising and unforgiving life on the streets. It represented neither the summit of their occupational aspirations nor a complete solution to their problems. Mainly it provided them with more money than other options immediately available to them. Squeegee work was seen as a better alternative, both financially and morally, to panhandling, stealing, drug dealing, and prostitution, and to legal employment in fast-food restaurants or in dreaded telemarketing.

Indeed, the fact that some individuals could make $50 on a good day does not bode well for liberal, anti-squeegee strategies that involve diverting them into existing or new legitimate low-wage jobs. The squeegeers also enjoyed the freedom of the job: they could establish their hours of work, and there was no boss or dress code.

What they wanted from a job, and what they found to a limited degree in squeegee work, makes them the deviant inheritors of the legitimate free-enterprise tradition, ultimately not very different from other maverick hustlers who work hard to make a living. Nonetheless, although their aggressive pursuance of a buck places them firmly in the North American mainstream, their willingness to reject conventional work rules simultaneously allows them to maintain a subcultural identity of resistance to low-wage employment.

STREET YOUTH AND JOBS

There is substantial agreement in the research literature that if street youth are ever going to escape the criminogenic clutches of street culture, they are going to do so through the restorative effects of paid employment. Hagan and McCarthy (1997), for example, argue that the experience of a paid job diverts homeless youth from the criminal culture of the street and facilitates the beginnings of more conventional transitions to adult life. Support for this optimistic prognosis comes in their two-city study from evidence suggesting that job-holding street youth do less "general hanging out," panhandling, foraging for food, drug dealing, and crime than the rest. At the same time, the researchers recognize the poor quality—low pay, low skill—of the jobs held by street youth. More importantly, street youth make the same observation but stick with those jobs because they see them as offering a steppingstone toward a more agreeable work-based lifestyle.

However, most homeless youth do not restrict their economic activities to either conventional work or deviant work—they combine elements of both. This has been made abundantly clear in another interesting Toronto-based study of the work strategies of homeless youth. Gaetz, O'Grady, and Daillancourt (1999) surveyed 360 homeless youth in 1998 and 1999. They asked their respondents about the different ways they acquired an income, and categorized their answers in terms of paid employment, social assistance, involvement in the sex trade, property crime, selling drugs, and panhandling and squeegeeing. As you will note, these monetary sources carry differing degrees of moral approval, with paid employment obviously a lot more acceptable than the others. Panhandling and squeegeeing were the most frequently cited means of making money, in some measure because even those who had paid employment (as telemarketers, general labourers, bike couriers) also partook of these activities.

Intriguingly, the researchers found that those who predominantly earned their money from each of these different sources had different social background characteristics and prior experiences. For instance, those in paid employment were more likely to have completed high school. Females were more likely than males to be on social assistance (because they had dependent children and could not afford to work). Those who relied on drug sales and property crime were primarily male and *least* likely to have left home because of physical and sexual assault. By contrast, those in the sex trade (prostitution, escort services, phone sex) were *most* likely to have left home for that reason. They were distinctive in other ways as well: they had left home at the youngest age, had been on the streets the longest, were the most likely to have grown up in a foster home, and received the least amounts of formal education.

In case anyone thinks that street youth *chose* the deviant informal economy over the conventional labour market, Gaetz, O'Grady, and Daillancourt are able to show that over 80 percent of their respondents are interested in finding regular paid work and would prefer that option to the more deviant ones, nor are they particularly selective (or picky) about jobs they are prepared to do. Asked why they continue with the "dirty work" (which is also often dangerous), they gave three main reasons: the need to survive (which encourages them to do anything to do so), the need to pay the rent, and their inability to get a regular job because of, variously, no work experience, no qualifications, no address, no telephone, and no appropriate clothes to wear to interviews.

STREET YOUTH, UNEMPLOYMENT, AND CRIME: FURTHER EXPLORATIONS

Toronto and Vancouver may be two of the largest Canadian cities, but they are not the only ones to have sizable street youth populations. Edmonton is another locus for them, and several investigations of their experiences with crime and unemployment and homelessness have been conducted there by Steve Baron.

The first of these was carried out in 1994 and covers much the same sort of terrain, with much the same sorts of results, as Hagan and McCarthy covered in their original Toronto study. In the first part of his study Baron explores how street youths' family, school, and (prior) criminal activities affected their current criminal behaviour. He found that negative family controls—where, for instance, parents did not know where their children were, or conversely, where control was coercive—increased the prospects of youth leaving home and facilitated criminal activity on the street. Having left home, the youths become immersed in a street lifestyle that revolves, to a greater or lesser degree, around criminal activity. The street provides plentiful opportunities for criminal activity of all kinds—interpersonal violence, property crime, alcohol and drug use, all supported by contact with like-minded others.

One of the more revealing aspects of this study is just how extensive the criminal activities of his respondents are. Two hundred respondents reported 334 636 offences in the previous year. On average, each respondent had committed 1673 offences. Baron suggests that his respondents are what Edmonton city police regard as "chronic offenders," part of the 3 percent of offenders who commit 16 percent of the crime in the city. On average, Baron's total sample made four drug deals and pulled off one property crime a day. Violent offences were conducted roughly at the rate of one or two a week.

Of the property crimes indulged in (20 percent of the total offences), stealing from cars was the most popular. Small electronic equipment—CD players, tape decks, radar detection equipment—were the preferred targets because they were easy to conceal and sell. Robbery from houses (break-and-enters) were also common, the prizes here being televisions, VCRs, and jewellery. Robbery was also the motivation for most of the violent offences committed by Baron's respondents. Drug sales were another important source of income. Indeed, drug offences of one sort or another comprised the largest number of self-reported crimes.

Most of Baron's respondents came from working-class backgrounds. However, contrary to what might have been expected, the small number of respondents who came from high-status family backgrounds were most likely to commit violent crimes, sell more drugs, and generally be more involved in criminal activity than their peers who came from more humble origins.

Further analysis showed that although youths from lower-status backgrounds were more likely to be on the streets in the first place, once there, youths from higher-status families were more likely to become serious offenders. Baron speculates that this is because higher-status homes encourage risk-taking in anticipation of legitimate entrepreneurial careers; what they have learned with regard to conventional economic activities is subsequently applied by street youth to illicit ones, such as drug dealing. Similarly, Baron suggests that higher-status families overpromote the importance of success.

As youths spend more time on the street and become more involved in criminal activities and drug use, they become more detached from conventional society. Their growing distance from "normal" society corresponds to a proportionate inclination to place responsibility for their predicament on society; and as street youth start to blame society, rather than themselves, for their homelessness and unemployment, a further restraint on criminal activity is removed.

Criminal solutions are also entertained with increasing regularity as it becomes apparent that legitimate labour market opportunities are not open to them because of their lack of qualifications. It is at this point that they make a rational choice (cf. Sullivan, 1989) to break into and enter homes and trade in drugs because these activities provide a more lucrative income than "straight" employment.

But again, the motivation for their crimes is not just economic, important though this is. Unemployment is frequently boring, often depressing because of the structureless nature of the passing days and weeks. In the absence of work and school, criminal activities provide structure for street kids' lives. They offer temporary relief from boredom and fund drug and alcohol habits. No less importantly, criminal activity gives street youth a sense of control over their own lives that has been eroded by the experiences of homelessness and unemployment.

But that said, it is important to remember that these conditions do not automatically result in criminal activity and that for those who indulge in it there are important variations in how deeply they are embedded in crime. What might account for these differences has not always been made clear in research that has relied heavily upon descriptive self-reports of the incidence and duration of unemployment rather than critical evaluations of the experience of being without work.

Fortunately, more recent Edmonton-based research carried out by Baron and Hartnagel has begun to correct this imbalance by exploring subjective interpretations of unemployment as well as objective measures of joblessness. Is it only those who feel angry and bitter about not having a job who resort to crime? Similarly, is it those who feel that joblessness is their own fault and, in any case, only a temporary situation who may be less likely to express their grievances in a criminal manner than those who blame governments and employers for a situation that they do not see ending in the near future?

These questions stem from attribution theory, a line of inquiry that suggests that how we react to the things that happen to us is influenced by how we make sense of them—particularly who or what we regard as being responsible for their occurrence. Baron and Hartnagel apply its insights to finding out more precisely what it is about unemployment and, more generally, life on the streets of Edmonton that stimulate a criminal response (1997). Their findings indicate that the youths who commit the most property offences are those who report the smallest incomes (an objective indicator of the sorts of impoverishment created by unemployment) *and* are most rejecting of the dominant meritocratic ideology that says that material wealth is a reward for hard work (a subjective measure of the fairness of the distribution of wealth in society). Similarly, among the long-term unemployed, those who blamed government, the economy, and private industry for their jobless state (as opposed to their own failings and inadequacies, such as lack of effort), were most likely to engage in property crime.

There was a similar interaction between objective and subjective labour market experiences and violent offending. Once again, it is the combination of long-term unemployment and rejection of the meritocratic ideology that is most generative of violent behaviour. Clearly some, though not all, excluded youth become sufficiently embittered by their experiences of poverty and joblessness that they resort to violence.

Baron and Hartnagel also offer a further examination of the relative import of background and situational determinants of criminogenic behaviour among street youth (cf. Hagan and McCarthy, 1997). They provide more evidence that homelessness and the deviant friendships facilitated by street culture are more conducive to crime than the "more distant background factors" of family and school. The one partial exception to this pattern is violent and aggressive behaviour. A self-reported early childhood experience of familial abuse has a greater influence on contemporary violent criminality than the more immediate pressures of impoverishment and homelessness. Hagan and McCarthy found a similar pattern in their two-city study. In both Toronto and Vancouver street youth inclined to violence and aggression have been that way from a very young age. Hagan and McCarthy conclude that such traits persist over a lifetime and are unlikely to either significantly improve or worsen because of the adverse circumstances of street life.

FAMILIES OR GANGS?

Before we close the chapter on street youth, I want to explore the connections between their lifestyles and gang activity. After all, gangs are associated with crime and so are street youth. A reasonable question to ask, therefore, is whether, or to what extent, the significant involvement of street youth in crime is a measure of their participation in gangs. Might one means by which gangs resolve the many problems facing street youth be a form of subcultural solution? Some answers are provided by Hagan and McCarthy's two-city study.

At the beginning of Chapter 3, I noted that whereas much adult crime is conducted individually, youth crime is characterized by its collective qualities. A similar distinction holds with regard to homelessness. Homeless adults tend to be loners, while homeless youth more readily involve themselves in group relationships. "Hanging out" with others—filling in time—is one of the main things that youth on the streets do

Interestingly, the vocabulary that homeless youth themselves use to describe their street lives owes more to the family than the gang. In interview situations, respondents would talk about their street families. Their choice of words hints at the range of services and functions that are supplied for them by group membership. The most important of these addressed safety and security needs, followed closely by those of food and shelter. Street youth are very much at risk from criminal victimization and do not, for fairly obvious reasons, have much recourse to police services for protection. Instead, they have to create their own security agencies, which they do by joining or forming alliances with other similarly circumscribed youths. In essence, street groups are *defensive* organizations. As one female street youth says of her social network, it was "just a bunch of friends that stuck together. Like, they watch each other's back for you … Otherwise, I probably would have gotten beat up, or whatever." Street groups were also more common in Vancouver than Toronto because homeless youth got less official protection there—another consequence of the West Coast city's crime-control policies

Female street youth were particularly vulnerable to criminal victimization. Their safety concerns led to an unexpected finding. Contrary to what virtually all previous research has found, more females than males in this study reported membership in street groupings. In one instance, Hagan and McCarthy came across an all-female group (in Vancouver) formed to deal with the shared problems of teenage pregnancy. By contrast, they found males on the street more inclined to be individualistic loners.

How successful were these street families at relieving the emotional and material pressures of street life? Hagan and McCarthy provide a mixed score card. They found that membership in a street family did not significantly reduce feelings of depression or other emotional needs. On the other hand, they were more successful at alleviating the material needs of their membership. Street families did facilitate successful foraging for food and shelter.

Finally, are street families gangs? Hagan and McCarthy provide an equivocal answer: on some criteria they qualify as such, on others they don't. Yes, street families are extensively involved in crime. Yes, some of them have individuals who assume leadership roles. But other vital defining characteristics were missing: street families rarely had any geographic base—they had no sense of territoriality, nor were they male-dominated or overpopulated by those from particularly "underclass" backgrounds.

Ultimately, Hagan and McCarthy draw back from viewing street families as gangs because those in them are no more likely to engage in collective criminal activity than street youth without group membership. It is a telling comment, worth repeating, that street youth rarely referred to their group affiliations as gangs or mentioned being part of a gang; instead, family imagery prevailed.

DROPOUTS AND CRIME

In the last chapter I looked at the dropout problem and how this might be perceived in terms of resistance to school. However, dropouts are also a subject of concern because dropping out has been linked to post-school increases in delinquency. That is, dropouts are routinely seen as being more delinquent than high school graduates.

Previous research on this issue has not, however, produced consistent results. Some studies (Schafer and Polk, 1967; Schreiber, 1963; Simpson and Van Arsdol, 1967; Thornberry et al.,

1985) report a positive association between dropping out and delinquency. Other research indicates that dropping out of school, in fact, reduces delinquency (Elliott, 1966; Elliott and Voss, 1974; Pronovost and Leblanc, 1980). The logic here is that students have removed themselves from the institutional source of the stresses and strains that encourage a delinquent response in the first place. To complicate matters even further, some researchers argue that rather than being a consequence of dropping out, delinquency may be a cause of it (Bachman et al., 1971, 1978).

However, all of this (exclusively American) research has concentrated upon the school factors and experiences that encourage or inhibit the delinquent careers of those adolescents who have dropped out of school. The usual research strategy is to track patterns of delinquency from the beginning of high school to the first year or two out of it. In fact, the best known of these studies only follows dropouts to the point in time when they would have normally graduated from high school anyway (Elliott and Voss, 1974). None of these studies therefore have very much to say about how experiences after high school might influence delinquency. In particular, they have nothing to tell us about the impact of labour market experiences upon dropouts' delinquent involvements. This is one of the issues concentrated upon in an Edmonton study of dropouts (Tanner, Hartnagel, and Krahn, 1995).

Many of the respondents in the Edmonton survey had encountered problems in finding and keeping paid work upon quitting school. A large number had experienced unemployment, and many more had to settle (temporarily, as they saw it) for low-paying, unskilled, and often part-time jobs. They found these experiences both psychologically dispiriting and economically punishing, just the sort of difficulties that might be expected to engender delinquency. In this part of the dropout study the connection between labour market activity and delinquency was examined. Measures of labour market activity included current employment status (full-time, part-time, or no job), total months unemployed since leaving school, and number of jobs held since leaving school.

Details of their illegal activities were gained in two ways. First, respondents completed a self-report questionnaire that asked about contacts with the police and convictions by the court, their participation in a range of crimes against persons and property, and the incidence and frequency of their drug and alcohol use. Second, they were invited to answer and discuss open-ended questions about these same events and experiences.

The findings from the self-report questionnaire indicated that 31 percent of respondents had been questioned by the police and 23 percent had been convicted of a non-traffic crime in the past year. These figures are significantly in excess of those students graduating high school in Edmonton who were surveyed at roughly the same time (Hartnagel et al., 1986). Eight percent of high school and 2 percent of university grads admitted being questioned by police; only 3 percent and 0.2 percent, respectively, acknowledged a non-traffic conviction. Clearly, high school dropouts, as a group, are more deviant than high school and university graduates. Between 7 percent and 26 percent of respondents reported involvement in particular types of crime over the past year. Generally speaking, there was an inverse relationship between the seriousness of the offence and the frequency of its occurrence. Thus, many more dropouts have been involved in stealing than in physical violence. Likewise, few respondents had been repeat offenders: for most offences, the vast majority of respondents (92 percent) reported three or fewer illegal acts. When it came to drug use, alcohol was considerably more popular than marijuana or other illegal drugs: 64 percent said they drank at least once a week, compared with 38 percent who reported smoking dope on a weekly basis and 13 percent who reported using non-prescription drugs at least once or twice per month over the past year. However, the more immediately important question is whether or not dropouts' deviant activities are intensified by their experiences in the labour market.

It was found that currently employed dropouts, particularly if they were male, were less likely than jobless ones to report involvement in property crime (stealing, break-and-enter). Although current unemployment was unrelated to the use of alcohol or smoking marijuana, unemployed dropouts were more likely to use non-prescription drugs. Similarly, the total amount of unemployment experienced by dropouts was unrelated to criminal activity, but linked to alcohol and drug use. Those dropouts who had the most experience with unemployment were most likely to report frequent use of drugs and alcohol. An unstable work history—as measured by the total number of jobs ever held—was also related to the use of non-prescription drugs, but nothing else, However, none of the measures of labour market activity is related to violent crime.

Why does unemployment have an impact upon dropouts' non-violent delinquent activity? One answer, coming from strain theory, is that those without jobs commit property crimes for instrumental reasons—because they do not have the money to buy the things they want or need. However, although those dropouts in the sample who reported being short of money were more likely to commit property crimes than those who did not report financial shortages, the relationship was not very strong. If economic hardship was an important stimulant of economic delinquency, then the shortage-of-money measure would have been a stronger predictor of that outcome.

That a shortage of money is seldom the direct cause of criminal behaviour is confirmed by interviews in which respondents were asked to discuss, among other issues, the connection between unemployment and crime. Many factors were seen as encouraging deviant activity, but boredom and excessive time on their hands figured most prominently in respondents' accounts. Unemployment, which destructures peoples lives (Jahoda, 1982; Burman, 1988), greatly exacerbated this problem, relief from which was sought in alcohol and drugs indulged in with others. To some degree, therefore, unemployed dropouts were involved in a network of retreatist subcultural activity familiar from Cloward and Ohlin's original conceptualization (1960).

MORE WORK, MORE DEVIANCE?

As we have just seen, crime and delinquency rank prominently among the undesirable consequences associated with unemployment. Hence it comes as something of a surprise to find some researchers arguing for a completely opposite account of the relationship between labour market activity and deviance—one that identifies an excess of work, rather than a shortage of it, as a source of deviance. What makes this thesis particularly intriguing is that it inverts conventional beliefs about the delinquency-reducing qualities of paid work.

In the seemingly endless quest for correctives to delinquent behaviour, paid employment has long been considered a potent antidote. You can probably predict the logic of the argument involved. For instance, it has been claimed that part-time jobs teach young people proper work habits, strengthen the work ethic, give them a sense of responsibility, and teach them the value of a dollar. Ideas of this sort have generated a variety of educational programs, particularly in the United States, designed to give young people early exposure to paid work while still in school. These programs have been guided by theories of delinquency. Without access to paid jobs, adolescents might turn to theft in order to acquire the goods and services that are so important to teenage life, an argument that comes from strain theory (Merton, 1938; Cloward and Ohlin, 1960). From the perspective of control theory (Hirschi, 1969), part-time jobs should increase the range of adolescents' conventional involvements, restrict the amount of time they have for delinquency, and create a pro-social learning experience.

However, the results of a study that I was involved with (Tanner and Krahn, 1991) found that far from reducing deviant involvements among adolescents, part-time work actually increased them. We surveyed over 2000 high school seniors in twenty-five high schools in Edmonton, Toronto, and Sudbury a month before they were due to graduate in June of 1985. We asked, among other things, about the part-time jobs that they held, participation in illegal activities, patterns of alcohol and drug use, and the illegal activities of their best friends. Our results suggested that those respondents who reported the most labour market activity also reported the largest amount of deviance—as measured by frequency of illegal activities (excluding traffic violations) and frequency of alcohol and drug use.

How can we explain what might be seen as a counterintuitive relationship between work and deviancy? We tested a number of possibilities: did a job provide an income that was then directed towards illicit drug purchases and use? No (working teenagers did have more money than those without jobs, but were no more likely to spend it on recreational drug use than those without jobs). Did a part-time job weaken the controls (financial and social) that parents are able to impose on teenagers? No (working teenagers were no less likely to be controlled than non-working ones). Are working teenagers more likely to have deviant friends? Yes! And where are they likely to meet them and presumably learn deviant motivations and rationalizations? At work! We concluded, therefore, that part-time jobs contribute to adolescent rule-breaking by providing a domain in which deviant definitions are spread. As Box observed: "[M]any adolescents willing to deviate are more likely to do so if they (know) ... that other peers have and still are deviating and are prepared to cooperate in further violations and refrain from displaying moral indignation should the individual decide to do it alone" (1981, p. 137).

Obviously, these findings do not support the contentions of those who believe that working while in school will keep young people out of trouble. On the other hand, we do not want to exaggerate the significance of these findings. First of all, the workplace is a less important determinant of adolescent deviance than other more traditional factors, such as gender, or the sorts of parental controls emphasized by control theorists. Second, the sort of deviance that results from labour force participation is not very serious. Much of it involves alcohol, the consumption of which ceases to be illicit once the legal drinking age has been reached. Indeed, both a part-time job and occasional alcohol use may be regarded as legitimate experimentation with future adult roles. As Matza and Sykes observed in their early commentary on subcultural theory, much juvenile delinquency is little more than a disturbing caricature of normal adult behaviour (Matza and Sykes, 1961).

Finally, we have focused upon school youth who work primarily to acquire spending money rather than to support themselves or their families. We strongly suspect that the effects of prolonged unemployment on crime and delinquency are much more serious for people in the latter situation than those resulting from the discretionary labour market participation of high school students.

WHATEVER HAPPENED TO YESTERDAY'S REBELS?

In the final part of this chapter I want to look at some of the adult consequences of adolescent wrongdoing. What happens in adulthood to those individuals who were deviant or delinquent in their youth?

This question is different from the ones usually asked by students of crime and delinquency. More often than not, the concern is with the causes and meaning of deviant youth behaviour, rather than the consequences of such behaviour. This has begun to change recently with the development of longitudinal research designs that allow investigators to track individuals over the course of their lives.

Initially, researchers in this area focused upon criminal outcomes and examined the relationship between juvenile delinquency and adult criminality. They wanted to know if juvenile delinquents grow up to become adult criminals. The answer, in most cases, is no. Although there are few adult criminals who do not have a delinquent past, most delinquents do not grow up to become adult criminals. Those who do, as you might expect, are the ones who as adolescents displayed most involvement with delinquency—as gauged by how young they were when they started, how often they offended, and the seriousness of their offending (Tracy and Kempf-Leonard, 1996).

More recently, however, researchers have switched attention to the connection between delinquency and teenage deviance and conventional adult economic activities and attainments—occupational success and failure, in other words. The first study I want to look at examines the delinquency–unemployment relationship, using data collected in London, England. It is an important study because it inverts the usual assumption that unemployment is responsible for increased criminality. John Hagan does not deny that this is the most likely sequence of events for adults. But for young people trying to make their way into the labour force, it may be the other way around (Hagan, 1993).

What reasons does he posit for believing that delinquency in adolescence leads to unemployment in adulthood? First, individuals are involved with delinquency before they enter the labour market. As we saw in Chapter 2, delinquent activity reaches a peak in the late teens and early twenties and declines rapidly from that point. On the other hand, significant labour force participation does not begin until early adulthood. Therefore, since delinquent experiences usually precede the search for full-time work, they may affect that outcome. Several American studies, for instance, have correlated adolescent delinquent activity with unemployment in adulthood. Similarly, Hagan's own previous work (to be described in a moment) has shown that, at least for some adolescent groups, delinquency weakens early adult occupational attainments. Early, and extensive, delinquent activity therefore has the potential to handicap individuals when they seek entry into the adult labour force. Second, adolescent deviance may be connected to adult unemployment because potential employers are reluctant to hire those publicly acknowledged to be delinquent: you don't need to be a labelling theorist to realize that possession of a criminal record does not help anybody find a job.

But other less obvious factors are also probably operative (Hagan, 1993). For instance, those individuals who, as adolescents, accumulated deviant contacts and put together deviant networks are going to have greater access to deviant economic opportunities in adulthood than conventional ones. Also, delinquent youth often have criminal parents. Having parents who are involved in crime and have criminal associations provides both criminal role models and prospects for illicit employment. Conversely, these networks and associations serve as a barrier to the "straight" or legitimate labour market. Just as contacts and connections made in adolescence can smooth the entry to conventional jobs, they can have a similar effect in the advancement of deviant careers.

Although this sequence of events has gone largely unnoticed in quantitative studies, several ethnographic accounts of adolescent subcultures have documented findings consistent with the view that delinquency predates unemployment. Indeed, we have already looked at some of them. Several of these studies focus on the drug transactions in which ghetto youth become involved. As adulthood approaches, they simultaneously find their access to straight jobs blocked and opportunities for drug-based enterprises multiplying (Sullivan, 1989; Anderson, 1990; Williams, 1989; Padilla, 1992). But the greater their involvement in criminal activities, the more they attract the attention of the police, making it more likely that their drug transactions would impede the transition to orthodox occupational careers.

Hagan is interested in explaining the dynamic whereby delinquent boys become adult criminals and an area that was one of high crime (cf. Shaw and McKay, 1942) in one generation continues to be so in the next. However, unlike the small-scale American ethnographies focusing upon minority youth (which conflate race and class), he uses quantitative longitudinal data from London, England, to explore the relationship between deviance and the labour market among the British working class.

The working-class individuals in question have been followed from adolescence to adulthood in data collected by West and Farrington (1973). The research began as a cohort study of boys born in the early 1950s who grew up in an impoverished inner-city, working-class neighbourhood. Roughly one-quarter of the sample had acquired a criminal conviction during adolescence, and approximately one-half had been unemployed by the age of eighteen. What bearing do these youthful contacts with the criminal justice system have upon adult employment prospects?

What Hagan finds is that an early, and heavy, involvement with delinquency and delinquent friends—a pattern described as "embeddedness" (Granovetter, 1985)—results in unemployment in adulthood. He also finds that parental involvement in crime (as measured by convictions) is a more important determinant of unemployment among young adults than is parental experience of unemployment. Hagan concedes that at the macro-level and among adults, unemployment probably does result in crime. But, for those in their teens and early twenties, the sequence is reversed, particularly in areas and communities where crime is endemic.

This focus upon the criminal networks shared by parents and their adolescent children goes some way to explaining pockets of conformity in high-crime areas. Hagan suggests that good boys in bad areas have grown up in families where, by luck or judgment, parents have managed to avoid official contact with the police and courts and the boys themselves have found non-delinquent friends.

Other studies concerned with the long-term impact of adolescent deviance have focused more specifically upon the role of schooling. Do negative school experiences, particularly if they involve academic failure, carry over into adult life? Is a deviant career in high school a harbinger of future adult criminality? Or, conversely, are its effects largely limited to the adolescent years? There have been several studies that have tried to answer these sorts of questions with the aid of longitudinal studies.

Marc Leblanc (1993) reported findings from one such study conducted in Montreal on the triangular relationship between schooling, juvenile delinquency, and adult criminality. Another "boys only" study, they looked at the consequences of juvenile delinquency for adult criminal behaviour, and the impact of school experiences upon both delinquency and adult criminal careers.

Leblanc et al. find that a wide range of school experiences (including tracking, bonding, and labelling) predict delinquency but that these same school experiences and variables have less of an influence upon criminal behaviour in adulthood. The one exception to this pattern is school performance: failing grades and a low IQ are predictive of criminal activity to come. Indeed, they argue that while self-reported delinquent behaviour in adolescence is a good predictor of adult criminality, a poor academic record in school is an even better one.

What do these findings tell us about schools, delinquency, and the future? Leblanc argues that they show that school factors that influence adolescent wrongdoing are not necessarily important determinants of adult criminality. I favour a slightly different interpretation. Unless unpleasant school experiences are combined with school failure, their impact is largely limited to the adolescent years. Such experiences produce (relatively superficial) flesh wounds rather than injuries that cause more serious long-term damage.

A second Canadian longitudinal study has looked at connections between school-based subcultural adaptations and conventional careers rather than criminal ones. Hagan (1991) tracked a sample first contacted in high school (in Toronto) through to young adulthood. While in high school the participants were surveyed about their deviant subcultural involvements. Their responses to the survey questions suggested that adolescents who were least controlled by parents and had the weakest attachment to traditional school values were also most involved in two distinctive subcultures: a subculture of delinquency and what Hagan refers to as a party subculture. The delinquent subculture included theft, vandalism, fighting, and running from the police; the party subculture embraced partying, rock concerts, dances, dating, driving around in cars, and drinking. As Hagan notes, it is only with the use of alcohol that the party subculture flirts with illegal behaviour. Clearly, by most people's definitions, the delinquent subculture represents a more serious brand of deviancy than the party subculture.

However, the main question driving Hagan's research involves the consequences, if any, for young adults of participation in deviant subcultures in adolescence. Do delinquency and partying interfere with their ability to achieve employment in the post-school labour market? To answer this question, Hagan surveyed his respondents for a second time in early adulthood. He found that for those individuals with middle-class social origins, both male and female, there was no significant long-term effect of identification with either subcultural adaptation. That is to say, their occupational attainments were not in any way impaired by excursions in adolescence into either delinquency or partying. Indeed, male middle-class partygoers found that their involvement in this subculture actually improved their occupational attainments! However, for those whose social roots lay in the working class, involvement in delinquency, but not partying, had a levelling effect upon occupational attainment in early adult life.

The results from this study suggest that middle-class adolescents are able to indulge in deviant leisure activities with greater impunity than their working-class contemporaries. Indeed, by engaging in delinquent acts, working-class adolescents diminish their future life chances. For working-class males, in particular, participation in delinquent subcultures is one of the experiences that lead to the reproduction of working-class status across the generations—a finding that echoes Paul Willis's argument about how working class males get working-class jobs.

Finally, let us turn to a study that I undertook with Scott Davies and Bill O'Grady (Tanner et al., 1999). Our data came from the American National Longitudinal Survey of Youth. Respondents were initially surveyed about a wide range of both serious and common delinquent activities, as well as encounters with police officers, in 1979 when they were aged between fourteen and seventeen. Twelve years later, when they were between twenty-five and thirty, those same individuals, males and females, were then asked about their labour market achievements: specifically, the jobs they got, their earnings, and their experience, if any, of unemployment.

What did we find? Those who reported the most delinquent activity in their youth were more likely to report lower occupational attainments and more unemployment. Most of the impact of delinquency upon labour market activity is indirect, particularly for females, in that those who have done less well in the quality of jobs acquired, income earned, and joblessness experienced have done so because delinquency has negatively effected their school performance, which, in turn, has made it more difficult for them to get good jobs.

However—and especially for males—some of the corrosive effects of delinquency is *direct*—that is, independent not only of grades and qualifications, but also of social class origins, racial background, and cultural resources available to them while growing up.

Why does delinquency have this effect? We suspect that there are two closely related reasons. First, those respondents who report most teen delinquency and contact with police officers also have criminal records and, given a choice, most employers will not willingly hire individuals with prior convictions—an argument consistent with labelling theory. Second, the most serious juvenile offenders will have been incarcerated; serving an institutional sentence will have had the effect of (a) making their existing job skills increasingly out of date, (b) hindering their acquisition of new skills and credentials, (c) rendering them particularly unattractive to employers (labelling again), and (d) cutting them off, on release, from all important informal sources of information about the availability of jobs in the community

The implications of our findings are twofold. First, they underlie parental warnings about staying out of trouble when young: early deviance, both major and minor, directly and indirectly, has a scarring effect on future life chances. Second, they cast doubt on the idea of benign or innocuous wrongdoing. That tradition, beginning with Matza (1964), argues that involvement in acceptable, if not respectable, teenage culture inoculates adolescents from involvement in more serious delinquency with more serious consequences (see Chapter 1). This assumption is not supported by our findings. Nor did we find any evidence that middle-class males, or any other subgroup, benefit occupationally from minor transgressions conducted in the past, as Hagan found in his Toronto study. Perhaps this is because our study focuses upon delinquent activity, rather than a "party subculture" that only skirmishes with illegalities.

YESTERDAY'S VICTIMS

Complementing our interest in what happens to delinquents when they grow up is a similar concern with the long-term effects, if any, of victimization. Although no one would seriously dispute that being robbed and attacked and so forth as an adolescent would be very distressing at the time, we are less certain about the longer-term effects of such events. The presumption is that there will be long-term consequences and they will be negative, but we cannot know this for sure because there has been little research on the topic.

Recently, however, this issue has been explored with Canadian data. Is victimization harmful in the long run? If so, why? These are the questions raised and answered by Ross Macmillan with information from two Canadian surveys—one longitudinal, the other cross-sectional (Macmillan, 2000).

His data provides, first of all, confirmation of the conventional wisdom—teenage victimization does create problems in later life. Second, he finds that the *timing* of victimization is crucial in that individuals who are victimized in adolescence experience more detrimental effects than those who are victimized earlier or later in life. Third, he has identified the domains of damage—lower educational attainments, poorer jobs, and lower incomes.

As with our study of the effects of delinquency, most of the negative impact of victimization is indirect: being a victim of assault or robbery results in a weaker attachment to schooling and reduced levels of educational performance that, in turn, lead to poorer jobs and incomes. Finally, underscoring the deleterious and enduring impact of victimization, Macmillan is able to show that even coming from a good home (that is, having loving, affluent, well-educated parents) and avoiding deviant subcultural entanglements in one's youth (staying clear of trouble) does not necessarily protect individuals from its scarring effects.

CONCLUSION

As we have seen, the tradition of street research went out of fashion in the 1960s. However, that trend has recently been reversed, for reasons that are not hard to trace. Young people have become the principal victims of recession and restructuring and find themselves at the front of unemployment lines or shut out of the job market completely. More young people are out on the street, homeless and hungry, potential recruits for deviant subcultures, and increasingly exposed to crime-producing conditions. We have noted that civic authorities have never relished the prospect of large numbers of out-of-work youth filling city streets or, more recently, shopping malls. In fact, these are precisely the sort of conditions most likely to provoke a moral panic about youth problems.

Similarly, some people believe that declining work opportunities for Canada's youth will remove an important barrier to deviant subcultural activities; no longer will they be able to hold on to the dream of personal advancement and upward mobility. When these hopes evaporate, so the argument goes, adolescents and young people will be provided with the motivation to become deviant. Extreme versions of this argument have been treated with some skepticism in this chapter.

Nonetheless, for all the overblown rhetoric about the dramatic consequences of an unresolved youth unemployment problem, there is little doubt that, as in the nineteenth century, young people are, in Harold Finestone's phrase, the principal "victims of change" (1976). In the United States, racial minorities rank prominently among those young Americans who do not have access to jobs, food, and shelter, and it is among their ranks, in particular communities, that serious subcultural crime and deviancy is most apparent.

No one is yet claiming that street kids and dropouts constitute a Canadian equivalent of the racially based underclass found in American cities, but it is clear from the research surveyed in this chapter that unattached youth are overrepresented in crime and delinquency. This does not necessarily mean that the opportunity to work will reduce deviance among the young. Toward the end of the chapter we discussed an opposite theory: that employment leads to deviance. However, I was careful to emphasize the contingent nature of these findings: the deviance in question was minor and the motivations for it unrelated to poverty and disadvantage. I do not think that they constitute a challenge to the more conventional understanding of the debilitating and deviancy-inspiring consequences of joblessness.

Finally, we examined some of the adult consequences of adolescent offending and victimization. Research indicates that delinquency can lead to both unemployment and poorer quality jobs in adulthood, and the experience of victimization can produce a similar effect. In most cases, the negative long-term effects of both offending and victimization derive indirectly via schooling. However, some effects of delinquency are direct—we think because of the reactions of significant others to the original delinquent behaviour.

NOTES

1. This discussion of changing employment patterns is taken largely from Hartnagel (1992) and Baron (1994).
2. For Australia, for example, see the study by Moore (1994).

C H A P T E R **6**

She's a Rebel? Female Deviance and Reactions to It

INTRODUCTION

You might be wondering by now if there are, or have ever been, significant numbers of female delinquents. Until fairly recently, sociological studies of crime and delinquency had very little to say about girls and women: female wrongdoers were conspicuous by their absence. All of the theories, and much of the research, that have been looked at so far are concerned primarily with male behaviour, written from a male perspective, and judged according to a male standard. If females make an appearance at all, it is as an afterthought or a footnote—a sideshow to a main event dominated by male rebels.

This neglect has been apparent from the very beginning of subcultural theory. Take Frederick Thrasher, for instance. His book, *The Gang* (1937), was over five hundred pages in length; less than a page is devoted to girls and gangs (Chesney-Lind, 1997, p. 18). Of the more than one thousand gangs that he observed and documented, only six were female ones and he regarded only two of these as genuine gangs. Shaw and McKay (1942) collected their data on delinquent activity with a similar disregard for gender. They compiled "delinquency rates" for more than sixty thousand delinquents studied in Chicago without mentioning that these delinquents were overwhelmingly male. The unstated assumption was that delinquency was primarily a male activity and a male problem. As the doyen of subcultural studies, Albert Cohen, was later to put it, "the delinquent is a rogue male" (Cohen, 1955, p. 140).

Nor is this neglect of female deviance confined to the subcultural theorists: the no less influential control theorist Travis Hirschi performed a magic trick in his book, the *Causes of Delinquency* (1969). As he put it (in a footnote!), "in the analysis that follows, the 'non-Negro' becomes 'white,' and the girls disappear."

The exclusion of girls from sociological theories of delinquency can, perhaps, partially be forgiven on the grounds that girls are more law-abiding than boys. However, this assumes that the official statistics of arrest and conviction are only measuring behavioural differences between male and female offenders—a dubious assumption, as will be seen in a moment. Moreover, even if girls commit fewer delinquent acts than boys, we still need to explain why this is so. Do theories developed with male delinquents in mind apply equally well to female offenders? If so, can they tell us why girls are less delinquent than boys despite their similar exposure to many of the same motivating forces—limited opportunities, deprived circumstances, and so on. And finally, if girls and young women participate less regularly in delinquent subcultures, does this mean that they do not face the same problems of adjustment that males face or that they respond differently to those same problems (Morris, 1987; Frith, 1985)? Some commentators, in fact, posit that what really needs to be explained about female delinquency is why it is not more frequent and extensive than it is. Marge Reitsma-Street (1999) has suggested that all theories of delinquency anticipate maximum delinquency from "those most abused, marginalized, and devalued by adults and societal institutions." Since this characterizes, in her opinion, girls' lives better than boys' lives, then the big failing of existing theorizing is that it is unable to account for the modest incidence and prevalence of female delinquency.

EARLY IDEAS ABOUT FEMALE DELINQUENCY

When girl delinquents have not been ignored, they have been mythologized and misrepresented. In fact, most of the early criminologists did both—assuming that because it was rare, female delinquency was profoundly different from male delinquency. Whereas male delinquents stole and robbed and destroyed property in groups, if not gangs, the small number of girls who became delinquent were assumed to be wayward and incorrigible, with a predilection for sexual activity. Girl delinquents have therefore been depicted as solitary sexual deviants whose condition is best understood in terms of personal pathology.

Although psychodynamic approaches of this sort dominated early interpretations of both male and female delinquency—and remain influential to this day—there is, within this basic paradigm, an important difference in how female delinquency is construed and responded to. This variation is a function of differing concerns about male and female delinquency. Male misbehaviour was seen as a threat to public order; female delinquents were a sexual problem (Murdock, 1982; Frith, 1985; Pilkington, 1994).

The origins of what has become a stereotypical view can be traced back to the pre-sociological theories of female delinquency touched on in Chapter 3.[1] Although he found fewer signs of atavism among female criminals than male ones, Lombroso nonetheless concluded that biological factors were responsible for both the lower volume of female criminal activity and the sexual content of what did occur. Biology rendered women more passive and nurturing than males to equip them for their caregiving role. When they deviated, they used deceit and cunning and were willing to misrepresent themselves—supposedly inbred female characteristics. Here we have the beginnings of a familiar stereotype: the femme fatale, a Lorelei-type figure luring boys and men into trouble. This identification of female deviance with "sexual matters" (Lombroso and Ferrero, 1895) was an early portent of future explanatory frames.

Another early messenger of this sexualized view of female deviance was W. I. Thomas, in his book, *The Unadjusted Girl* (1928). Like many studies of that era, it focused on the deviant careers of known offenders. Thomas looked at the case records of girls brought before the Cook County Juvenile Court in Chicago. He found that most of them had been arrested for prostitution and for being suspected carriers of venereal disease. Given the climate of the time—his data-gathering took place during the First World War—it is not surprising to find that Thomas took this as evidence that female delinquency was basically a sexual problem. Nonetheless, it was insidiously cultivated by social pressures: young working-class girls became "working girls" in order to secure valued consumer goods (money and clothes, for instance). At least in retrospect, this argument can be seen to anticipate something of Merton's later discussion of innovative deviant behaviour: the "wrong" means are chosen in pursuit of the "right" goals.

More importantly, the willingness to use sex as a form of cultural capital was attributed to weak familial social controls that, in turn, were a product of social disorganization in the big cities. The solution to this problem was seen by Thomas to lie in the interventionist activity of the family court. Like other commentators of his day, he saw in the developing family court an opportunity to counter the immoral behaviour of largely immigrant, working-class girls. If intervention came early enough—in the form of probation—the problem could be nipped in the bud.

Prognostications about deviant sexuality similarly colour other pre-war accounts of female delinquency. In the 1930s, for instance, Sheldon and Eleanor Gluek, pioneers in the study of delinquency, researched 500 institutionalized young offenders in Massachusetts. Among the voluminous amounts of information that they collected was the detailed sexual history of the female delinquents, but not of the males. This may be partially defended on the grounds that many of the girls were incarcerated for prostitution. But for the remainder, details of their sexual past was deemed relevant only because they were female (Pollock, 1978, p. 43).

Post-war studies continued this practice of investigating female delinquency with institutionalized samples. Again, the identified delinquencies are assumed to be largely sexual ones, a consequence, more often than not, of biological and psychological pathologies. For example, Cowie, Cowie, and Slater investigated 318 girls housed in a British juvenile institution in 1958. Most of them were there for offences that the authors called "sex delinquencies," a category that also included such status offence staples as a need for "care and protection," "being refractory," and "being beyond control" (Cowie, Cowie, and Slater, 1968, p. 67). The authors also go out of their way to emphasize the differences between male and female delinquency: "The nature of delinquent offences among girls is completely different to the delinquent offences committed by boys. A large part of the delinquencies of girls consist in sexually ill-regulated behaviour of a type not to demand social sanctions in the case of an adult" (Cowie, Cowie, and Slater, 1968, p. 43).

To some degree, Cowie et al. are modernists who emphasize psychological and sociological factors in their explanation of female delinquency. They do pay some attention to the home and family circumstances that encourage delinquency. Nonetheless, for the most part, their work reflects nineteenth-century beliefs about delinquent sexuality. Once again, anatomy is practically destiny since they argue that "sex chromosome construction is one of the basic factors determining the liability to delinquency."

The early sociological subcultural theories dealt with female delinquency by ignoring it. If they less readily resorted to biological or psychological arguments, it was because they understood delinquency as a group activity of working-class males. Since the ideas of Albert Cohen are so integral to this approach, it is worth considering why he thinks that the study of delinquency is the study of the "rogue male."

Cohen was one of few early subcultural theorists to recognize the existence of female delinquency. However, he also claims that his formulation of gang delinquency does not apply to girls. He exempts girls from his analysis on the grounds that since their wrongdoing is of a sexual nature, it is pursued individually rather than collectively. He accepts that girls, too, have problems of adjustment but because they are not chasing the same goals as boys, their mode of adaptation is also different. Unlike males, whose status is determined by jobs, education, and income, female status is attained by marriage to the "right" man. Relationships with males therefore affect not only the goal attainment problem that girls have, but also the solution that they adopt:

> In short, people do not simply want to excel, they want to excel as a man or as a women, that is to say, in those respects which, in their culture, are symbolic of their respective sex roles ... Even when they adopt behaviour which is considered disreputable by conventional standards, the tendency is to be disreputable in ways that are characteristically masculine and feminine. (Cohen, 1955, p. 138)

According to Cohen, working-class girls who reject conventional status attainment goals do so individually via permissive sexual activity rather than gang delinquency. Although Cohen is right to question the applicability of his conception of delinquent subcultures to girls, it is not for the reasons that he emphasizes. As will be seen in the next section, female delinquency is characterized neither by its solitary nature nor its sexual content.

THE REALITY OF FEMALE DELINQUENCY

Of course, there is one potentially obvious reason why social researchers have found it easy to either ignore female delinquency or treat it as an individual sexual problem: girls could be missing from subcultural theories because their contribution to delinquent behaviour is insubstantial. In other words, the criminological literature might provide a faithful reflection of the reality of female delinquency.

Needless to say, this is a relatively easy proposition to test with the available data sources. Indeed, it has been tested and found wanting! This becomes evident when we revisit some of the terrain covered in Chapter 2. Drawing largely on a recent comprehensive review of what (American) police statistics and self-report studies reveal about the nature and extent of female delinquency, I will reiterate and expand upon the points made earlier.

It is unambiguously clear from the reviews of Chesney-Lind and Sheldon (1992) and Chesney-Lind (1997) that young female offenders are less likely to become known to the police than young male offenders. American police statistics indicate that for every girl arrested, four boys are arrested—a ratio of 1 to 4.

Canadian UCR reports tell a similar story. In 1999, of those youths charged by the police, 77 percent were male and 23 percent female (Tremblay 2000). Likewise, two out of every ten offenders appearing in youth court in 1998–99 were female (Carrière, 2000).

Self-report studies—American and others—reveal smaller, but still significant, differences between the sexes (Chesney-Lind and Sheldon, 1992; Chesney-Lind, 1997; Mawby, 1980). It has been argued that some of the gender gap in self-report studies is attributable to the greater reluctance of girls to admit wrongdoing in personal interview settings. And, indeed, there is some evidence to support this proposition (Morris, 1965; Gold, 1970). At the same time, most self-report surveys involve the completion of an anonymous questionnaire rather than a more intimate personal interview; in these settings of greater anonymity, there is no evidence that girls are any more reticent than boys about revealing their indiscretions. Although there may be some dispute about the size of the gender gap, there is little doubt that male adolescents break more rules than girls.

Is female delinquency different in character from its male counterpart? One way of answering this question is to look at the nature of the offences for which female young offenders are arrested. According to the UCR survey for 1997–98, both male and female youth are charged most frequently with theft under $5000. One-third of female youth are charged with this offence, compared with one-fifth of male youth. Following a long way behind is common assault, at 14 percent the second most frequently occurring offence for which female youth are charged.

The official data sources also make clear that girls are much less likely than boys to be arrested for crimes of violence or more serious property crimes, such as burglary and robbery (Mawby, 1980; Chesney-Lind and Sheldon, 1992; Chesney-Lind, 1997). Add to this the fact that boys are also more likely to be apprehended for possession of stolen goods, vandalism, and weapons offences, and it is not hard to see why they, rather than girls, are the focus of much of the public's alarm about street crime.

On the other hand, there are offences for which girls are much more likely to be arrested than boys. For instance, in 1993, 253 girls were arrested in Canada for prostitution, compared with only 53 boys (Canadian Crime Statistics, 1993). No less tellingly, American police statistics cited by Chesney-Lind and Sheldon and Chesney-Lind show that running away from home is more likely to result in arrest for females than males. Indeed, whereas nearly 20 percent of all female arrests are for running away, this figure is a minuscule 4 percent for males. Chesney-Lind and Sheldon suspect a similar gender gap also holds for incorrigibility, unmanageability, and truancy—the other so-called status offences. These infractions, although not technically illegal, do allow for the arrest of young people for breaching parental authority. As a category, status offences loom large and negatively in the lives of American teenage girls, as we will see in a moment.

As these comments suggest, it is more than possible that arrest statistics reflect police behaviour as well as adolescent behaviour. To what extent are gender differences in delinquency a function of selective policing? The results from numerous self-report investigations substantiate the argument developed in Chapter 2 and repeated here. First, female delinquency—like male delinquency—is more common than police and court statistics indicate. Second, most of the wrongdoings of adolescent girls—like the wrongdoings of adolescent boys—are (relatively) benign in nature. Third, the major difference between male and female delinquency is largely one of volume: boys engage in more delinquent behaviour than girls. This pattern is such that it has encouraged some prominent researchers (cf. Hindelang et al., 1979) to insist that it is the quantity of deviant behaviour in which they engage, rather than its content, that separates the boys from the girls. This argument is valid up to a point, but becomes less accurate with respect to status offences. Although girls are not significantly more likely to *report* committing more status offences (running away from home, for instance), they are more likely to be *arrested* for them.

There is one further dimension to delinquency in which males and female differ quite significantly. Although the majority of delinquent boys and girls do not grow up to become criminal adults, boys are more likely to do so than girls. Boys are more inclined, therefore, to extend delinquent involvements developed in adolescence into adulthood.

Evidence on this score comes from longitudinal studies, mainly American ones. One of the best known of these studied the records of arrest of all youths, male and female, born in Philadelphia in 1958 who lived in that city between the ages of ten and seventeen (Tracy, Wolfgang, and Figlio, 1985). Some 33 percent of the males in this cohort had been arrested before their eighteenth birthday compared with only 14 percent of the females. In addition, the males were arrested for more serious offences and were arrested more often than the females, whose involvement in delinquency throughout adolescence is consistently more casual and episodic.

Consistent with this last point, it is recognized that girls are considerably more likely to terminate delinquent activities earlier than boys. Moreover, findings from several American studies show that this is the case regardless of the sorts of illicit activity in which they have been engaged. Ageton (1983) tracked a national sample of girls over time in the United States, beginning when they were between the ages of eleven and seventeen, and ending when they were between fifteen and twenty-one. She noted, in particular, that age brought with it a decline in assaultative behaviour.

The same pattern is also found with female status offenders. Datesman and Aickin (1985) looked at the career patterns of a sample of young offenders, both male and female, who had been brought before the juvenile court in Delaware for status offences. Over a three-year period, the researchers noted that apprehension for a status offence marked not the beginning of an escalation into more serious offences, but the beginning of the end of their involvement in deviant activity. Even if they did make a return trip to the family court, it was most likely to be for another status offence rather than something more serious.

Two comments can be made about the findings from this study. First, they can be seen as supporting the contentions of both court officials and some academic advocates of deterrence theory that early intervention on the behalf of "at-risk" adolescents discourages any further and more serious delinquent activity. Insofar as this is the case, it also counts as evidence against the labelling perspective that argues—as we have seen at several points in the book—that early contact with police officers and the juvenile court system predicts more intensive deviant involvement at a later date.

Second, and conversely, perhaps these findings could just mean that deterrence is most effective with individuals least committed to deviant activity, among whose ranks you might want to include female status offenders. Indeed, to anticipate a criticism that will be made in the next chapter about prison-based deterrence programs for young people (in particular, "Scared Straight"–type programs and boot camps), it seems highly dubious to claim that adolescents who are essentially non-criminal in the first place have been brought back on track because of early court intervention. Given the trivial nature of their offences, it is equally plausible to argue that they would have made a natural progression from delinquent to conventional careers.

ARE GIRLS AND WOMEN BECOMING MORE DEVIANT?

I began this chapter by noting the perennial absence of females from theory and research on crime and delinquency. Ironically, after being ignored or misrepresented for decades, female deviance recently has more recently become headline news (Mawby, 1980, p. 525)—and not just because news stories that manage to link "women" and "sexual behaviour" have proven to be a winning combination for those in the business of selling newspapers.

Instead, this somewhat belated interest in female deviance has come about because it is believed that girls and women are engaging in more criminal activity, particularly violent crime, and are becoming more involved in gang activity. As one magazine headline put it, "Sugar and Spice and Veins as Cold as Ice—teenage girls are closing the gender gap in violent crime" (Pearson, 1998, pp. 26–27). In this regard, the murder in 1997 of fourteen-year-old Reena Virk in Victoria, B.C., has done much to concentrate the nation's attention on the violent tendencies of teenage girls.

Needless to say, it is the mass media that have lead the way in documenting apparent changes in female delinquency and interpreting its behavioural content as meaner and nastier than ever before. A common strategy is to provide a provocative headline ("GIRLS IN GANGS"), give a brief summation of the story's thesis in a subheading ("teenage girls are commiting more violent, gang-related crimes as they learn to copy male behaviour"), and illustrate the article with a (posed?) photograph of knife-wielding gang members, and conduct short interviews with adult experts (*Toronto Star,* December 10, 1996). The better articles also include a selective sampling of Statistics Canada data, seemingly confirming the story line that girls are becoming more violent and aggressive—just like the boys.

Current concerns about girls and gangs and violence is a continuation of older speculations about the effects of changing gender roles. Some criminologists have argued that as women abandon, or add to, their traditional domestic roles, their patterns of crime and deviance will more closely resemble those of men. This has been referred to as the liberation hypothesis, and was originally developed in the 1970s to explain the link between rising female crime rates and increased female labour market participation. As women begin to free themselves from the clutches of patriarchal control and gain more economic power, the argument went, they have started to involve themselves more frequently in crime (Adler, 1975; Simon, 1975).

This thesis—in its original form, clearly more applicable to adult women in the workplace than to teenage girls in school or out on the streets—has not been well supported empirically. Nonetheless, versions of it have found their way into more contemporary accounts of female delinquency. And, to be fair, it is not hard to find statistical evidence consistent with media portrayals of increasingly violent and aggressive school girls. For example, 1998 UCR reports indicate that for the ten years between 1988 and 1998, girls aged twelve to seventeen were charged with violent crimes at twice the male rate, and in 1998 the violent crime committed by girls represented a greater proportion of all female youth crime (23 percent) than the violent crime committed by boys (20 percent).

However, media reports of rising female crime rates, particularly violent crime, emphasize the size of the increase rather than the small number of incidents involved. To illustrate what I mean, it is worth bearing in mind that ten incidents in one year, compared with five incidents the previous year, is an increase of 100 percent! When we apply this observation to Statistics Canada data, we find that between 1986 and 1990 there was a 29 percent increase in the number of female young offenders charged by police—the numbers rose from 18 336 to 23 610, more than double the male increase of 14 percent (Conway, 1992, p. 11). However, what the Statistics Canada data also show, but the newspaper headlines do not, is that the rise in the number of young females charged notwithstanding, only 18 percent of those charged overall were female. This means, of course, that over 80 percent of teenage wrongdoers arrested during that four-year period were male! It is true, as we noted earlier, that the size of the gap between male and female delinquency rates is narrowing. But when 77 percent of those charged by police are male (1999 figures), the two rates are still a long way from converging.

Also, insofar as girls are becoming more involved with violent crime, it is an involvement that centres on common assault, its least serious variant, the variant most likely to be subject to increased reporting and recording in times of zero tolerance. The latest statistics indicate, for instance, that among adolescents charged with a violent crime, girls are more likely than boys to be charged with common assault. The gender gap in violent teenage crime is narrowing because girls are now being arrested for the types of relatively minor offence that police officers used to overlook when the perpetrators were female.

Although some commentators have been tempted to explain alleged changes in female crime and delinquency in terms of the liberation hypothesis, both contemporary and historical statistical evidence showing consistent differences in rates and types of male and female criminality suggests that such theorizing is in advance of the facts. Nevertheless, it is ironic to encounter an argument that, in effect, predicts that greater economic and social opportunity for girls and women will result in more crime and delinquency, when those same conditions are assumed to reduce crime and delinquency in males.

Finally, we might want to remind ourselves that moral panics about a "new breed" of young and violent female criminal have the effect of distracting attention from problems and issues arguably more worthy of our attention. In the case of female violence and aggression, moral panics cause us to overlook situations where girls do genuinely behave worse than boys. For example, studies of bullying at school routinely concentrate upon its physical manifestations. Doing so shows bullying to be very much a male problem. However, if the conception of bullying is broadened to include less direct and more verbal abuses as well, girls are revealed as significant perpetrators of violence. As two researchers have put it, "the degree of aggressiveness exhibited by girls has been underestimated in prior studies, largely because forms of aggression relevant to girl's peer groups have not been assessed" (Crick and Grotpeter, 1995, p. 719).

A Canadian pioneer in exploring this reconstituted view of female violence is psychologist Debra Pepler. She suggests, on the basis of observational studies of school playgrounds, that girl aggression is mainly emotional and focuses on the spreading of false rumours, verbal abuse, and premeditated manipulation. This behaviour is much more common among girls than boys, is difficult to see, and even more difficult to prevent. Its effects, though, can be devastating. One incident involved three twelve-year-old girls spreading a false story that a classmate was pregnant. Within twenty-four hours, the whole school and the victims' parents had heard the rumour (*Globe and Mail,* October 23, 1999).

GIRLS, GANGS, AND SUBCULTURES: FOLK DEVILS IN DISGUISE?

Although the official police and court data fail to confirm media portrayals of vicious female fighting gangs, there are other issues pertaining to young women and subcultures that might be better explored with qualitative research methods. It is to these other questions and this data-gathering technique that we now turn.

If female delinquency is both more common and less distinctive than once supposed, does this also mean that it is committed collectively rather than individually? Are girls really missing from delinquent networks and delinquent groups and uninvolved in, for instance, punk and skinhead groups? Does the "natural rapport" that is said to exist between male sociologists and male subcultural participants (which causes the former to identify with and romanticize the latter) completely explain why female gang delinquency has been overlooked?

Anne Campbell has tried to answer these questions in a field study of girl delinquents in New York City. Her focus is on the deviant activities of Puerto Rican girls, their motivations for becoming gang members, and the roles that they play in gangs (1984, 1990a).

She begins by noting that in New York City there has been a female presence in gang life ever since the early 1800s (Asbury, 1927). However, from the very beginning, the role of girls in gang activity has been limited and circumscribed, heavily influenced by conventional notions of approved female behaviour. Campbell cites a study from the 1940s (Bernard, 1949) showing that while there was a growth in female gang activity in New York in that era, virtually all of the female gangs and gang members were affiliated with male gangs. The roles they played were those of girlfriend to prominent male members, a generic source of sexual favours, or carrier of drugs and weapons (chosen because they stood less chance of being searched by male police officers). They were, in effect, the ladies' auxiliary of the criminal underworld. Similarly, during the Second World War female subordinates would entice off-duty GIs into side streets, where they would be rolled by male gang members (Campbell, 1984, 1990a).

Little seems to have changed since then. According to Campbell, most female gangs are still primarily tied to male gangs and their members. All-girl gangs are unusual, and where they have existed (in New York and other large American cities), they formed as the female equivalent of a local male gang, from whom they often derived their name. Older readers will find these names—the Shangrila-Debs, the Robinettes, the Chandelers—very reminiscent of those used by the "girl groups," popular music performers in the late 1950s and early 1960s. This is probably because the girl gangs and girl groups shared similar origins in the loose neighbourhood-based associations formed in childhood and early adolescence in inner-city areas.

The gang members that Campbell is describing are not typical working-class girls. They are drawn, instead, from the most deprived and disadvantaged segments of the working-class: members of ethnic minorities who make up an inner-city underclass, with minimal access to good jobs and reasonable incomes, and lacking the basic educational qualifications to lift themselves out of the ghetto. The future that they face is one of unemployment, poverty, domestic work, uncertain relationships with male breadwinners, and exclusive responsibility for child care. For these girls

> the gang represents ... an idealized collective solution to the bleak future that awaits. The members construct for themselves at a rhetorical level, an image of the gang that counter-

points the suffocating futures they face … the members tacitly
conspire to portray the gang to themselves—as well as to
others—in a particular romantic light. (Campbell, 1984, p. 173)

Talk, more often than action, is therefore of drugs, drinks, and
parties. The reality is of long days spent on street corners not
doing much of anything. Toughness in the face of threats to reputation and turf is an important value, though, once again, more of
this is verbalized than actualized.

Campbell's point here is that the exaggerated stories, the tales
of drugs and partying that gang girls tell to prying journalists and
academic researchers are not just intended to fool or mislead investigators. She also suggests that by romanticizing gang life they
are—deliberately—fooling themselves: for a few brief moments
they are able to pretend that their lives are more exciting and
meaningful than they really are. In essence, this is what the British
subcultural theorists (see Chapter 3) are referring to when they
talk about "magical" (as opposed to real) solutions to problems
facing deprived and disadvantaged inner-city youth.

Gang members refer to themselves and their compatriots as
"sisters" or "home girls"—names chosen deliberately to convey a
sense of collective cohesion. Attacks from rival gangs or the intru-
sion of the police also strengthen gang solidarity. The gang is particularly important for these girls because their family lives were
often underscored by parental divorce. Moreover, prior to joining
the gang, "home girls" were often isolated individuals poorly connected to their schools and communities because of frequent
changes of address, truancy, and early school leaving. Gang membership, therefore, provides marginalized underclass girls with a
sense of belonging and identity.

According to Campbell, recruitment into the gang comes
through ties of friendship and family connections and departure
from it coincides with the end of adolescence. Sometimes their exit
is precipitated by the birth of a child; on other occasions, relationships with males that remove them from street life are established.

Thus Campbell paints a picture of female gang delinquents
engaging in tentative, short-term, subcultural solutions to their
problems. The girls are not, however, radicals: they are neither
feminists in training nor potential political militants, although
they have sometimes been described as both. Campbell summa-
rizes the goals and aspirations of the girls in the gang as follows:

The gang is not a counter-culture but a microcosm of
American society, a distorted mirror image in which power,
possessions, rank, and role remain major issues but are found
within a subcultural life of poverty and crime. Gangs do not
represent a revolutionary vanguard rejecting the norms and

values of a capitalist society that has exploited them. When gang members talk of politics, they talk of the American Dream, of pride in their country, of High School Equivalency diplomas. They want better welfare and health benefits, they want more jobs, but they don't want revolution. Gangs exist not in an anomic vacuum where sex roles are forgotten and anything goes, but in a subculture deeply embedded within the value system of Western capitalism. Girl members as women want to be American, to be free, to be beautiful, to be loved. These girls subscribe to the new woman's dream, the new agenda: No more suffering or poverty. No more lonely, forced "independence," living alone on welfare in a shabby apartment. First, a good husband; strong but not violent, faithful but manly. Second, well-dressed children. Third, a beautiful suburban apartment. Later for the revolution. (Campbell, 1984, p. 267)

In a sequel to her study of female subcultural delinquency, Campbell has made some interesting observations about gang delinquency in general and female gangs in particular (1990a). She notes, first of all, that (rather like other youth problems) there are cycles of interest in gang delinquency: in some eras it is a hot topic, in others it seemingly disappears from view. We are currently in a high-profile phase for reasons discussed in Chapter 5: in the United States, if not elsewhere, gangs have flourished as a new urban underclass has begun to develop. Nonetheless, Campbell is not sure that the new conditions of permanent urban atrophy have changed the content of gang behaviour much. For all the new-found attention that they have received from both the mass media and sociologists, the new gangs are very much like the old ones. Nor is she convinced that female gang members are always very different from "the rest of us," the very real circumstances of poverty, homelessness, and unemployment notwithstanding. However, female gang members have been depicted as the "villains and folk devils of the yuppie era." By emphasizing differences in values and beliefs between gang girls and non-gang girls, female gang members are turned into contemporary folk devils.

FEMALE STREET YOUTH, GANGS, AND VICTIMIZATION

In Chapter 2 it was suggested that concerns about predatory behaviour by youth are rarely matched by concerns about youth victimization. This imbalance, only recently recognized by findings from victimization surveys, is particularly important for female youth.

Surveys of adults consistently show that although males generally outnumber females as victims of crime, this is not true with regard to sexual assaults that take place in the domestic environment. Studies that focus on adolescent girls and young women similarly reveal that sexual victimization in the home is a particular problem for them, as well as an important stimulus for distinctive patterns of female offending.

The body of research on this topic, reviewed by Chesney-Lind (1997), indicates that girls are more likely to be sexually abused than boys, and that the abuse starts at an earlier age and is more likely to be instigated by (male) family members, often stepfathers, who see young females as sexual property. Moreover, exploitative opportunities are increased because of societal norms that encourage home-centred routines for girls. The consequences of this abuse are both immediate and longer term: psychological stress and problematic behaviour—disruptive conduct in school, running away from home, and early marriage.

Moreover, if girls and young women are successful in extricating themselves from coercive domestic environments, they face legal approbation from the very authorities—police and courts—whose job it is to provide care and protection for young citizens. As Chesney-Lind explains, status offences, combined with the legal rights given to parents to control their children, mean that the criminal justice system forces girls to either stay in an unhappy and unsafe home environment or face judical punishment, including institutionalization, if they should run away. In effect, the law criminizalizes female victims' coping strategies. Those who are not returned to the parental home—this is assuming that adult family members want them back—are "free" to drift onto the streets, where, of course, they are exposed to a variety of criminogenic situations and provided with ample situational motivations for criminal activity.

Research conducted in Hawaii and reported on by Chesney-Lind also indicates that female street youth are often doubly angry: they are bitter that their experiences of abuse at the hands (literally) of parents had forced them to leave home in the first place; and they are further embittered that, through the provision of the status offence category, they had been defined by the juvenile court as delinquent. Rather than discouraging them from further wrongdoing, the intervention of juvenile court personnel helped to confirm developing deviant identities.

Although virtually all researchers find that male street youth outnumber female ones, young women have attained a certain prominence and visibility within the street youth community. Moreover, although abuse and maltreatment by parents is a common cause of leaving home and becoming homeless, it is particularly important for female runaways, according to McCormack, Janus, and Burgess (1986). In a Toronto-based study, they found that sexually abused female street youth were more likely to have stolen money, food, and clothes, used illicit drugs, and prostituted themselves than either non-sexually abused female runaways or male runaways. (This finding is similar to Gaetz, O'Grady, and Daillancourt's discovery [1999], discussed in the previous chapter, that it is sexual victimization in the home that orients female street youth toward the sex trade.)

Comparable findings have been reported on by Moore and Hagedorn in their qualitative study of Los Angeles gang women (1996). They note that because it is more acceptable for boys to be "out on the streets," young male gang members tend to come from conventional working-class families; girls are more likely drawn from "underclass" (visible minority) backgrounds and families that were violent and sexually abusive. Moreover, family violence and sexual abuse predicted heroin use among female gang members but not among male gang members. Indeed, several studies suggest that female street youth and gang members are self-recruited from much worse backgrounds than their male counterparts.

Finally, the emerging results from longitudinal surveys are also now beginning to document linkages between the sexual victimization suffered in girlhood and adult female criminality (see the discussion in the previous chapter). Widom (1988, cited in Chesney-Lind, 1997) reports that women who experienced sexual abuse in their youth were more likely than non-victims to become involved with crime as adults. Males chart a similar course, though the connection is less strong. Furthermore, whatever early childhood abuse males suffered was most likely to result in violent criminality in adulthood, whereas female victims more typically end up commiting property crimes and public order offences—loitering, for example.

THE ORDINARY WRONGDOING OF ADOLESCENT GIRLS: EXPLAINING FEMALE DELINQUENCY

Girls in gangs and out on the streets are, of course, the part of the young female population most likely to be involved with crime and deviance as both offenders and victims. What of more ordinary, typical girls? What explains the near-universal finding that girls are less involved—collectively and individually—in delinquency than boys? There are two schools of thought as to how adequate explanations of female delinquency might best be developed, although they are not as different as they might at first appear.

The first approach begins with the assumption that since most female delinquency is similar to most male delinquency, and varies more in quantity than quality, it can be explained by the same variables and factors used to explain male delinquency. Thus the same subcultural, strain, and control theories can account for why girls are less delinquent than boys. According to this argument, gender-specific theories of crime and deviance are not required (Box, 1983).

This is not a view shared by scholars influenced by feminist ideas. They argue that it is unreasonable to expect that theories developed on the basis of assumptions about male behaviour and tested exclusively with male adolescents will prove equally applicable to female deviants. Although not wholly rejecting male-oriented theories, feminists are not convinced that our understanding of female deviance is advanced by, as Chesney-Lind and Sheldon (1992) put it, "adding gender and stirring." What is needed, they argue, is a theory or set of theories that takes full consideration of the differences, as well as the similarities, between growing up female and growing up male.

However, despite the differing ideological starting points, both mainstream and feminist approaches to explaining female deviance end up emphasizing the same extended family of concepts that relate to the nature of the female gender role. Borrowing from Mawby (1980), these can be identified as follows:

1. *Expectations of Appropriate Behaviour*
   Boys are expected, even encouraged, to court danger and, within limits, break some of the rules. Girls, on the other hand, are not expected to take risks, nor is their deviant behaviour as likely to be tolerated.

2. *Social Control*
   Boys are accorded more freedom than girls, whose activities and whereabouts are more closely monitored.

3. *Opportunity*
   A summation of the two previous points: the expectations of proper female behaviour and increased surveillance of their activities means that girls have fewer opportunities to become involved in delinquency.

4. *Career Models*
   Closely related to the first point: girls are (still) less likely than boys to anticipate careers in the paid labour market. They are instead expected to focus their ambitions on marriage and

family. Not encouraged to strive for the top jobs in society, they are not disappointed when they fail to get them and do not, therefore, respond to failure by turning to delinquency.

5. *Attitudes*

Again, because of the accumulated effects of the previous factors, girls are more extensively committed to pro-social attitudes than boys. In particular, they are more supportive of conventional attitudes to law-and-order issues.

Most attempts at explaining female delinquency, or its absence, focus on the above characteristics of the female gender role, concentrating in particular upon the effects of socialization experiences in the home and school: power-control theory, self-control theory, and routine activity theories all recognize the importance of internally and externally imposed restraints and circumscribed opportunities in limiting the scope of female delinquency.

However, prior to the development of these theories, some studies did draw on strain and subcultural theories by arguing that male and female adolescents have different ambitions that, if frustrated, result in deviant outcomes. Boys strive for occupational success; girls are primarily interested in getting married and raising a family. Indeed, it is because of the presumed existence of distinctive female goals that some investigators have asserted that girls do not involve themselves in same-sex peer-group activity. They insist that from early adolescence onward, girls are primarily interested in securing a mate—an essentially competitive enterprise not furthered by close relationships with female rivals (Campbell, 1990b).

If—as Albert Cohen and the other early subcultural theorists believed—girls are oriented toward domestic rather than occupational goals, then it is in that context that they will encounter blocked aspirations and status frustration. According to this gendered version of strain theory, girls who are unsuccessful in the pursuit of love and marriage might turn to delinquency. However, Canadian research by Sandhu and Allen (1969), comparing delinquent and non-delinquent girls, found that the former were less likely to be striving for the goal of marriage, were less interested in that institution, and anticipated fewer barriers to realization of these goals than non-delinquent girls. They had no need to react against a goal that they had little interest in achieving.

A similar Cohen-inspired hypothesis—that girls denied access to marriage will hit back by turning to delinquent sexuality—has also been refuted. Empirical research suggests that sexual rebellion is not very common because neither delinquent girls nor delinquent boys are any more supportive of sexual delinquency (such as promiscuity) than non-delinquent females and males. As Campbell's ethnography (among others) shows, indiscriminate sexual activity is neither cause for celebration nor an alternative source of status among working-class girls. It cannot therefore become a female equivalent to male gang delinquency. In fact, the girl in a male gang faces a real quandary: if she is sexually promiscuous she faces rejection by the very males in whom she is most interested. But if, on the other hand, she imitates and replicates male behaviour, she runs the risk of condemnation as a tomboy (Campbell, 1990b).

FEMINISM AND DELINQUENCY

As a body of knowledge, feminism contains a number of ideas that conflict with traditional assumptions about female behaviour. There have been several attempts to explore the connections between a feminist orientation and female deviance. One hypothesis is that female delinquents are gender rebels—the argument being that girls (and women) who are least supportive of expectations surrounding appropriate female behaviour will be more delinquent than more traditional girls.

For instance, James and Thornton (1980) examined the relationship between feminist attitudes and delinquency among 287 female adolescents in the United States. They found that feminism had little immediate impact upon status offences. For more serious aggressive and property crimes, pro-feminist values did have an effect—but in the opposite direction to that proposed by the theory. That is, those girls and women *most* supportive of feminist ideals were the *least* enthusiastic about delinquency. Rather than providing a vocabulary of motivation for deviant activities, feminist beliefs, at least in this study, acted as a suppressant or antidote to them. The authors found that even when factors encouraging deviant activity were present—when opportunities for it were plentiful and parental social controls lax—those girls who aligned themselves ideologically with feminism were the least interested in delinquent solutions.

Similar conclusions have been reached in other (largely American) studies. Cernkovich and Giordano (1979) examined the attitudes of girls in high school and juvenile justice institutions toward traditional sex roles and career paths. On balance, they found that rather than being at the cusp of female liberation, delinquent girls are more likely to hold traditional sex-role attitudes and behave traditionally, and that although delinquency was associated with a rejection of marriage and family, there was no evidence that those traditional goals were being replaced by aspirations for typically male jobs.

Further evidence that feminist attitudes and beliefs discourage delinquent activity comes from an examination of male and female high school students in the American Midwest (Figueira-McDonough, 1984). No matter how they were operationalized, feminist principles failed to rate as significant precursors of delinquency. They did, however, emerge as significant predictors of high career aspirations and, through them, high grades. And as virtually all sociological theories of delinquency emphasize, adolescents of either sex who recognize the intimate connection between educational success and future life chances tend to be less delinquent than adolescents who are unable or unwilling to make this connection.

Feminism, of course, would be an even more important suppresser of delinquent values if it were attractive to larger numbers of girls (not to mention boys!). However, Figuiera-McDonough found—as have other researchers before and since—that adherence to feminist principles is not equally distributed among the young female population: they were the preserve primarily of relatively privileged, middle-class, white females. It, of course, remains a moot point as to whether black and other minority girls would have abandoned their delinquent activities had they been more committed to feminism.

The idea that most, if not all delinquency, is an expression of male (as well as working-class) values and interests has also influenced how some theorists have constructed their images of female delinquency. In particular it has been proposed that delinquent girls might be more similar to boys in their characteristics, values, and beliefs than conforming girls.

Is gender bending linked to delinquency? According to Chesney-Lind and Sheldon (1992), studies that have systematically examined this argument have produced "decidedly mixed results" (1992, p. 74). Cullen, Golden, and Cullen (1979), for example, administered a "masculinity scale" (a series of stereotypically masculine traits such as aggression, independence, objectivity, dominance, competition, and self-confidence) to a sample of university students. They found that although females who scored high on the masculinity index were indeed more delinquent than other females, males were still more delinquent than females. In other words, factors additional to attitudinal androgeny are responsible for the gender gap in deviance.

Other investigations of the masculinity hypothesis have been less persuasive. Norland, Wessel, and Shover (1981) administered a similar masculinity scale to high school students and found that various measures (leadership, competition, aggression, ambitions) were related to minor status offences but not to the more serious violent and property crimes.

These findings may be seen as counterintuitive in that the "masculine traits" fail to predict the sort of serious offences that might have been best expected to predict. Even worse, the females in the sample who possessed the masculine traits were less delinquent than females not so endowed (an anomaly not very satisfactorily explained by the researchers with the argument that the "masculine" girls were more likely to have non-delinquent friends!).

And the findings only get more complex. Employing the same data set, but using a different conception of masculinity, Loy and Norland (1981) found that girls who identified least with both traditional female gender expectations and traditional male gender expectations were more comprehensively delinquent than other girls. On the other hand, males identified as "traditionally masculine" were the most delinquent subgroup in the sample—particularly with regard to aggressive behaviour. In other words, "real men" become "real delinquents."

Gender, Schooling, and Resistance

Other research on female deviancy has focused more explicitly on its contexts and domains and upon how behaviour is influenced by gendered prescriptions of appropriate sex-role behaviour. The bottom line is that even in those domains known to be conducive to delinquency, girls are still less likely than boys to respond in a deviant manner. For instance, with regard to school and delinquency, we find that school failure, poor grades, and low commitment generate more delinquent activity among boys than girls. My own study on youth culture and the high school, discussed in Chapter 4, is only one of a number of studies that have made this discovery. Rankin (1980) reports similar findings for the United States, as does Arthur Stinchcombe in his earlier study of rebellion in high school (1964).

School has also, of course, figured prominently in British subcultural theories of resistance (see Chapters 3 and 5). How does gender fit in with resistance theory? To answer this question, we must first recap the main outlines of this argument.

Resistance theorists look to Paul Willis (1976) for their inspiration. They contend that rebellious working-class subcultures in school challenge the principles and ethos of capitalist schooling. However, their anti-school behaviour—truancy, smoking, clashes with teachers, and so on—lead to a poor academic performance and, in due course, a marginal position in the labour force. In the process of contesting schooling, working-class youth reproduce themselves as future members of the manual working class.

Resistance theorists acknowledge that an exaggerated sense of masculinity drives this dual process of resistance and reproduction. They recognize that this dynamic may be less applicable for working-class females: it is well understood that in a classroom setting girls are often less openly confrontational than boys, and that resistance is less dramatically disruptive and antagonistic when girls are involved (McRobbie, 1981; Davies, 1984; Apple, 1985; Griffen, 1985; Gaskell, 1985; Lees, 1986).

Resistance theorists have therefore had to amend their basic argument to take account of behavioural differences between male and female working-class youth. What they have produced is a theory that interprets gender traditionalism as a form of resistance. Working-class girls adopt an exaggerated display of femininity—a precocious use of make-up and other elements of adult style and substantial interest in the culture of romance. An excessive interest in boys, marriage, and children is incompatible with the pro-school role and therefore becomes a cultural expression of school rejection. Thorne (1993), for example, in her ethnography describes how cosmetics, boy talk, and "exaggerated teen femininity" are part of the female cultural repertoire used to challenge parental and school authority. However, as with the subcultural activities of their male counterparts, these anti-school behaviours of working-class girls ensnare them into early marriage and youthful motherhood, thereby ensuring that existing patterns of class and gender relations are reproduced.

Resistance theorists are arguing, in effect, that gender traditionalism among working-class girls is a form of dissent. According to this formulation, we would therefore expect traditional females (particularly working-class ones) to be more deviant (or resistant) than less traditional ones.

The resistance perspective of female incalcitrance has been tested by Scott Davies as part of his exploration of schooling and deviance in Ontario, examined in Chapter 4. The first data set that he uses is a large (3300) survey of Ontario high school students.

Davies uncovers a pattern of findings that is at least partially consistent with claims about gendered resistance. He finds that female underachievement in the scholastic domain is associated with domestic traditionalism (as measured by expectations of early marriage and responses to a series of questions involving traditional attitudes to gender roles). As Davies suggests, young women's adoption of traditional femininities can be a coping strategy for dealing with a lack of school success and marginal chances of being independent breadwinners, especially in the context of a peer-culture that values their sexual attractiveness over their abilities (1994b).

Yet this finding only partially confirms resistance theory because the relationship between underachievement and traditionalism holds for both middle-class and working-class girls. It is not, in other words, a class-specific response to schooling among females. This finding, coupled with evidence that a poor academic performance correlates with school rebellion (or resistance) for males of all class backgrounds, convinces Davies that what is primarily being reproduced through scholastic underachievement and deviant involvement is less a class culture as such than conventional forms of masculinity and femininity (1994b). For both male and female adolescents, a poor academic performance in school leads to traditional gender roles and identities.

Davies has pursued this line of inquiry among high school dropouts in Ontario (1994a). Again, he finds that male and female deviants do not necessarily travel the same route to a dropout destination. In particular, what distinguishes the females from the males is that prioritizing domestic concerns leads to early leaving for the former but not the latter, who are more likely (in contrast to the girls) to report disruptive behaviour as precursive of dropping out. This finding underscores the conventional wisdom about the greater and more public disruptive qualities of male anti-school behaviour, and provides support for the argument that it is traditionalism that leads to early school leaving for girls. Again, the two-track route to dropping out—rebellion for boys, marriage and motherhood for girls—does not relate well to class. Indeed, Davies reports that many anti-school phenomena are as strongly linked to gender as they are to either class or in-school variables and experiences.

Davies's results are, as he fully recognizes, similar to those American studies that find that "traditional" girls are more delinquent than non-traditional ones. However, in the interpretation of resistance theory, female underachievers, dropouts, and delinquents are the "progressives" of the adolescent world—a view that strains credibility to a breaking point. Indeed, an opposite argument is considerably more compelling: because they are more likely to hold liberal or radical views, non-traditional females challenge the prescribed norms of capitalist society. Moreover, progressive females—radicals who contest gender inequalities in society—are far more likely to be found inside educational institutions—universities and the like—than among the ranks of high school dropouts or unemployed street youth.

GIRLS, LEISURE, AND DEVIANCE

Earlier in this chapter I mentioned that female peer-group activity—or rather the absence of it—has often been singled out as a reason for the underrepresentation of girls in delinquent behaviour. Because of the reluctance of parents to allow their daughters to roam the streets and shopping malls of their communities, girls spend more time at home than boys; they are more involved in a "bedroom culture" than a street culture, and correspondingly less likely to get into trouble (Murdock and Phelps, 1973; Frith, 1985).

One interesting study that does not necessarily disprove this thesis has suggested that some refinement to it is in order. Conducting her research in Boston, Morash (1986) found that what distinguishes female and male adolescent leisure activity is not that girls are uninvolved in peer-group activity, or that female subcultures lack solidarity or cohesion. Instead, the critical source of variation was that among the girls, delinquency was less likely to be a focus of group activities.

Another American study has similarly suggested that it is the quality of peer-group interactions rather than the quantity of them that limits female delinquency. Giordano, Cernkovich, and Pugh (1986) interviewed 942 male and female adolescents. They found that whereas male peer groups encourage the sort of risk-taking behaviour that often leads to delinquency, female groups stress qualities that discourage it, such as caring, self-disclosure, trust, and loyalty.

This is not to say that there are not restrictions placed on female interactions that affect patterns of deviancy and conformity. All the evidence suggests that there are, and that they derive from the greater controls exercised by parents on female behaviour. Parents have different expectations of appropriate sex-role behaviour for boys and girls. As a result, parents monitor the activities and companions of the latter more closely than the former. Girls are restricted about when, where, and with whom they can go out and when they must return. They also—unlike boys—have a role in the domestic division of labour; they have to help with chores around the house, look after younger siblings, and do the shopping. Girls therefore spend more time at home than boys (McRobbie and Garber, 1975; Frith, 1978a). Conversely, of course, they have fewer opportunities to be out on the street, where the action—and the delinquency—is. (This is one important reason why, as Murdock and Phelps [1973] have shown [see Chapter 4], girls who rebel against schooling become involved in pop media culture: because parents have ensured that they have only limited access to a neighbourhood-based street culture, they turn to the pop media.)

Gendered leisure is also an important focus of recent applications of routine activities theory. Jensen and Brownfield (1986) find a strong connection between offending and victimization in two different American surveys of teenagers: those who report most of the former also report much of the latter. They explain the overlap in the sorts of leisure orientations and activities that lead to both—partying, driving around in cars, spending evenings out with friends, what the authors refer to as "the mutual pursuit of fun." Conversely, other recreational activities—staying home, going shopping or out to the movies, for instance—reduce the risk of both offending and victimization.

Crucially for the present discussion, it is girls who are least likely to pursue criminogenic leisure routines. It is they who are most likely to have home-centred lifestyles or engage in safe recreational activities. However, what is left unanswered—indeed, because of routine activity theory's preoccupation with the situational inducements to crime and deviance, largely unasked—is *why* it is that young males and young females have different opportunities for entering more and less risky leisure environments.

Part of the answer lies in the effects of parental controls and socialization. The import of these factors has been made apparent in another application of routine activity theory. Riley (1987), in a nationwide survey of fourteen- and fifteen-year-olds in the United Kingdom, found that much of the greater male than female self-reported offending (he did not look at victimization) was explained by the more public leisure activities of the males, activities that provided more opportunity for criminal wrongdoing. But he also found that although female offenders did have more public, peer-group oriented and less parentally supervised lifestyles than female non-offenders, girls overall were less delinquent than boys even when the girls were involved in leisure pursuits free from adult supervision. This suggests—echoing the American findings of Morash (1986) and Giordano et al. (1986)—that parents control, first of all, which leisure environments girls and boys are permitted to enter and vicariously influence behaviour once specific leisure domains have been entered. Pro-social directives have, in other words, been internalized and are operative even in the physical absence of parents.

How parental controls channel opportunities for youthful deviance is also shown to good effect in another British study conducted in Sheffield (Mawby, 1980). The first part of Mawby's investigation of self-reported delinquency shows that girls held more conventional attitudes toward law-and-order issues than boys (for instance, they were less critical of the police). Presumably these pro-social attitudes reduce girls' involvement in deviancy.

However, not all of the gender differences in the Sheffield study can be explained by attitudinal variations. Interestingly, boys who had positive opinions about the police still committed more delinquent acts than girls whose views were more critical. (Likewise, a study by Jensen and Eve [1976] in the United States found that the relationship between gender and delinquency remained after other self-reported behaviours and attitudes had been controlled for. Thus, even girls who experience poor relationships with parents, have a weak attachment to the law, underperform in school, and overcommit to youth culture are less delinquent than boys who enjoy more positive experiences in all of those domains.)

Mawby found that the experiences that shaped the differing involvements of boys and girls in delinquency as both offenders and victims could be traced back to control and opportunity factors that affected their routine activities. Girls were less vulnerable to personal victimization than boys largely because they were physically absent from situations and domains where they could become victims of crime.

In turn, their exclusion from crime settings is related to their being more protected than boys; the after-school-hours movements of girls, for instance, are more strictly monitored than those of boys. Thus, girls, on the one hand, are prevented from entering settings that might lead to their victimization and, on the other, are restrained from making the anti-school contacts that might accelerate the drift (cf. Matza) into more serious delinquent commitments (Mawby, 1980).

Other findings from Mawby's survey reinforce the argument that control affects opportunity, which in turn shapes the local geography of teenage crime. Respondents were asked where they were most likely to play. Girls replied by identifying their home. Boys, by contrast, reported that they played (or hung about) on deserted land (1980, p. 540). Quite obviously, girls who stay at home to play are less vulnerable to personal crime (except, of course, from other family members) than boys who hang about in unsupervised areas of the city.

Similarly, where they played (or hung about) directly influenced their delinquent patterns. Girls and boys were equally likely to commit common thefts in peoples' homes and at school— because these are two domains that boys and girls equally inhabit. However, boys were more likely than girls to commit offences at the site of outdoor play activities—theft from construction sites and breaking into and entering empty buildings. Mawby therefore concludes that girls have a lower rate of delinquency than boys because parental controls and diminished opportunities influence where girls spend their leisure time.

The two British studies also highlight the often complex relationship between leisure activities and delinquency (cf. Agnew and Petersen, 1989). From Mawby's study we can conclude that the leisure routines that boys pursue have an effect upon their encounters with crime—as both offenders and victims—that is relatively independent of whatever pro-social attitudes they might have developed. More specifically, risky leisure routines neutralize the positive effects of pro-police sentiments. Conversely, Riley's study suggests that pro-social socialization insulates girls from trouble even when pursuing risky leisure activities.

CONTROL AND OPPORTUNITY: NEW DIRECTIONS

Control and opportunity are obviously two vital and closely entwined variables explaining diminished female involvement in deviance. How they work to suppress female deviance is apparent in two recent Canadian studies.

POWER-CONTROL THEORY: GIRLS JUST WANT TO HAVE FUN[2]

"Power-control theory" has become an influential explanation of common (that is to say, minor) delinquency. It is a product of integration, a synthesis of traditional control theory and contemporary Marxian class analysis, and it has evolved through a series of surveys of Toronto high school students and their parents (Hagan, Gillis, and Simpson, 1979, 1985, 1987).

It is important to emphasize that Hagan et al. depict common delinquency as fun and pleasurable, an activity rooted in leisure ambitions rather than the desperation and frustrations engendered by lack of opportunity. No less important, they argue that young males and females are not granted equal access to enjoyable, but deviant, leisure activities. Gender and the class background of parents determine how much freedom—to have a good time, take risks, and, on occasion, get into trouble—teenagers have.

Hagan et al. begin with the now familiar observation that growing up female is a more constricting experience than growing up male. However, Hagan et al. also argue that the amount of power (or authority, cf. Dahrendorf, 1959) that parents exercise in the workplace influences the amount and type of control that they exert at home on their teenage children. But, contrary to what you might expect, those parents who are most controlling at work are most likely to excuse the miscreant behaviour of their own children—particularly male children—at home. The interaction of (parental) social class and gender means that, predictably enough, boys are more free to deviate than girls and, less predictably, middle-class adolescents are more free to deviate than working-class ones. The most free of all are upper-class males. (Think here, for example, of the Kennedy family in the United States and the large amounts of deviant sexual and drug-related behaviour they have been allowed to indulge in without official sanction.)

The earliest application of power-control theory indicated that while class was a weak correlative of common delinquency, the gap between male and female delinquency rates was largest in families headed by employers: those who had most control (because they were owners) in the workplace. More recent versions of the argument have addressed the connection between family power structure and delinquency. Respondents are categorized as coming from either egalitarian or patriarchal families.

Egalitarian families are ones in which both husbands and wives have authority (control) over others in the workplace. In contrast, patriarchal families have a male head who exerts control at work while control at home resides in the hands of his wife, who monitors the activities of their children. The prediction—subsequently borne out by further analysis in Toronto—is that the more egalitarian the power relationship between parents, the more similar the delinquent profiles of their sons and daughters. Further refinements to the theory have built upon the same theme. Authority relations at work spill over and shape authority relations in the home and, in situations where parents enjoy equal amounts of control in both the employment setting and domestic domain, the gap between male and female delinquency is narrowed.

Several attempts have been made to replicate the power-control concept. Some aspects of the theory have successfully withstood retesting while other parts of it are in the process of refinement. Singer and Levine (1988) conducted a partial replication among suburban adolescents and their parents in the United States. Some of their findings were consistent with those of Hagan et al. Girls were more controlled than boys, mothers were more controlling of their daughters than their sons, boys were bigger risk-takers than girls and less easily deterred from doing so than girls. On the other hand, many of the key precepts of power-control theory were reversed in this study. For instance, all of the aforementioned findings were more pronounced in egalitarian families than in patriarchal ones, and, in egalitarian households, boys were more delinquent than girls. Shoemaker (1990, p. 267) thinks that this study offers "mixed support" for power-control theory. However, since the parts of the theory that are discounted constitute its defining elements, this might be seen as an overgenerous interpretation (on this issue, see Chesney-Lind and Sheldon, 1992, p. 97; and Chesney-Lind, 1997).

Other researchers have disputed the claim of Hagan et al. that girls are more frequently subjected to parental, particularly maternal, control than boys. Hill and Atkinson (1988), in a study conducted in Illinois, argue that the sexes differ not in regard to the amount of control they receive from parents but in the form that it takes. Girls, for instance, were more subject to curfew regulations, whereas boys were required to conform more closely to a parental dress code.

There are two additional critical comments that need to be made about power-control theory. First of all, it is designed to explain the common delinquencies of ordinary adolescents. Although class may have a positive effect on trivial and episodic offending (as Hagan et al. claim) or no effect at all (as Jensen and Thompson counter, 1990), this pattern is unlikely to be repeated when the focus is on serious or repetitive delinquency. Power-control theory, at least as it is presently constituted, is likely to underpredict the sorts of violent and aggressive adolescent behaviour that most adults find disturbing.

Second, Hagan and his colleagues have got themselves into trouble with some feminists for suggesting that egalitarian homes and female-headed households are particularly conducive to female deviance. In this sort of family setting women are frequently working outside the home. Chesney-Lind and Sheldon infer from this that power-control theory is blaming increases in female delinquency on working mothers. A variant of the increasingly discredited emancipation thesis (see earlier discussion), it is also at odds with statistical evidence that shows an inverse relationship between female labour force participation and rates of female crime and deviance (Chesney-Lind and Sheldon, 1992).

GENDER AND SELF-CONTROL

In Chapter 3, I mentioned that control theory has now been transformed into self-control theory. This is the brainchild of Gottfredson and Hirschi (1990), who claim that all deviant conduct, regardless of situation or setting, is activated by one factor: low self-control. This same variable is also responsible, so they say, for all the known variations in, and correlates of, crime. Thus, young people commit more crime than older people and poorer people commit more crime than richer ones because the young and the poor lack self-control. The same principle holds for gender—the gap between boys and girls and men and women in terms of crime rates is explained, say Gottfredson and Hirschi, by the greater inability of males to exercise self-control: it is their greater inclination to risk and impulsivity that causes them to behave badly and get into trouble

How valid is this argument? Lagrange and Silverman set out to test this thesis in a study of a wide range of delinquent behaviour among Edmonton high school students (1999).They dutifully recognize that there are other reasons why girls are less likely to become involved in disreputable activities than boys, not least of which is that parents provide their daughters with fewer opportunities to do so. Accordingly, to find out whether self-control has a further, and independent, suppression effect on female delinquency requires controlling for the opportunity variable.

Their results indicate that even when girls are afforded the same freedoms as boys, they are still less likely to get into trouble, a pattern, moreover, the researchers are able to attribute to various measures of self-control. They therefore feel safe in concluding that boys are more delinquent than girls in large part because they exhibit lower levels of self-control; in particular, they are less averse to risk.

However, neither opportunity nor self-control explained all the gender variance in teenage crime in their Edmonton sample; the researchers conclude with the observation that "there is something about being male or female" (p. 62) that contributes to the gender gap in crime. What that "something" might be is not considered by the authors.

Finally, we need to remind ourselves that it is not just adults who control the opportunities and routines of girls: the same role is also played by their male peers. Girls are often missing from, or subordinated in, deviant youth cultures because of the exclusionary practices of their male members. Some researchers have suggested that male gangs and groups do not always relish female participation—except as ancillaries to their own activities or as objects of their sexual goals. There is little reason to believe that delinquent males are any more welcoming and less sexist than non-delinquent ones. Sexism is therefore another reason why girls—even when motivated to do so—are infrequent members of deviant subcultures.

Illustrating this point is Daniel Wolf's description of the treatment that girls and women receive at the hands (often quite literally) of the male members of an Edmonton-based motorcycle gang, the Rebels (1991). As he tells it, bike gangs are likely to be one of the last outposts of male chauvinism, where the aspirations of the women's movement are entirely unheard of. Women are not, and cannot be, permanent members of the Rebels motorcycle club, nor do they participate in the decision making or policy formulations of the club. The roles that are ascribed to them involve either straightforward sexual exploitation (as a communal "broad") or sexually stereotyped "ol' ladies" and "mamas."

According to Wolf, there are two main reasons why bikers marginalize women. First, the psychological appeal of the motorcycle gang resides in its ability to furnish a highly masculine image that would be diluted by a female presence. Territorial claims are hardened and unwanted competition with outsiders reduced when bike gangs are able to project a public image of toughness. The prospect of a coed bike gang weakens the deterrent effect. Second, women threaten group cohesion and solidarity because they are an alternative focus for bikers' loyalties. Permanent liaisons are therefore discouraged. As one of Wolf's informants told him, "There are no biker weddings, only ex-biker weddings" (Wolf, 1991, p. 138).

Skinheads are also illustrative of how female entry into and membership in subcultures is conditional and limited, with participants relegated to secondary, often sexualized, roles. According to Young and Curry (1997), whose work we encountered in Chapter 5, European skinheads involved in "football hooliganism" deploy female accomplices as weapons carriers when the police began cracking down on their activities and instigators were forced to smuggle weapons into the football grounds. In their own study, female skinheads—"chelseas"—were allocated the clerical and domestic chores when it came to the job of making special skinhead suspenders or organizing mail-order deliveries from the United Kingdom of skinhead albums and CDs, magazines, and clothes.

The males in the crew were also supporters of what has been referred to as the Madonna or whore syndrome when it came to their sexual and romantic relationships. For them, the female world was divided up into "crew sluts," suppliers of quick and easy sex, and those who might become more regular partners—the chelseas. Though neither role seems obviously very attractive, the girls in the group claimed to derive benefits from their skinhead associations. However, the only example proffered by the authors is a protective one: being in the company of male skinheads enhanced their feelings of safety and security on downtown streets.

The fact that both male skinheads and their female consorts commit to essentially traditional gender roles—unflinching masculinity on the one hand and supportive femininity on the other—encourages the authors to conclude that regardless of whatever it is the subculture resists, it is also in the business of reproducing the existing gender order.

RESPONDING TO GIRLS: PATERNALISM AND THE DOUBLE STANDARD

As I noted at the start of this chapter, most of the historical and contemporary concern about the problem of delinquency and youth crime has focused on the behaviour of males. This is because the public and collective nature of their subcultural activities poses more of a potential threat to law and order. Concerns about the deviant behaviour of female adolescents have, by way of contrast, targeted sexuality and its control (Murdock, 1982, p. 64; Frith, 1985, p. 67; Pilkington, 1994).

Not surprisingly, therefore, much of the early thinking about female deviancy rested on images of delinquent sexuality (Campbell, 1990a; Chesney-Lind and Sheldon, 1992; Chesney-Lind, 1997). This view was, however, by no means restricted to the theoretical musings of largely male criminologists. A similar assumption was shared by many members of the criminal justice system, where it has had a huge impact upon the way in which girls have been dealt with by the police and the courts.

BRIGHT LIGHTS, BIG CITY

This has been made evident in a historical study of what Carolyn Strange refers to as Toronto's "girl problem" (Strange, 1995). Her focus is upon the impact that the growing presence of young, single, wage-earning women had on the moral sensibilities of civic leaders in Toronto a century ago. This was a time when large numbers of young women were leaving their small-town and rural homes and migrating to the big city in search of jobs, money, and independence.

These young women were often referred to as "working girls"—in modern times a euphemism for prostitution. Although working girls were not prostitutes, the phrase does convey the sorts of concerns that a patriarchal society had about the emancipated lifestyles that employment in factories, offices, and department stores afforded rather more easily than the alternative—domestic service.

Much of this concern centred on leisure. The financial rewards of wage labour allowed young females access to the pleasures of the dance hall, movie theatre, and skating rink—often in the company of men and to the accompaniment of alcohol. From the vantage point of the city fathers, moral reformers, health experts, and so on, these were the conditions that led to moral depravity and compromised the women's futures as wives and mothers. Working girls were viewed as a "moral menace" whose activities beyond the workplace required tight control.

Control strategies were a mix of the conciliatory and coercive: supervised (chaperoned) dances and after-work clubs at the more enlightened end of the spectrum, arrest and incarceration at the sharp end. Any young female worker suspected of prostitution was liable to imprisonment and, indeed, a similar fate—an indeterminate reformatory sentence—was also possible for participation in any leisure pursuit regarded as morally dubious—such as skating arm in arm with an unknown male!

The Juvenile Delinquents Act of 1908 provided the legal justification for the regulatory strategies. But it has to be emphasized that the legislation was not just responding to those who had become "fallen women"; it was also used as a means of dealing with young, single women deemed at risk of meeting that fate. As Strange points out, most of the early inmates of Ontario's correctional institutions were not there because they had hurt anybody or stolen anything or were pursuing deviant careers as prostitutes; they were there because they had offended patriarchal notions about what constitutes appropriate behaviour for persons of their age and gender.

However, police, courts, and social workers were not the only active agents in this regard. Strange emphasizes that the committal records of receiving institutions indicate that many of the cases were initiated by the girl's own parents. Poor families, in particular, were dependent on the cheap domestic labour provided in the household by their daughters. Those young women who chose to buck this fate, preferring instead to create their own more autonomous lives in the city, therefore often came to the attention of moral reformers via the controlling efforts of their own families.

It was noted in the opening chapter that since its inception in the nineteenth century, the juvenile court has been invested with powers over young people that are by no means limited to those who break the law. A paternalistic concern with the moral well-being of children and youth gave rise to a category of misbehaviours that are commonly referred to as status offences. These offences have a special relevance for female adolescents because historically it is for "incorrigibility," truancy, "moral depravation," and the like that girls, rather more frequently than boys, have been referred to the juvenile court. Likewise, girls have often been punished more severely—with custodial sentences—for violating moral codes rather than the Criminal Code. Status offences are, according to one American expert, often little more than a convenient cover or code for acts of sexual deviance. As he puts it, "The categories of 'ungovernability,' 'loitering,' 'immoral' or 'indecent conduct,' 'runaway,' and similar designations are frequently the preferred charges, particularly if the court has a policy to avoid stigmatizing an individual with a sex offence" (Reiss, 1960, p. 309).

Girl offenders are viewed and treated in this way because our society has established different standards of sexual behaviour for males and females. Adolescent males who engage in sexual activity find their behaviour justified—or even lauded—as "sowing wild oats"; adolescent girls who do the same are condemned as "loose" and "immoral." This double standard exists as a reflection of the different sort of threat offered by male and female deviants: the former are seen as a threat to public order, the latter, as a threat to patriarchal domesticity.

THE POLICING OF GIRLS

The perception that boy and girl delinquents pose different kinds of threat similarly affects how they are policed. I noted in Chapter 2 that even if police discover or are made aware of crime, they do not necessarily act on that information and make an arrest. Instead of arresting an offender, they may decide to deal with him or her informally—cautioning the individual about his or her future conduct, for instance. This is what is known as police discretion that has long been recognized as an inevitable aspect of law enforcement: it is simply not possible for the police to uniformly enforce all the laws and regulations on the statute books on every occasion. It is also not always desirable to arrest each and every wrongdoer. For some offenders—particularly young, first-time offenders—being stopped and lectured by a police officer is enough to deter them from further wrongdoing. In the judgment of the police officer, no good purpose will be served by arresting them. Indeed, the officer may even agree with those criminologists who argue that charging adolescents only turns minor deviants into major ones.

As these comments suggest, the street-level decision making by police officers is not arbitrary: it often follows certain implicit, informal rules. In particular, the decision to forego arrest is most likely to be exercised when the offence is not serious or when evidence or witnesses are lacking and a conviction therefore unlikely. Situations in which discretion is deployed for essentially legal reasons are unproblematic. However, there is reason to believe that in their encounters with juveniles, police officers are also influenced by more subjective, extra-legal factors.

American research has shown how decisions made by police officers are determined not only by the seriousness of the offence, but also by the personal demeanour of the offenders—the way they dress and their attitude toward the arresting officer (Piliavin and Briar, 1964; Black and Reiss, 1970). This means that disrespectful young offenders who have half-shaven heads and wear scruffy jeans, leather jackets, or grunge clothing are more likely to be arrested than polite and contrite adolescents who wear more conventional clothing. Some clothing styles and patterns of behaviour are, in other words, seen as "signs of trouble" and might, therefore, provoke a booking. More controversially, there is some (largely American) evidence to suggest that skin colour, combined with demeanour, also counts as justification for arrest (Smith, 1982).

Might gender also be one of the factors affecting police decision making? It is conceivable that girls are perceived more positively than boys by police officers. On the one hand, the different socialization experiences of males and females are such that girls stopped by the police will be more demure and respectful (see Mawby (1980). Boys, particularly in group settings, are more likely to be defiant and aggressive in their dealings with the police. On the other hand, police officers in public settings feel less threatened by girls than boys and therefore more inclined to leniency.

American research on police reactions to female offenders provides qualified support for these propositions. One study of males and females arrested for drug offences indicated that if—and only if—female offenders displayed stereotypically female behaviour (breaking down in tears, expressing anxieties about their children's well-being, or claiming to have been led along by more willful males) their chances of escaping arrest increased. However, failure to produce these gendered characteristics resulted in arrests for females no less frequently than for males (DeFleur, 1975).

Other American research has shown how the double standard makes girls more or less liable to arrest in different situations. Monahan (1970) found that girls were more likely than boys to be released for illegal acts, equally likely to be arrested for running away, but more likely to be arrested for sex offences. Indeed, this seems to be part of a pattern whereby girls are treated with leniency when committing "male" crimes but are punished more severely when transgressing the expectation of appropriate female sex-role behaviour. Moreover, a more recent American field study of police encounters with crime suspects found that the age of the offender had no bearing on police discretion with males, but did influence how female suspects were dealt with: the younger they were, the more likely they were to be arrested. According to the researcher, the police adopt a deliberately interventionist stance with young female offenders in order to deter them from further defiance of sex-role norms (Visher, 1983).

It is also the case that police officers sometimes react to changes believed to be taking place in society. In effect, they may end up policing the shifting nature of gender roles. For example, although there is little empirical evidence to support the idea that female emancipation has increased violent and predatory female deviancy, police officers on the beat are unlikely to have read that literature. They are rather more likely to operate on the assumption that they are now dealing with a new type of female offender and act accordingly. Perhaps they have learned—from the newspapers and television—about emancipated women and girls and have used this knowledge as the basis for their interactions with juveniles. This would appear to be the case with two police officers interviewed in one British study:

> I think girls are very much more violent now. We see them in here. I'm not surprised by it and I suppose it's mainly due to Women's Lib. and that lot. Much more violent than five to ten years ago, much more assertive.
>
> It's regrettable that girls now think they've got to be like the boys. Girls were much nicer five or so years ago. I blame the Equal Pay Act myself, it's been a major cause of crime, not only did it lead to more women going out to work and consequently neglecting their children ... increasing juvenile crime in this way, but women themselves are less satisfied with their lives ... equal pay forced prices up ... therefore more women had to go out to work. Career women ... it's all wrong. If women are content it would solve a lot of problems. (Gelsthorpe, 1986, p. 130)

As these comments suggest, people frequently act on their perceptions. If policemen think that the position of girls and women in society is changing and now justifies more punitive policing, their beliefs are going to have an impact on arrest rates. Whether these perceptions are accurate or not is another matter entirely.

GENDER AND THE COURTS

As I have previously noted, status offences have been a controversial feature of the juvenile justice system in Canada and the United States. Feminists and others critical of the functioning of the juvenile justice system have long argued, with good reason, that the existence of status offences has contributed to the less-than-equal treatment of young male and female offenders.

There is considerable evidence that in a variety of places and over considerable periods of time girls are significantly more likely than boys to be charged by the police and prosecuted by the courts for behaviour that is not criminal for adults. Under the status offence category, therefore, girls have been disproportionately arrested for truancy, incorrigibility, and so forth (Chesney-Lind and Sheldon, 1992; Chesney-Lind, 1997)).

Since status offences have formally been eliminated under the Young Offenders Act in Canada, it is reasonable to anticipate changes in the numbers and sorts of offences for which young people in general, and girls in particular, are apprehended and dealt with. Such is not the case, however. This has been made apparent by findings from several studies that have sought to explore gender differences in the treatment of young offenders in the immediate post–Juvenile Delinquents Act era.

One of the first of these was conducted by Marge Reitsma-Street (1993). She compared and contrasted sentences dispensed by the youth court for both female and male young offenders before and after the implementation of the Young Offenders Act. She found, in the first instance, that the majority of both male and female offenders are charged with minor breaches of the law and that the new act has not changed that pattern. Typically, female delinquents in Canada (as elsewhere) are charged with minor theft. On the other hand, she also found that there has been an overall increase in the number of young females charged since the introduction of the Young Offenders Act. Reitsma-Street suggests two possible explanations. First, in a climate of zero tolerance and in the name of gender equity, there is a greater willingness to charge female adolescents in minor assault cases. Second, there has been a substantial increase in charges laid against female youth for noncompliance with youth justice administration decisions. For instance, nearly 24 percent of the total charges laid against young females in 1990–91 were for offences against the administration of youth justice. These include

- failure to appear in court,

- leaving a residence without adult permission, and

- breach of probation.

Since 1984, there has been an annual increase in charges against the administration of justice, from one in twenty in 1985–86 to approximately one in four in 1990–91. These charges are also laid against young males, but not so readily. Adults are not charged for breaking these administrative rules; vestiges of paternalism have not, therefore, been completely eliminated from the juvenile justice system. Moreover, these rules are applied more readily against young female offenders than male ones.

Doob and Meen report similar findings (1993). In their examination of the workings of a Toronto court, they found that from the end of the application of the Juvenile Delinquents Act to the implementation of the Young Offenders Act there had been a doubling of charges involving minor violations of what are referred to as administrative and order maintenance offences. Failure to appear in court is an example of the former and charges of mischief or breach of probation are examples of the latter. Although these are not status offences as the term is usually understood, they are not the sort of serious delinquent activity commonly understood as criminal.

The new legislation notwithstanding, adolescents, especially female ones, are still being brought before the courts for largely minor age-specific offences. The explanation for this lies in the fact that, reflecting continuing uncertainties about appropriate juvenile justice philosophies, the Young Offenders Act still affords considerable discretion to police and courts when handling young offenders. As a result, paternalism still prevails in the juvenile courts, and, as in the past, it is primarily directed against girls. For example, a judge in a southwestern Ontario jurisdiction recently

> ... committed a thirteen-year-old female to a period of secure custody not in response to the serious nature of the crime she committed—a "breach of probation"—but out of concern for the fact that the girl had been involved in street prostitution and her history included many serious risk factors for subsequent disturbance.... (Leschied and Jaffe, 1991, p. 167)

The Young Offenders Act has also been examined from the point of view of possible gender bias in another study of the family court in southwestern Ontario. Sandra Bell (1994) surveyed young people and their parents appearing in an Ontario provincial family court. What she was trying to find out was whether judges sentenced young offenders strictly on the legal merits of cases before them—as indicated by offence seriousness, prior criminal record, and number of charges—or, instead, allowed extra-legal variables such as class, race, and gender to influence their decision making.

Her findings are surprising from a legal point of view. None of the legally important variables predicted length or type of sentence very well. On the other hand, they did support the claim of feminist scholars that girls are more subject than boys to judicial paternalism. Bell found that the offender characteristic that correlated best with sentencing outcomes was gender: young female offenders receive lighter sentences than their male counterparts. Two other gender-related factors also affect sentencing: young offenders from families with a female head and those appearing in court with their mothers received less severe sentences.

Further explanations provide more support for feminist hypotheses. In particular, Bell finds that female offenders only benefit from judicial leniency when charged with traditional crimes against persons and property. If charged with order maintenance, administrative, and age-specific offences such as obstructing justice, disturbing the peace, mischief, truancy, and loitering—offences that clearly resemble the now eliminated status offences—then judicial leniency was not forthcoming.

She concludes by suggesting that despite the intentions of some reformers, the new youth court created by the Young Offenders Act is used—as in the past—as an agency for controlling adolescent behaviour that is deemed problematic but is not necessarily criminal. Adolescents are still referred to the courts because other institutions—notably the family and the school—have failed to curb what is seen as antisocial behaviour.

CONCLUSION

Throughout much of the twentieth century women and girls have been missing from debates about crime, delinquency, and youth culture. When they have made an appearance it has been as isolated sexual delinquents. How are we to understand their absence? Are they really uninvolved in deviant peer-group activities? Or are they there and simply ignored or overlooked by male researchers who prefer to identify with the more romantic male rebels (McRobbie and Garber, 1975)?

Researchers who have focused on highly visible deviant youth cultures have concluded that although girls are present in subcultures, their roles are marginal and traditional: they are present as girlfriends or supporters of male group members. As such, their participation in subcultural activity is contingent upon the largesse of the males. As McRobbie and Garber put it, "[a] girl's membership of the group was dependent on the boy she was with—it was always tentative, easily resulting in her expulsion from the group, depending on the state of her relationships with the boys" (1975, p. 216). Illustrating this point are the highly unequal relationships between the male members of the Rebels motorcycle club and the female members documented in Wolf's ethnography (1991).

More recently, however, girls have figured more prominently in media accounts of crime and delinquency. However, stories of violent and aggressive gang activity are not well supported by either official data sources or findings from sociological research.

And what of more ordinary non-gang female delinquency? Are girls only peripherally involved and then only as sexual deviants? Research suggests otherwise. Female delinquency is both more common and less distinctive than routinely believed. Girls commit less delinquency than boys, but they indulge in the same sort of minor property offences. They are inclined to commit fewer violent personal crimes but are more likely than boys to be arrested for status offences.

Students of female delinquency therefore increasingly identify a twofold task for themselves: explaining the reduced volume of female teenage deviant behaviour and explaining why female sexual behaviour, under the guise of status offences, is so tenaciously policed by parents and law enforcement officials. Answers to the first of these two questions have revolved around the effects of socialization and social control—girls have weaker motivations and more limited opportunities than boys for becoming deviant. Risk-taking behaviour is less likely to be encouraged by parents who are also more likely to monitor their daughters' activities and friendship patterns. Girls spend more time at home, both by themselves and with female peers, and are therefore less well placed for entering more deviant external domains, such as the street or shopping mall.

Girls' lives are more tightly controlled than boys' (hence less characterized by delinquency) because of paternalism. Paternalism, in turn, is responsible for a double standard that tolerates behaviour in boys that is condemned in girls. The research literature shows that police officers and juvenile court judges share, along with parents, the paternalistic presuppositions that allow for the double standard. Paternalism also affects girls' contacts with the criminal justice system. They are particularly vulnerable to apprehension by the police for status offences. Moreover, the police are often made aware of status offending through parents who report their runaway or incorrigible daughters to them. Thus although girls may be less likely to be charged by police or punished punitively by the law for traditional crimes against property and persons, they are more likely to be dealt with seriously for infractions of rules pertaining to appropriate female behaviour.

NOTES

1. This section, and others in this chapter, draw heavily on the work of Chesney-Lind and Sheldon (1992) and Chesney-Lind (1997).
2. I am indebted to Ron Gillis for this summation of power-control theory.

C H A P T E R 7

From Delinquency to Youth Crime: The Young Offenders Act and the Response to Juvenile Offenders in Canada

INTRODUCTION

For most of the previous century, juvenile offenders in Canada were dealt with under the terms and conditions set out by the Juvenile Delinquents Act. Originally passed in 1908 and amended several times, it established the legal principles by which successive Canadian governments responded to the problem of juvenile crime. In 1984 it was replaced by the Young Offenders Act (YOA). Why was a change in juvenile justice legislation deemed necessary? What was wrong with the previous act? What factors and forces encouraged the development of new thinking about juvenile justice policy in Canada? And why has the YOA proven to be so controversial, so much so, in fact, that it too is scheduled for replacement by new youth justice legislation? The purpose of this chapter is to address these important questions about the development and trajectory of the juvenile justice system in Canada. It will also examine the effectiveness of various programs designed to prevent, control, and rehabilitate delinquent youth.

In order to carry out these tasks, it is necessary to go back to the beginning and examine the ideas and assumptions about delinquency that were influential when the Juvenile Delinquents Act was first enacted, and how those ideas have evolved over time. The Juvenile Delinquents Act was formulated according to a positivist philosophy (Corrado and Markwart, 1992). It assumed that various aspects of adolescents' social environment were responsible for their delinquent behaviour. These negative environmental influences were wide ranging and included inadequate moral training, hunger, poverty, and poor schooling. Adolescents learned the wrong lessons from these influences; countering them required the active intervention of a special juvenile justice system whose prime purpose was rehabilitation—a goal that was to be met by the development of the probation service—an emphasis on the informal handling of juveniles, and treatment-oriented custodial sentences (often of an indeterminate length).

The conviction that delinquent behaviour was caused by negative—and correctable—environmental factors led to what has been called a welfare model of juvenile justice and a concomitant focus upon the offender rather than his or her crimes. This model of juvenile justice has prevailed throughout most of the twentieth century, not only in Canada but also in other parts of the English-speaking world.

ORIGINS OF THE YOUNG OFFENDERS ACT

The origins of the YOA are to be found in criticisms of its predecessor and the welfare model of juvenile justice on which that act was based. During the 1960s dissatisfaction with the juvenile justice system increased, precipitated by two major developments. First, recorded levels of juvenile crime were rising dramatically. As the post-war baby boom generation moved into adolescence—the peak years for crime (see Chapter 2)—the incidence of delinquency began to increase. Second, it was discovered that many juvenile offenders, like their adult counterparts, were repeat offenders—recidivists. High rates of delinquency and recidivism were not a good advertisement for a juvenile justice system that claimed to be rehabilitating young law-breakers (Burrows, Hudson, and Hornick, 1988; Bala, 1988).

A growing disillusionment with the juvenile justice system's ability to restore young offenders also served to refocus attention on other, competing justifications for criminal sanctions, particularly deterrence and incapacitation. If as a society we were not able to lower rates of delinquent behaviour by rehabilitation, then perhaps we should be paying more attention to preventing its occurrence in the first place or, failing that, limiting its appearance in the future by more regular use of incapacitative sentences. However, these goals could not be met because the penalties available under the Juvenile Delinquents Act were seen as doing little to discourage further offending or keep offenders off the street for very long. The act was seen, increasingly, as being too soft on juvenile crime.

Although the public was critical of the Juvenile Delinquents Act because it was insufficiently punitive, other critics found fault with it because it afforded too few legal protections for young criminals. The welfare orientation of the Juvenile Delinquents Act was seen as leading to civil rights abuses. A growing children's rights lobby—spearheaded by lawyers, social workers, and probation officers—argued that because of the emphasis upon the offender rather than the offence, many youths appearing before the juvenile court were denied the full range of due process consideration available to adults (Burrows, Hudson, and Hornick, 1988).

In particular, they did not like the use of indeterminate sentences. The only legal guideline given judges when sentencing young offenders was a vague one—their obligation to act in "the child's best interests." As a result, getting into a correctional institution was often considerably easier than getting out; once there, offenders were only released when probation officers and other prison officials judged that they had been rehabilitated. This policy resulted in an uneven application of justice. For example, two juvenile offenders in two different provincial jurisdictions or institutions could serve custodial sentences of very different length for roughly similar offences. Even worse, juvenile offenders could spend more time in a correctional institution than adult offenders who had committed the same offence but received a specific sentence upon conviction.

There were other ways, too, in which juvenile justice was unevenly meted out. The fact that different provinces set different upper age limits for juvenile delinquency contributed to variation in sentencing patterns. For instance, in one province a sixteen-year-old would be punished as a juvenile, while in another, a sixteen-year-old offender would be punished (more severely) as an adult. And because the emphasis of the juvenile court was on the informal dispensation of justice, young offenders often had their cases heard without the benefit of legal representation.

A heightened concern with potential civil rights violations partially explains why status offences became an increasingly controversial and contentious aspect of the Juvenile Delinquents Act. A number of commentators (Bernard, 1992, for instance) have pointed out that the existence of status offences gave the state extensive and intrusive provision to intervene into young people's private lives. Adolescents could be arrested simply because parents regarded them as incorrigible or because they had established undesirable sexual liaisons. Chesney-Lind (1997) demonstrates, as we have seen in the previous chapter, that in the United States parents are often responsible for bringing their female children into contact with the criminal justice system, reporting them to the police for these very reasons. The inclusive nature of status offences also meant that adolescents could be arrested without a more specific charge being laid. Under the Juvenile Delinquents Act, and legislative provisions like it, adolescents were charged with committing a delinquency rather than a particular offence (Griffiths and Verdun-Jones, 1994, p. 604).

Ultimately, as they were intended to do, status offences criminalized adolescents for behaviours that were legal for adults. What made this policy increasingly unacceptable was research informed by the labelling perspective indicating that the more early and formal contact that juveniles have with the police and courts, the more likely they are to become involved with crime as adults. Status offences were not only unduly paternalistic, their existence increased, rather than diminished, the probability of future law-breaking.

With hindsight, it can be seen that the welfare-oriented Juvenile Delinquents Act was under attack from both ends of the political spectrum. Conservatives grew to dislike it because it was ineffective in curtailing the rise of juvenile crime, while liberal and left-wing reformers in the legal and "caring" professions worried that the civil liberties of young offenders were threatened by its paternalistic mandate.

Indeed, even without the above criticisms of the Juvenile Delinquents Act, it seems unlikely that it could have endured much longer once the Canadian Charter of Rights and Freedoms was proclaimed in 1982. It was felt that the act—characterized by its disregard for due-process considerations and by provincial variations in the handling of juvenile justice issues—would not be able to rebuff court challenges to its legality (Hylton, 1994, p. 234).

After a number of false starts, the YOA was passed in 1984. It established the legal principles for juvenile justice in Canada for young people between the ages of twelve and eighteen, although each province is given the constitutional right to create its own administrative organization to enact them.

Many of the provisions of the YOA attempt to redress the criticisms directed at its predecessor. Hence there is now a uniform maximum age limit—seventeen—for juvenile offenders. Legal protection—the right to a lawyer, more stringent rules about the gathering and presenting of evidence in court—for young offenders has been established as a principle. Indeterminate custodial sentences have been replaced, originally by a three-year maximum term, more recently extended to five years. And status offences have been abolished. Other highlights of the act include the raising of the age of minimal criminal responsibility from seven to twelve and a prohibition of the publication or broadcasting of the names of those charged under it.

MODELS OF JUVENILE JUSTICE

Most commentators agree that—like similar initiatives in juvenile justice legislation in the United Kingdom and parts of the United States—the philosophical intent of the YOA represented a shift away from a welfare model of juvenile justice (Reid-Macnevin, 1988). What it is shifting toward is more complicated (and debatable) because two other philosophies and models of juvenile justice have clearly influenced the thinking behind the new act. These are a justice (or due-process) model and a crime-control model.

Justice models derive not from positivism, but from the neoclassical school of criminology that says that individuals engage in crime of their own free will; some people decide that criminal activity is more rewarding than non-criminal behaviour. If we want to reduce crime, we should make it a less attractive alternative: criminals and delinquents should be made accountable for their choices. The purpose of the criminal justice system is therefore to ensure that criminals are punished in proportion to the severity of their crime, and that due-process considerations govern the application and administration of these legal principles. The crime-control model is more concerned with the safety and well-being of law-abiding citizens than with the treatment or civil rights of the offender. It emphasizes community protection, which is to be achieved by long custodial sentences that, it is believed, both incapacitate and deter.

Some commentators see the YOA as an amalgam of all three models drawing in roughly equal measure from each (Reid and Reitsma-Street, 1984). Others insist that it is best viewed as an example of a modified justice model. Corrado and Markwart (1992), for instance, advocate the latter perspective. The major point of departure of the YOA from its predecessor, as they see it, is that the former is predicated upon the idea of individual responsibility and accountability for wrongs done, whereas the guiding principle of the Juvenile Delinquents Act was that responsibility and blame for juvenile misconduct rest fairly and squarely with negligent and deficient parents and the community at large.

However, the YOA is not entirely based on the justice model—if it were, the juvenile justice system would be indistinguishable from the adult criminal justice system—because it retains the axiom that juvenile offenders are more reformable than adult offenders. Similarly, it employs the same rhetoric regarding informal disposition and diversion as was evident in the Juvenile Delinquents Act.

WHAT'S WRONG WITH THE YOUNG OFFENDERS ACT?

Unless you have been living on another planet for the past fifteen years or so, you will realize that the YOA has not been received by the general public or the mass media as the shining light of a radically improved juvenile justice system it was intended to be. In fact, it has been the focus of so much critical attention that it is hard to believe there was once a time when it was lauded by its sponsors and supporters on Parliament Hill, and seen by the criminal justice field as marking the beginning of a "new era" of juvenile justice administration in Canada. What has gone wrong, or is thought to have gone wrong, with this once-heralded legislation?

Some of the criticisms that the YOA has engendered have been relatively minor and involve problems of implementation. For example, the provinces complained that they had not received promised financial resources from the federal government. On the other hand, the provinces were accused of failing to implement some of the new act's more treatment-oriented provisions. Those charged with the task of making the act work at the provincial level felt that it was an increasingly complicated piece of legislation. Amendments were introduced to deal with these criticisms.

These amendments have done little or nothing to cool debate about the act, which remains as controversial as ever. Indeed, following an American pattern, juvenile justice has now become part of everyday political discourse in Canada; for the first time, it became a central element in the 1993 federal election campaign (Hylton, 1994, p. 234). Why and how has "youth crime" become politicized?

According to its more friendly critics, the problem with the YOA is that it has had difficulty in meeting different, and in some cases contradictory, objectives (Archambault, 1991, p. ix). Infused by principles from three distinct models of juvenile justice, it is not surprising that the various goals of the act occasionally clash. For instance, custodial sentences that "fit the crime" (justice model) will also protect the community (crime-control model), but will they rehabilitate young offenders and smooth their reentry into society (welfare model) (Burrows, Hudson, and Hornick, 1988)?

However, most criticism of the YOA has not been of this subtle and temperate variety. Indeed, it has often been virulent and has emanated, as you might have guessed, from the framework of the crime-control model whose principal champions are often connected with police organizations or victims' rights groups and—certainly in Alberta and Ontario—the governing provincial political party. A good example of police claims-making about the lamentable failings of the YOA is provided in Carsten Stroud's book, *Contempt of Court: The Betrayal of Justice in Canada* (1993). Stroud, an ex–police officer, is withering in his dismissal of legislation that the police apparently refer (sarcastically) to as the Youth Protection Act. Another high-profile lobbyist against everything that the YOA stands for is Gordon Domm, also a retired police officer, who heads an organization called the Citizen's Coalition, a lobby group for, in Domm's words, "punishment people": "The pendulum is starting to move in our favour. For the last 30 years, the anti-punishment group has had control. They have made a mess of things. Now it is our turn, the punishment people. Punishment works" (Addario, 1993).

Other anti-YOA interest groups and claims-makers have even closer connections to the police. The Canadian Resource Centre for Victims of Crime has made it its job to monitor incidents of violent crime and supply information on them to politicians and the mass media. This organization is headed by Scott Newark, whose activities, and those of the resource centre, are paid for by the Canadian Police Association and a police publishing group (Corrado and Markwart, 1994, p. 345).

It need hardly be stated that the law-and-order lobby group believes that the legislative prescriptions of the YOA do not do enough to control, punish, or deter young criminals. Given this starting point, it is not hard to predict the specific nature of their criticisms. These involve, by and large, a rejection of all of the main provisions of the act. Maximum custodial sentences are seen as too short, while setting the minimum age of criminal responsibility at twelve is believed to allow those under that age to commit crimes—including violent crimes—with impunity. A variant on this theme concerns what has been called the "Fagan factor," after the character created by Charles Dickens in *Oliver Twist*. The suggestion is that adult criminals employ children as their agents of crime because they are immune from prosecution under the YOA. They also argue that treating seventeen-year-olds as young rather than adult offenders entitles them to the sort of lenient punishment that does nothing to protect society or deter young people from committing more crimes; that the publication ban on the names of young offenders removes an important opportunity to shame them, and thereby deter them from further wrongdoing; and finally that the transfer of young offenders to adult court—where sentences are more severe—should be made more frequently and automatically.

From their perspective, the police feel that the new-found concern for young offenders' rights is excessive and that it interferes with their priorities: crime control and community protection. They do not like being obligated to advise young suspects of their legal rights before questioning. They also object to the requirement of a written waiver or the presence of a lawyer or parent before a confession is sought.

The police are similarly dubious about the encroachment of defence lawyers into youth court proceedings. The arrival of defence counsel signifies a growing adversarial culture that young offenders—particularly seasoned ones—will exploit to their advantage. In particular, young offenders will now learn, through their defence lawyers, that there is a distinction to be made between legal guilt and factual guilt.

HAS THE YOUNG OFFENDERS ACT INFLUENCED YOUTH CRIME?

The common thread underlying most of the specific criticisms of the act is that it has led to an increase in youth crime, particularly violent youth crime. This claim was initially fueled by official data showing that rates of youth crime reached their highest-ever recorded levels in 1991. Tellingly, those who make this argument fail to explain why rates peaked in that year, rather than the mid-1980s, when the legislation was first ushered in. Equally significant is the fact that much less attention was paid by the critics to the subsequent decline in youth crime rates documented by the official statistics throughout the remainder of the 1990s. Moreover, what, in retrospect, was a short-term "hump" in Canadian youth crime rates in the early 1990s was also evident in other countries—and not therefore explainable by the workings of the YOA (Carrington, 1999). This is not to say that nothing about youth crime has changed since the introduction of the YOA. The more important question, though, is what—and why.

Part of the answer is that some of the increase in youth crime incidents was an artifact of the changed legislative procedures created by the act. Previously, in some provinces sixteen- and seventeen-year-olds were treated as adult offenders, and therefore, when arrested and charged, contributed to adult crime rates. Now, by contrast, all sixteen- and seventeen-year-olds count as young offenders, a change in legal status made more important once it is understood that police officers are commonly less inclined to show leniency to older rather than younger teens. Required to handle older teens—sixteen- and seventeen-year-olds—as young offenders (rather than adult ones), police have responded to them in the same way that they have often responded to older teens in the past—by arresting them instead of releasing them with a warning (Carrington and Moyer, 1994).

Other, more recent research by Carrington suggests, however, that there has also been a real shift in police practices since the passage of the YOA; more specifically, police officers are now showing, under the influence of zero tolerance policies, less discretion to all young offenders (Carrington, 1999). The proportion of young people apprehended by police officers has not changed with the YOA, but the numbers arrested and charged has—more of them being formally processed, in other words. Several examinations of youth court statistics have revealed similar indications of increasingly punitive sanctioning of young offenders throughout the 1990s.

Doob and Meen (1993) collected data from Toronto youth courts involving young offenders under the age of sixteen. The information came from two post-YOA periods (1984–86 and 1989–90) and was compared with data collected during the last two years of the Juvenile Delinquents Act (1982–84). Doob and Meen found that the pattern of disposition changed over time: the implementation of the YOA corresponded to an increasing use of custodial sentences. However, they also discovered that, although there are more of them, the length of these custodial sentences has become shorter in the post–Juvenile Delinquents Act era. As well, the authors found that the seriousness of the charge is more strongly related to the severity of sentence under the YOA than it was under the Juvenile Delinquents Act. Doob and Meen take this as evidence that judges have been encouraged to prioritize the offence, rather than the offender, when passing sentence.

That the YOA has led to more custodial sentences (although not necessarily longer ones) is also apparent from other comparisons with its predecessor. Corrado and Markwart (1992), after comparing data from the youth court surveys of 1986–87 and 1988–91, conclude that the range of offences for which a custodial sentence is deemed appropriate has broadened under the YOA. Although it is certainly the case that all serious offences receive custodial sentences, most of those juveniles in receipt of custodial sentences have not committed violent crimes. This Corrado and Markwart construe as evidence that a process of tightening up the judicial response to young offenders is under way.

Schissel, in another overview of trends in official juvenile crime rates, reaches a broadly similar conclusion. He notes that despite the YOA's articulation of diversion and alternative measures as policy objectives, more offenders have been handled formally—by arrest and institutionalization—since the legislation was enacted in 1984 (1993, p. 18). Again, like Corrado and Markwart, he argues that rather than making the juvenile justice system more lenient, the YOA in practice imposes more control on adolescents than its predecessor.

Even programs that have rehabilitative goals have resulted in a more punitive handling of juvenile offenders than in the past. Take, for example, Ontario's alternative measures program that began in April 1988 (Leschied and Jaffe, 1988). This program is aimed at first-time offenders who face a minor charge. Designed to prevent less serious, and therefore "reformable" offenders from coming into contact with the justice system, it circumvents the formal court system by having those charged sent to a probation officer or a community agency where they might do some form of community service or receive counselling. While participation is voluntary, it does require an admission of guilt and acceptance of responsibility for the wrongdoing from the young offender. If the youth denies the charges, the case goes to the youth court. Successful completion of the alternative measures program is rewarded by a withdrawal of the original charges and any record of conviction.

On the face of it, this looks like a laudable attempt to prevent the possible transformation of minor juvenile offenders into hard-core adult criminals. Good intentions notwithstanding, however, there are problems with this initiative. In particular, it increases, rather than decreases, the amount of contact that young offenders have with the legal system. Compare the present arrangement with what happened in the past. Previously, juveniles would have benefited from police discretion—they might have been released with a warning for a minor offence or, if they were brought before the court for a non-serious offence, they might be given an absolute discharge. Now, they are obliged to admit their guilt and undertake some form of community service, which will probably be interpreted as a punishment for the wrongdoing. It is hard to see how the effects of this diversionary program will be any less detrimental to young offenders than those of more traditional approaches to juvenile justice.

Thus while the YOA is routinely condemned for ushering in an unconscionably lenient era of juvenile justice policy, in practice the effect has been the very opposite. As Carrington and others point out, the guiding principles of the YOA emphasized informal response (by both police and courts) as the best means of dealing with youth crime. This advice has not been heeded. Of all the provinces, only in Quebec has there been a decline in the formal processing of young offenders under the YOA. Whereas that province had the highest recorded rates of youth crime under the previous act, it now has the lowest. This is because of provincial legislation, introduced in 1979, that pioneered innovative diversionary strategies for young offenders. Ironically, of course, the increase in police charges and custodial sentences in other Canadian provinces (step forward, Alberta and Ontario) is seen as evidence that the YOA is fatally flawed and therefore needs replacing.

Another related complaint about the YOA is that it has done little or nothing to curb the problem of repeat offending. It is true that a substantial number of young people appearing before the youth court are making a return visit. According to 1998–99 youth court statistics, some 42 percent of cases heard by the youth court involve recidivists. However, this is a familiar pattern not unique to the YOA. Other studies carried in other eras and other jurisdictions also show that both youth and adult courts are sentencing people that they have sentenced before. While recidivism is a disturbing fact of criminal justice life, it is not a unique consequence of the YOA.

Nor is there much evidence that the nature of youth crime has been transformed in the YOA era. Minor property crime still predominates, as we saw in Chapter 2. This has not prevented, however, violent crime from becoming the main focus of critical debate. Statistics do indicate that since 1986 there has been a sizable increase in crimes of violence among young people. But before we conclude that this increase justifies all fears about the nefarious effects of the YOA, we should remember what was said in the earlier chapter: the Statistics Canada category of violent crime covers a broad spectrum of offences that range from homicide to common assault. And it is worth reminding ourselves of the inverse relationship between the seriousness of an offence and the frequency of occurrence. In 1998, for instance, two-thirds of female youth and 46 percent of male youth charged with a violent crime were charged with common assault. Whether schoolyard scuffles and the minor pushing and shoving officially defined and classified as "assault" is really what the public has in mind when it thinks of teenage violence is, as I have mentioned, extremely debatable. Moreover, we must not lose sight of how the official statistics are put together. Most policing is reactive. Police officers often intervene in situations only at the request of members of the public; the police rely upon citizens' reporting criminal incidents to them.

At a time when adults are very sensitive to the growing seriousness of juvenile crime—the media reminds them of the problem all the time—they are perhaps increasingly inclined to make their fears known to the police. As a result, the police handle many incidents that in the past neither they nor the public would have paid much attention to. Thus, much of the apparent increase in violent teenage crime is of the less serious sort that in more tolerant times would not have been reported to the police in the first place.

Generally speaking, academics have been more sympathetic to the YOA than other groups in society. However, there are dissenters in the ranks, academic experts who are prepared to entertain the possibility that the YOA has not always provided an appropriate response to youth crime.

In their commentary on the YOA, Corrado and Markwart (1994) acknowledge the huge gap that exists between public beliefs about a serious youth crime problem and academic discussions that tend to deny such beliefs much objective validity. They try to bridge that gap by suggesting that crime control critics correctly interpret the act as too soft on serious young offenders, while the academics are right in believing that the act is too punitive to the considerably more numerous non-serious offenders. They concur with critics who insist that the small number of serious habitual criminals are currently treated too leniently by the youth court: too few are transferred to adult court and insufficient use is made of long custodial sentences. But they also argue that the fact that large numbers of youths who commit non-violent property offences or breach probation regulations receive custodial sentences suggests a continuing belief in incapacitation and deterrence. Hence, as Corrado and Markwart put it, the paradox: the YOA is both too soft and too hard. They suggest that this paradox is responsible for the radically divergent interpretations of the act proffered by the general public and academic experts.

The public, with and without the assistance of the mass media and special-interest groups, are mainly concerned with violent street crime. Criminologists, on the other hand, while not denying the meanness and nastiness of violent and aggressive adolescent behaviour (I am thinking here about the murders of Reena Virk and Dimitri [Matti] Baranovski), stress its atypicality. The differing emphasis of the two constituencies creates different perceptions of the YOA. Moreover, public anger provoked by a small minority of high-profile cases during the tenure of the act has been turned into a more general rejection of the act as a whole. As the authors put it, since the act is seen to be soft in a few cases, then surely it must be soft on all youth crime (Corrado and Markwart, 1994, p. 362). More recently, Corrado (1999) has stated that he believes there has been a real increase in youth violence, with the exception of murder, and that, although none of this increase can be attributed to the YOA, the legislation nonetheless has done little to counter this upward trend.

Finally, we need to emphasize that the furious debate about the YOA involves a piece of legislation that has been in effect for fewer than twenty years. Thus any and all commentary about its responsibility for worsening patterns of youth crime is based on a very short period; concentrating analysis and interpretation on year-to-year fluctuations in crime rates may conceal longer-term trends in the opposite direction, an important point that has been made to good effect by Ted Gurr (1989). He has demonstrated that, in both Western Europe and the United States, there has been a gradual overall decline in violent behaviour over the past several hundred years. However, this downward trend is not apparent when crime rates are compared on a yearly basis or even over several decades. On this argument, therefore, it is simply too soon to know what, if any, effect the YOA has had on youth crime. Moreover, we are unlikely to ever know because there are plans afoot to replace it with new youth justice legislation.

WHAT'S NEXT? REPLACING THE YOUNG OFFENDERS ACT

Predictably enough, virtually all discussion of change to the YOA up to and including suggestions that it be replaced involve stiffer sanctions and the elimination of judicial leniency for young offenders. At the vanguard of this trend is the Canadian Alliance Party, which has quickly and easily managed to politicize juvenile justice in Canada. The party is now in the vanguard of the law-and-order response to the problem of juvenile crime.

There are interesting parallels here with the United States and the crack issue. Not only did Reagan's Republicans take a highly publicized "hard line" on illicit drug use in the 1980s, they forced politicians of all ideological stripes to do likewise. Those who were seen as being soft on drugs risked electoral failure (Reinarman and Levine, 1989). Something similar has happened with juvenile justice in Canada: all major federal political parties, the NDP included, now favour a more punitive response to young offenders. Hence, in 1995 a set of amendments to the YOA emerged that have a familiar ring to them: All youths aged sixteen or seventeen charged with serious crimes of violence are now automatically transferred to an adult court (previously offenders aged fourteen and up could be, but did not have to be, transferred to a senior court) and the maximum sentences for first and second degree murder were increased to ten and seven years respectively. The original maximum custodial penalty was three years.

As Corrado and Markwart had earlier (1994) pointed out, many of these amendments are predicated on the assumption that treating young offenders as adult offenders will provide more security for the public because offenders will then be exposed to more severe adult sanctions. Such is not necessarily the case, however. In practice fewer institutionalized young offenders than adult ones receive remission for good conduct or are paroled. Thus, even when sentenced to a nominally light prison term of one year, many young offenders do more time than adult offenders who, although they might have received a longer term of incarceration in the first place, are able to earn substantial reductions in their sentences. Indeed, a three-year YOA sentence (the original maximum for crimes other than murder) is often equivalent to an adult sentence of between six and nine years in terms of actual time served.

In addition, it cannot be assumed that bringing fifteen- or sixteen-year-olds before the adult court will automatically produce more realistic (read "severe") institutional sentences. As Corrado and Markwart observe, young, and perhaps first-time, adult offenders are prime candidates for a more sympathetic hearing and hence a lighter sentence. There is real doubt, in other words, that redefining young offenders as adult ones will result in the more severe prison sentences favoured by the law-and-order advocates.

Nonetheless, it is unlikely that future changes in juvenile justice legislation will involve the abandonment of incapacitative and deterrent-based sentences. At the very least, harsh retributive punishments allow governments to show the electorate that they are doing something about crime. Moreover, punitive measures for dealing with young offenders satisfy the urge for retribution and revenge at the heart of symbolic justification for criminal sanctions (Garland, 1990).

Federal politicians are currently debating new legislation to succeed the YOA. The youth criminal justice bill, introduced in March 1999, is the Liberal government's attempt to strike a balance between demands for more punitive measures to protect society from young predators and the recognition that such strategies may unnecessarily criminalize non-serious and non-habitual young offenders. The putative compromise solution prescribes a differential response to major and minor offenders. The small number of serious and persistent offenders will receive adult-style custodial sentences, the age at which a young person may receive an adult sentence will be lowered to fourteen, and the prohibition on identifying young offenders will be removed Meanwhile, the more numerous and less habitual minor offenders will be treated more leniently.

CYCLES OF JUVENILE JUSTICE

Little of the critical reaction to the YOA that has prevailed since its introduction is unique to Canada. In fact, much of it is understandable in terms of Thomas Bernard's analysis of juvenile justice policy over the past two hundred years (1992). He argues that periodic reforms of the justice system emphasize either lenient treatment or punitive crackdowns. The United States—like Canada and other English-speaking liberal democracies—is, as you might have guessed, in the midst of the second, punitive phase of the cycle.

Bernard begins by making what is by now a commonplace observation that both the general public and important opinion makers in society believe that rates of juvenile crime have reached extraordinarily high levels and have done so, in large degree, because legislative measures are too lenient. The only way to remedy this situation is to introduce tough new legislation that does not mollycoddle young criminals. However, Bernard says, we have been here before, three times in fact in the past two hundred years, and our current desire to deal more punitively with delinquents is embedded in a historical cycle that is hard to break.

The origins of this cycle can be traced back to a time (approximately two hundred years ago) when judges and juries had more harsh than lenient measures at their disposal for dealing with young criminals. Forced to choose between, for example, capital punishment or no punishment at all, they choose the latter. When juvenile crime rates start to increase, blame is inevitably placed upon the leniency of the justice system. Policymakers act on these criticisms by developing a separate justice system for juvenile offenders. The defining characteristics of this new juvenile system are an emphasis on probation rather than incarceration and treatment rather than punishment—the philosophical "building blocks" of the welfare model of juvenile justice. The subsequent legislation—the Juvenile Delinquents Act in Canada—is then heralded as providing a solution to the delinquency problem. These hopes, however, are quickly dashed. Juvenile crime rates do not suddenly decline; indeed, they may continue their upward climb. Explanations are sought, and quickly found, in the failings of the legislation: it is declared too lenient, not offering sufficient punishment or deterrence for young criminals. These criticisms lead to demands for newer, tougher measures that will punish, incapacitate, and deter delinquents. As we move into the new millennium, most governments are being encouraged to introduce—or, more accurately—reintroduce, increasingly tough penalties for juvenile offenders. In Bernard's view, we are at a tightening-up phase in the cycle of response to juvenile crime and about to repeat a long-established process.

Bernard is not alone in noting the cyclical nature of ideas about juvenile justice. Lundman (1993) similarly notes, for example, that today's "solutions"—more secure, punishment-oriented conventional facilities, more frequent "short, sharp shocks"—were part of yesterday's problem that was to be swept away with reforms that focused on rehabilitation. Only a short while ago, rehabilitation was the paramount objective of the juvenile justice system, with diversion, probation, and treatment-oriented community programs its favoured strategies. Once again, however, the pendulum has swung and more punitive policies are back in vogue.

As we saw in the opening chapter, one of the main motivations for periodic crackdowns on juvenile crime is the belief that it is a worse problem today than ever before. Bernard, like Geoffrey Pearson (see Chapter 1), suggests that the myth of the "good old days" is a powerful force in driving the juvenile justice cycle. How does this myth work? How can such an idea have an effect upon the trajectory of juvenile justice policy? Bernard argues that the explanation lies in the essential optimism of the myth: if we can believe that were was once a time when delinquency was not the serious problem it has become, then all we have to do is find out what our predecessors did right in the battle against juvenile crime. Once we have rediscovered the historical remedy, there is nothing stopping us from applying, or, more accurately, reapplying, the same solutions to our own considerably more serious delinquency problem.

The trouble with this thesis is that its optimism derives from the erroneous assumption that in the modern world the causes of delinquency are simply and easily identified. Accompanying this simplistic view of the origins of delinquency is the belief that it is a problem that can be quickly, easily, and cheaply solved. In contemporary terms, it results in get-tough policies with regard to juvenile offenders, the most recent manifestation of which is "boot camp," to be discussed in a moment. But before boot camp there was *Scared Straight*.

SCARED STRAIGHT

On March 5, 1979, a documentary film called *Scared Straight* was shown on national television in the United States. Hosted by Peter Falk (best known as the star of *Colombo,* a then-popular television detective show), the program was a documentary of an encounter session at Rahway Prison in Newark, New Jersey, between long-term adult prisoners, many of them lifers, and local teens. The project—initiated by the inmates themselves—was designed to discourage young people from embarking on lives of crime. Both the project and the documentary proved to be enormously popular: the television program was a ratings hit and later won a best documentary award at the Academy Awards.

Scared Straight was well received and influential because it apparently demonstrated a simple, quick, (and cheap) method of steering delinquent adolescents away from criminal activities. The documentary claimed that of the seventeen persistent and seriously delinquent adolescents featured, sixteen were still straight three years later. Moreover, these "reformed" juveniles were presented as being merely the tip of the iceberg; of the close to eight thousand adolescents who had visited Rahway prison, nearly 90 percent had subsequently managed to stay clear of further trouble with the law. This success rate was unparalleled in the history of juvenile correction programs, and it is easy to see why the program was celebrated and much imitated.

What happened behind the prison bars that caused delinquent adolescents to rethink their ways? In essence, the juveniles were exposed to what has been referred to as the "pains of imprisonment" (Sykes, 1958). They were shown the appalling physical conditions to which prisoners had to adapt and survive; they were party to (temporarily) the unpleasant sights, sounds, and smells of prison life. And this was just the beginning. The visitors were then introduced to a group of about twenty cons who spared little in providing a graphic account of the horrors of prison life, with particular emphasis upon the physical brutality and emotional deprivations involved. The lifers were, of course, trying to paint a grim picture of the "costs" of crime. In so doing, they were basing their project on the assumptions of deterrence theory.

Deterrence theory derives from the classical school of criminology. It is predicated on the idea that criminals and delinquents are rational human beings who have willingly decided to engage in criminal acts because the anticipated rewards of crime outweigh the costs of potential apprehension and punishment. From the point of view of juvenile justice, the best way of preventing adolescents from engaging in rewarding delinquency is to make sure that the costs of doing so are sufficiently high that it is simply not worthwhile to pursue delinquent careers.

Punishment is, of course, the cost of crime that the state uses to deter future delinquent behaviour. Three aspects of punishment are reputedly responsible for the deterrent effect: the certainty, severity, and celerity (swiftness) of its administration. The certainty of punishment indicates the probability of a wrongdoer being caught and sanctioned for the delinquent act, severity of punishment refers to the amount or intensity of punishment, and swiftness of punishment directs attention to the length of time between the commission of a delinquent act and punishment for it.

Reference is also made to a distinction between specific (or individual) deterrence and general deterrence. The former refers to the sanctions that deter a particular offender from repeating his or her criminal activity; the latter refers to sanctions designed to discourage others in the community from engaging in similar criminal behaviour.

Like most applications of deterrence theory, the Scared Straight program is based primarily on the severity principle: telling young and impressionable people about the miseries of prison life—sodomization, murder, suicide—will make them so fearful that they will immediately abandon their delinquent pursuits. Despite the glowing reports and optimistic expectations, evaluation research has not supported the claims made by Scared Straight sponsors nor have other similar programs managed to scare delinquent adolescents straight. The first note of skepticism was sounded by James Finchenauer, whose suspicions about the claims of success for Rahway's Juvenile Awareness Project prompted him to evaluate the program experimentally (1982). His findings make interesting reading. First of all, he was able to show that the encounter sessions with the lifers group did not change adolescents' perceptions about the realities of prison life: that is, it had no effect upon their beliefs about the severity of punishment. Second, he could find little evidence to support the contention that exposure to a maximum security prison and its inmates did anything to reduce the incidence of juvenile delinquency. In fact, it made things worse. Finchenauer compared a group of kids who had gone to Rahway with a control group similar in all respects except that they had not visited the prison. Six months after the prison visit, 41.3 percent of the experimental group had committed a new offence, compared with 11.4 percent of the control group. Far from deterring delinquency, the glimpse into the hellish world of a maximum security prison seems to be have encouraged it.

Although similar deterrence-based programs with juvenile offenders have not produced these contrary results, they have not produced the positive effects that their advocates expected of them either. Such programs do not appear to be able to scare adolescents straight.

Those most directly associated with the Scared Straight program were disappointed and upset when confronted with the evidence that it did not work, but criminologists were not really surprised. Other studies of deterrence, particularly those that looked at the severity of punishment, similarly have failed to document any substantial deterrent effect. In the particular case of the Juvenile Awareness Project, severe punishment took the form of shock tactics. However, whatever jolts and shocks the youthful visitors to Rahway received in their encounter with the lifers faded away very quickly. Over the longer haul, what happened to those adolescents—whether they remained "ordinary kids" or "became more delinquent"—was influenced by other, more enduring prior factors in their lives—such as the quality of family relationships and opportunities for education and employment.

Two further questions remain. First, how was the original television documentary able to claim success rates so high that other researchers have been unable to replicate them? Second, how is it that involvement in Scared Straight–type programs might increase, rather than diminish, delinquent behaviour among adolescents?

The answer to the first question was revealed when Finchenauer embarked on his evaluation of Rahway's Juvenile Awareness Project. He found that the adolescents who participated in the project and appeared in the television documentary resided in a small, middle-class suburb in New Jersey. The community did not have a serious problem with delinquency, nor were the kids who took part, as volunteers, seriously delinquent. In other words, most kids who went to Rahway were not seriously or frequently delinquent in the first place and therefore did not need to be scared straight. As Finchenauer points out, kids who are not delinquent prior to exposure to the Scared Straight program, and who remain non-delinquent afterwards, cannot be credited as successes of the program!

The second question, why being yelled at and psychologically abused by serious adult criminals in an oppressive and intimidating institution might make adolescents more, rather than less, inclined to delinquency, is less easily answered. Finchenauer suggests two possibilities, though he readily admits that both are speculative. First, the effect of aversion programs like Scared Straight might be to romanticize lifers—to turn them into "outsiders" or outlaws deserving of the admiration of young, impressionable minds. Second, the harassment that the young prison visitors experience may be interpreted by them as a challenge—an invitation to prove to themselves and to others that they are not intimidated by the prison culture to which they have been exposed (Finchenauer, 1982, p. 170).

Nonetheless, while the Scared Straight program, and others like it, may have little or no positive impact upon crime rates, they are very important for the messages that they convey and reflect about the crime problem. The television documentary depicts crime as a simple problem that is easily remedied by severely punishing its perpetrators—mean and vicious individuals who have chosen crime as a lifestyle. Little or nothing is said about the social factors that might have contributed to their criminal behaviour in the first place. The film also offers quick, easy, and cheap (the price of a bus or subway ticket to Rahway) solutions to the crime problem where more familiar techniques of prevention and rehabilitation of criminals have failed (Cavender, 1981). Finchenauer has described this package of beliefs about juvenile justice policy as the "panacea phenomenon." As exemplified by *Scared Straight,* panaceas usually involve dramatic and punitive measures that promise an imminent end to delinquent behaviour. They fail to deter, according to Finchenauer, because they are premised on the assumption that a problem as multifaceted and complex as delinquency is resolvable by a quick fix. Nonetheless, the appeal of panaceas, particularly deterrent-based ones, remains strong in an era of growing fears about teenage crime.[1] This brings us, appropriately enough, to boot camps.

BOOT CAMPS

Most of us probably have some idea of what correctional boot camps, or shock incarceration programs as they are officially known, are all about; they have become a favourite topic of television news documentaries, and many newspaper articles have now been written about them. As their name suggests, they are modelled after basic training programs used in military organizations. They expose young criminals, for a relatively short period of time, to military-style basic training techniques characterized by a strict daily regimen of hard physical activity and subservience to authoritarian decision making imposed by drill sergeants.

They have become popular because of their assumed ability to prevent juvenile offending: the experience of spending time in a strict learning environment is believed to discourage further offending. A large part of their appeal is, therefore, based on an assumed deterrence effect. Research also indicates that members of the public will only support shorter sentences for offenders if they are carried out in a harsh and intensive correctional environment. They are, in addition, favoured by politicians and taxpayers on financial grounds. Boot camps are cheaper than more conventional juvenile institutions because offenders spend less time there—the right lessons having been learned more quickly than in prison.

How do we know if boot camps work, if they are successful or not? In other words, how do we go about evaluating their efficacy? The standard procedure is to compare the reoffending or recidivism rates of individuals who have been given boot camp sentences with those who have been confined in more conventional juvenile prisons. Needless to say, the only place where it has been possible to carry out this sort of comparative analysis is the United States—because the United States is the only nation to have deployed boot camps in sufficient number.

Doris MacKenzie has conducted the most thorough evaluation yet of boot camps operating in eight states (MacKenzie, 1995). All the camps under investigation shared the same hallmark qualities of military discipline, drill and ceremony, and rigorous daily activity. However, some performed better than others when compared with local juvenile penal institutions. In four of the states, boot camp was no more and no less effective at preventing recidivism than prison. In another three states, boot camp graduates were less likely to have reoffended (in the three-month follow up period) than those who had served a prison term. And in one state, boot camp was considerably less successful at reducing further offending than prison.

These are, obviously, pretty mixed results, the variability of outcome making it difficult to conclude definitively whether boot camp works or not. However, a closer examination of the workings of particular boot camps provides some helpful clues as to why some are more successful than others.

Mackenzie found that the (relatively) successful camps devoted significant amounts of time (at least three hours a day) to treatment or counselling programs. They also provided intensive post-release supervision in the community. By contrast, the less successful camps concentrated more or less exclusively on the military aspects of the experience—drill and inspections and so forth. This finding encourages her to conclude that, first, unless boot camps provide remedial help as well as more practical job-finding skills, they are unlikely to ever be very effective. Second, she suggests that the relatively successful camps would be more successful if they ceased to model themselves on military institutions and extended their use of counselling programs.

This less-than-ringing endorsement invites speculation as to why boot camp is unlikely ever to become a very satisfactory antidote to juvenile crime. It has been suggested, for instance, that the experience may induce psychological states not conducive to long-term law-abiding behaviour. Being repeatedly shouted at by a drill sergeant does little to increase confidence or improve self-esteem—two factors supportive of a pro-social personality.

Indeed, other research has shown that the custodial and militaristic culture of the camps increases levels of aggression among both inmates and guards (Morash and Rucker, 1990). While a willingness and ability to act aggressively may be vital to the "profession of arms," for most other jobs, not to mention marital and family relationships, it is probably a negative life skill. The confrontational nature of the boot camp experience and the use of summary and humiliating treatment have also led to claims that boot camp constitutes "cruel and unusual punishment," and there have been proven cases of inmate abuse in several boot camps in the United States.

Finally, there is also the possibility, as with Scared Straight programs, that boot camps—having been widely promoted as "escape-proof," high-security custodial institutions—will offer hardened young offenders the wrong sort of challenge. Some reluctant participants might be keen to embarrass law enforcers and their political paymasters. And this is precisely what happened on the eve of the official opening in 1997 of Ontario's first, and so far only, experiment with this sort of response to juvenile wrongdoing, Project Turnaround (referred to as a "strict discipline" institution, not a "boot camp"), when two young male inmates escaped. A recent internal evaluation of Project Turnaround has shown it to be no more successful than American boot camps.

NOTHING WORKS?

What makes current arguments for a crackdown on juvenile crime so persuasive, and boot camp and Scared Straight–type programs attractive remedies for delinquency, is that rehabilitation has increasingly been abandoned as a worthy or realizable goal. The restoration of young offenders has been replaced by an emphasis upon deterrence and retribution because it is widely believed that attempts at rehabilitation have failed.

The collapse of the rehabilitative ideal—the idea basic to the original conception of a separate juvenile justice system—was occasioned, in large measure, by the publication in 1974 of an article titled "What Works?" Written by Robert Martinson, the paper evaluated the results from a wide range of treatments and programs designed to rehabilitate offenders. He looked at studies of the impact of imprisonment, correctional system–based programs, community-based programs, group-based programs, and those that were tailored to meet the needs of individual offenders. Martinson concluded that none of them worked very well. It made little difference how long offenders spent in prison, what sort of prison program they were in (or not in), or whether they received probation rather than a custodial sentence. Regardless of the treatment or program examined, rates of recidivism remained high. Martinson's findings were widely interpreted as concluding that, in terms of the rehabilitative goal, "nothing works." They were seized upon, particularly by conservative critics of the criminal justice system, as an important justification for abandoning the restorative ideal.

It is not, however, a view that has gone unchallenged. Thomas Bernard, for one, feels that the justice system has received a bum rap, and that, in reality, it is far more effective than it is ever given credit for. In fact, Bernard reverses what has now become the received wisdom, and argues that the system of juvenile justice is in fact more successful than it is given credit for (1992).

Bernard argues that the contrary perception stems from the fact that all assessments of treatments and programs for juveniles begin with the acknowledged failures of the system. Youths in correctional institutions are their starting point. It is easily discovered that at a much earlier time, in an encounter with a police officer, the decision was made not to charge the individual. Subsequently, that individual is involved in another arrest situation, but this time he or she is charged. However, the probation officer uses his or her discretion to direct (or divert) the offender away from the youth court and away from formal processing. Informal handling is rewarded by another delinquent act, which is responded to, not by a custodial sentence, but a probation order. The next time that he—it usually is a he—commits an offence, he is (finally) locked up.

At this point—as an official statistic of failure—the inquest into "what went wrong" begins. The problem, it turns out, is that at each and every stage of the justice process, the offender was treated too leniently. Had firmer measures been taken earlier on—by the police, by the courts—all of the subsequent trouble could have been avoided—or so the conventional argument goes.

But there is another side to this particular coin: what about all those kids who interpreted leniency by the police, probation officers, and courts for what it is—a chance, maybe a last chance, to mend their ways and break with their delinquent past. These are the kids—far more numerous than the high-profile failures of the system—who have learned the lesson that delinquency is not worth it. These are the kids who, in Bernard's phrase, have made the "rational choice" to get out while the going is good. They responded positively to a dressing-down from a police officer or a spell on probation and never came into contact with the criminal justice system again. It must be not forgotten that most juvenile delinquents do not grow up to become adult criminals; the reason for this is that lenient strategies work more often than they fail.

He also critically examines measures of success and failure in the juvenile justice system. On the assumption that most people would count institutionalization as indicating failure and that substantial numbers, if not a majority, would define a probation order as failure, Bernard calculates that currently the American system of juvenile justice operates with a failure rate of 18 percent. That is, for every one hundred juveniles who come into contact with the police, eighteen of them end up on probation or serving a custodial sentence. But if eighteen out of a hundred young offenders are failures of the system, conversely, eighty-two of them qualify as successes. Yet unlike the failures of the system, who are easily counted, the successes, those who make the adjustment to non-criminal lifestyles, remain invisible.

Bernard is therefore not convinced that attempts to curb or, better still, prevent delinquency are doomed to failure. He is not alone in this belief; Richard Lundman thinks the same way. On the other hand, neither researcher believes that different treatments and programs are equally effective in tackling the problem. Lundman (1993) has recently evaluated the efficacy of various attempts to control and rehabilitate delinquent juveniles. What follows is his verdict on the relative effectiveness of different attempts designed to reduce the scope of the delinquency problem. He begins by looking at those programs that do not have a very good track record. In addition to Scared Straight–type programs, he gives failing grades to area projects and institutionalization.

AREA PROJECTS

Chicago has figured prominently in the study of urban delinquency. It was in that city that data on delinquency was first systematically gathered and where the first attempts at sociological explanation were launched. It has also been the site of several experiments in delinquency control, experiments that began with that prominent member of the Chicago School, Clifford Shaw.

After identifying a number of high-delinquency areas within the city, the concentration and persistence of which was explained in terms of "social disorganization" (see Chapter 3), Shaw sought to alleviate the problem. He proposed community action: those who lived in the areas were to assume responsibility for crime control and prevention.

The result was the Chicago-area project, which began in 1932 and ran until the early 1960s. Its rationale for delinquency reduction derived from the logic of Shaw's own beliefs about delinquency causation: eliminate the sources of social disorganization and the motivations and opportunities for delinquency will decline. More specific applications of this philosophy involved the creation of local self-help groups that sponsored recreational programs for neighbourhood youth, counselling sessions, and the assignment to neighbourhood street gangs of detached youth workers who also worked as advocates at police stations and in the courts for those adolescents who had gotten into trouble with the law.

What kind of impact has this type of treatment had? Unfortunately, it is hard to provide a definitive answer to this question because, according to Lundman, the Chicago-area project has never been properly assessed or evaluated, even though all those who were prominently involved extolled its virtues many years after the project was wound up.

Nonetheless, it has inspired other programs in other American cities. Employing paid, professional social workers rather than relying on members of the community, these attempts at delinquency prevention and control have not been very successful. Not only are these restorative projects (such as the Cambridge-Somerville youth study) unable to prevent delinquency, they are also very costly. Lundman concludes that "leaving these juveniles alone almost certainly would have been just as effective and far less expensive" (1993, p. 244). For the largest portion of the twentieth century, we knew what the major correlates and probable causes of delinquency are in the inner city, yet all of our knowledge of these factors—high infant mortality, few jobs, lousy schools, poor health care—has done little or nothing to prevent the reproduction of crime and delinquency in those areas. Perhaps if the organizers of such projects had been empowered to provide jobs, housing, and food, they would have been better placed to rid the areas of their criminogenic conditions.

INSTITUTIONALIZATION

Long prison terms are often justified in terms of the principle of deterrence. However, institutionalization also appeals on the grounds of incapacitation: if they are locked up, juveniles cannot be out on the streets committing crime.

It is well known that a small number of adolescents are responsible for the majority of offences in a community. (For recent Canadian data on this point see Hagan and McCarthy, 1997, and Baron, 1994.) From some points of view, the community would be best served if these chronic offenders could be identified at an early age and then placed out of harm's way in secure penal institutions. According to this argument, the problem of repetitive delinquency is best solved by incapacitating those who are most inclined to be repeat offenders.

What are referred to as "cohort studies" are useful for testing this assumption. Indeed, I have already had reason to discuss some of the better (and better-known) cohort studies in delinquency. In order to demonstrate how they work and how they fit into the incapacitation argument, let us again refer to Wolfgang et al.'s longitudinal study of delinquents in Philadelphia (1972). The researchers traced the delinquent careers of nearly 10 000 males born in the city of Philadelphia in 1945 who lived in that city between the ages of 10 and 18. Of that number, 627—6 percent of the total sample—committed nearly 52 percent of the 10 214 offences recorded over that period. Had all first-time offenders been put away until they were 18, two-thirds of the total number of subsequent recorded offences would not have taken place. Clearly, locking up all adolescents who drifted into delinquency would have done much to solve the delinquency problem.

What makes this policy less reasonable and attractive (although perhaps not completely unacceptable to some law-and-order enthusiasts) is the fact that many kids gave up their delinquent ways after their initial involvement in delinquency. More specifically, over half of the cohort members who had committed one delinquent act never went on to commit another one (or if they did, were never caught). In other words, they aborted their delinquent careers without any need for institutionalization. Incarcerating all first-time offenders on the grounds that some of them would go on to become chronic offenders would be morally unacceptable to most people. Indeed, it is a fundamental tenet of our criminal justice system that punishment be administered on the basis of an offence or offences that individuals have committed in the past, not on what they might do in the future.

In addition, the vast bulk of even chronic delinquents are not dangerous and aggressive. The serial delinquents in Wolfgang et al.'s cohort studies (they began another one in the same city based on persons born in 1958) are predominantly minor property offenders. Given that keeping people in institutions is a very expensive business and that the vast majority of frequent delinquents do not cause bodily harm, the case in favour of incapacitation is very much weakened.

One way out of this moral and legal impasse would be to develop a reliable method of forecasting which adolescents are most likely to grow up seriously delinquent and target them for institutionalization. The problem is that doing this is notoriously difficult. As Wolfgang et al. (1972) acknowledge, even copious background information about first-time offenders does not tell us how or when they are going to strike next. Predicting delinquency is even more difficult than forecasting the weather.

But Lundman's (1993) analysis is not just another litany of failed ventures. Some attempts at controlling delinquency do work or can, at least, be shown to work better than other curative endeavours. As far as minor property offenders are concerned, he concludes that the less treatment they receive the better. Hence, he recommends that they, and status offenders, be diverted away from the criminal justice system: lectures, warnings, and cautions work better and are considerably cheaper than other, more interventionist strategies.

Routine probation is the next frequently used sentencing option for juveniles and has been for a considerable time. Lundman recommends a continuance of this practice with most adolescent property offenders. Given that most probation officers have very heavy case loads—they are responsible for supervising a large number of clients—it is interesting to consider why Lundman regards it is a relatively effective strategy.

One clue is provided by Mark D. Jacobs's ethnographic study, *Screwing the System and Making It Work* (1990). Jacobs suggests that the benign effects of probation have little to do with the quality of supervision that delinquents receive—probation officers are sufficiently busy that they have little time for this on an ongoing basis. Instead, he suggests that in the course of compiling a pre-sentence report, probation officers accumulate valuable information about offenders and their offences. As a result, they are able to make fairly good judgments about which juveniles on probation are likely to be good risks. In addition, a probationary sentence serves as a warning: if offenders fail to abide by the conditions of probation—principally keeping out of trouble with the law—they face a return visit to the court and a possible custodial sentence. Finally, according to Jacobs, at least some of the probationers receive a considerable amount of care and attention from their probation officers. Examples given by Jacobs include providing rides to school and work, acting as a coaching partner in childbirth classes for a female teenage probationer, and offering opportunities to "hang out" at the probation office. Little of this counts as expert advice or in-depth counselling, but it is enough to keep some moderately delinquent adolescents on the straight and narrow.

Jacobs concludes that while routine probation is not always successful, it is no less effective than more focused community-based probation programs that emphasize restitution. Finally, probation is a sentence that can quickly and easily be evaluated if adolescents fail to comply with its demands: those who cross the divide between moderate and chronic delinquency can be returned to court for more intensive intervention.

Lundman (1993) also recommends that community treatment programs be expanded to include most property offenders. Such programs represent a halfway house arrangement between the (relatively) informal supervision and sporadic assistance associated with routine probation and institutionalization in custodial facilities for juvenile offenders. His rationale is quite straightforward: community treatment is no less effective in reforming chronic property offenders than prison, it is considerably cheaper, and it does not compromise the community protection role of the criminal justice system. One reason why such treatments are successful is because, again, there are restrictions on who is included and who is excluded from the programs. For instance, one of the better-known American programs is the Provo (Utah) experiment. Candidates for the experiment had, on average, seven previous arrests, more than enough to put them behind bars in a custodial institution (a state training school) if a community-based program had not been available. However, those whose prior records included violence against persons were specifically excluded from the program, as were offenders deemed to be psychologically disturbed.

Lundman acknowledges that a small number—a very small number—of juvenile offenders are a serious threat to both themselves and the community. Invariably, they make habit of causing physical and emotional harm to others. Although it is a moot point as to whether they will ever be successfully rehabilitated in prison (not the best place to achieve that goal), the community is protected from their predatory behaviour for at least the time that they are locked up.

And what is the role of deterrence? Lundman shows that some research suggests incarceration reduces delinquency, and not just because the most notorious delinquents are physically prevented from law-breaking because they are behind bars.

Several studies have shown that chronic offenders are significantly less likely to reoffend the year after institutional release than had offended the year before incarceration. However, what is considerably more doubtful is whether the lessons of imprisonment—that crime doesn't pay, prison is a hellish environment, and other elements that make up the deterrence package—stay with young offenders for very long. Research that follows young inmates released back into the community does not track them very long, usually for little more than a year. Those studies that have used longer periods as the basis for their evaluation of success and failure find that the deterrent effect (and possibly the rehabilitative effect) of institutionalization wears off very quickly.

Over the long haul, the (relative) advantages of community-based programs over imprisonment became more apparent. Finally, as I have mentioned before, imprisonment is a costly business. Lundman, writing in 1993, estimates that one year's imprisonment costs American taxpayers something like $25,000. For that kind of money, you could send two or three needy children to a reputable day-care centre and, who knows, prevent delinquency from occurring. It is to the issue of prevention that I now want to turn.

PREVENTING DELINQUENCY

One of the limitations of the public policy debate about youth crime is that often the only solutions ever offered to the problem are legal ones. It is assumed that only active intervention by the courts and correctional system will rehabilitate or deter juvenile offenders. This perspective is organized around the need to curtail delinquency once it has occurred. However, there is an old adage suggesting that prevention is better than cure. Not only might preventing crime be a more effective (and cheaper) policy than reacting to it afterward, this approach does not rely on the law for its utility. For regardless of how radical the provisions of the new legislative efforts are, it is unlikely that levels of youth crime will decline very significantly. To reiterate: the causes of delinquency are sufficiently complex to make it exceedingly unlikely that legal initiatives will by themselves make much of an impression on youth crime rates.

Given the failure of deterrence-based policies to significantly lower rates of juvenile crime, why not give crime prevention strategies another chance? This is the advice offered by Corrado and Markwart, who suggest early intervention on behalf of problem families within the community (1994).

Evidence from several of the cohort studies that have been discussed in this book indicate that in some communities, different generations of the same family are often involved in crime. The work of Farrington et al. (1986) and Hagan (1993) (as well as Rutter et al., 1979) suggests that parental criminality predicts children's criminality in a process of criminal "embeddedness."

Breaking down the criminal networks and associations of young people in high-crime areas and replacing them with more conventional opportunities have been recommended as one strategy for preventing delinquency. Needless to say, this is easier said than done. Moreover, it is unlikely to succeed unless attempts to improve the quality and quantity of paid employment available in the community are prominent on the agenda.

LESSONS FROM ELSEWHERE: THE FRANCOPHONE ALTERNATIVE

Although Canada generally lines up alongside those nations that take a tough crime-control approach to young offending, note should be made of the Province of Quebec's exceptional approach in this regard. From at least the 1950s, Quebec has pursued juvenile justice policies that prioritize rehabilitation over punishment and has been the Canadian leader in successful experiments with diversion programs, as previously observed. Coincidentally or not, it is France that has, internationally, advanced policies and programs most different from those favoured by much of the Anglo-Saxon world.

Jim Hackler and his colleagues have compared the administration of juvenile justice in Alberta with that in France (1987). Their concern (confirmed by some of the data discussed in this chapter) was that the YOA legislation would increase the number of young people dealt with formally by the juvenile justice system (largely through the maximum age requirements), resulting in the incarceration of more juvenile offenders. Hackler et al. question the need to lock up so many young offenders and the basis for their skepticism derives from observations about the French system of juvenile justice.

Statistics indicate that, when matched for size, Alberta institutionalizes many more juvenile offenders than comparable jurisdictions in France. The authors calculate that the province of Alberta locks up approximately ten times as many juveniles per capita as the city of Paris. Moreover, although evidence on this is not definitive, Hackler et al. feel that these differences stem not from the more delinquent nature of Alberta's adolescents but from the ways in which delinquent behaviour in the two societies is responded to. Explaining these variations is the main thrust of Hackler et al.'s analysis.

The key difference between the two systems is that judges in France reserve closed or secure custody sentences for juveniles who have actually broken the law. Adolescents are not, for instance, institutionalized for refusing to stay in a rehabilitative residential facility. Similarly, social workers in France do not have the power to forcibly detain or confine young offenders in a juvenile care facility. The French authorities cannot, in other words, keep a juvenile locked up "for his own good!"

In contrast to Alberta, there is a much clearer distinction between punishment and restoration in the French system. The minority of serious youth offenders in France are sent to prison, where retribution is the order of the day. But for the rest—the overwhelming majority—the thrust of the administrative response is toward helping young people to see the error of their ways.

The hallmark of the French system of juvenile justice is, as Hackler et al. see it, flexibility. Unless and until young offenders refuse to take advantage of the help being offered to them, French judges refrain from sending them to punishment-oriented institutions. This flexibility reduces some of the problems characteristic of the North American system of justice. In France, the criminal justice system is invoked when social service provisions have failed.

In brief, Hackler et al. argue that the French experience is modest testimony to the benefits to be gained from adopting a policy of limited intervention with regard to juvenile offending. In North America, youth problems are created or aggravated by defining those who run away from juvenile institutions as criminal, or by institutionalizing those who have failed to abide by rules of probation imposed on them. Offering help, rather than punishment, may be the better way to reduce levels of criminal activity among youth.

Conclusion

To say that the YOA has been a controversial piece of legislation is a significant understatement. In a very short period of time it has become the focus of everything that many people think is wrong with how we deal with the problem of youth crime in this country. Why and how has the act become a sounding board for so many people's concerns about the state of Canadian juvenile justice? How legitimate are the complaints that are frequently made about the legislation?

I have tried to answer these questions by tracing the evolution of Canadian juvenile justice policy from the Juvenile Delinquents Act to the YOA. I noted that the latter act and its predecessor were informed by differing legal objectives and philosophical ideals. More importantly, critics and defenders of the YOA draw on different, and competing, models of juvenile justice when interpreting the effectiveness of the new act. Liberal-minded supporters of the YOA have been under unrelenting attacks from an influential law-and-order lobby that uses high-profile cases to illuminate their basic argument that the legislation is too soft on delinquents.

I also emphasized that this claim is by no means unique to Canada, and that currently the urge for more retributive justice is widespread throughout the Western world. Not long ago, however, rehabilitation was seen as the best hope for reducing levels of juvenile crime in society.

As several experts have noted, views on how the juvenile justice system might best be reformed have oscillated over the course of history. The Canadian reaction to the YOA is part of a broader international swing of the pendulum that has resulted in a more punitive response to juvenile crime. This shift has, arguably, gone furthest in the United States, where the pressure to solve the juvenile crime problem is most intense. A desperate public mood has permitted draconian measures, such as Scared Straight–type programs and boot camps, that do not work. However, not all attempts at reducing the scope of the delinquency problem are unmitigated failures. In the last part of this chapter we looked at some of the programs that do work, some that might work, and strategies that appear to be working elsewhere.

NOTES

1. The Scared Straight project exemplifies an interesting irony. Although the mass media are regularly indicted as a cause of crime, they are also on occasion invoked as a remedy for it (Surette, 1992, ch. 6). According to Surette, the television documentary was so popular it was shown to groups of youths as a substitute for the real prison experience. As Surette puts it, "if you didn't have a real prison and convicts handy, a media image of one would apparently suffice" (1992, p. 154).

   Other contexts of youth deviance have played a similarly contradictory role. Sport, for example, has often been linked to violent and aggressive behaviour among young people (Goldstein, 1986; Waddington, 1992). On occasion, though, those looking for solutions to the youth crime problem have turned to organized sport. A recent example is basketball. Amid the media reports of violence at high school basketball games is the occasional story of how diverting inner-city youth from the streets to the basketball courts might reduce levels of criminal activity. One such program is called Midnight Basketball, originally developed in a small town outside Washington, D.C. (Christie and Macleod, 1995). According to an article in the *Globe and Mail* (n.d.), its incipient introduction into Canada is an attempt to impart important "life skills" to inner-city youth.

CHAPTER 8

Summary and Conclusions

This book has offered an account of adolescent deviance in Canada and other advanced, urban industrialized societies. I begin this final chapter by briefly summarizing the main arguments and findings presented in the preceding chapters and highlighting some of the more important conclusions. I then conclude both the chapter and the book with a brief commentary about the implications of these findings for social policy.

SUMMING UP

The study of deviance entails an examination of both deviant behaviour and reactions to that behaviour. The chronologically young have probably always been disproportionately involved in rule-breaking behaviour, but it is only in relatively modern times that their infractions have emerged as a distinctive problem of youth, warranting the legal designation of delinquency.

The problematic status of young people—something we now take for granted—is directly attributable to the great social and economic changes of the nineteenth century. Rapid urbanization turned rural inhabitants into city dwellers and transformed agricultural labourers into factory workers. Many people, but particularly young people, became displaced as a result of this process. The moral and economic certainties of the old rural order were replaced by the harshness and unpredictability of the factory system and city life. It was in this context of extreme social rupture that adolescence became recognized for the first time as a separate and unique stage in the life cycle. Not coincidentally, the discovery of youth led to growing concerns about a crime problem among the young.

As a number of commentators have emphasized (Bernard, 1992; Pearson, 1983; Gillis, 1974), the first delinquents were young people who, excluded from the early factories, were left to roam the streets of Victorian-era cities in Western Europe and North America, scratching out an existence by begging, thieving, and prostitution. By the end of the nineteenth century, what in contemporary terms would be understood as youth gangs were a common feature of those cities. The association between adolescence and deviance had been firmly established in the public consciousness, and it remains to this day.

There is, in fact, a repetitive quality to much of the public debate about youth and crime. One of the recurring claims made about young people is that they are particularly vulnerable to antisocial tendencies. Their vulnerability means that the young, more than any other group in society, are seen as susceptible to all manner of corrupting influences. Many of these have, in one way or another, involved leisure, particularly mass leisure. From the dime novels (or "penny dreadfuls," as they were called in Britain) and music halls of the late Victorian era to more recent concerns about the mass media and violence, popular entertainment has consistently been linked to delinquency and deviancy. Much of the leisure activity of young people in contemporary society is conducted publicly and collectively and with conspicuous attachment to distinctive hair and clothing styles that do not always meet with adult approval. For many people, the signs and symbols of teenage leisure spell trouble.

This perception is reinforced by the dogged tendency of the mass media to devote large amounts of time and newsprint to the most dramatic forms of youth deviance, presenting events in a stereotyped manner. Inevitably, the real or true nature and dimensions of youthful deviance is overlooked or distorted as a result of media coverage of delinquency or, as it is increasingly called, youth crime. The impression is conveyed, however unintentionally, that all young people can be judged by the disreputable standards set by the few who hit the news headlines.

Lest this argument be misinterpreted, I am not implying that the behavioural components of adolescent deviance are unimportant or that the willingness to define certain rule transgressions as such is simply a matter of caprice. Least of all am I suggesting that we can dispense with the need to explain those behaviours that many people find disturbing.

In many instances, it is not hard to see why the activities in question are regarded as deviant or delinquent: stealing, drug and alcohol use and abuse, violence at school and elsewhere, and prostitution are judged by many people—and not just powerful or influential ones—to be wrong. The issue is not so much why these behaviours are deemed deviant or delinquent but why they are so frequently subject to overreaction. The answer to this question I have proposed is that the focus on youth reflects a range of anxieties about changes in society that in and of themselves have little to do with youthful (mis)behaviour (Taylor, 1982). Moral panics are a consequence of public apprehensions about real, but poorly understood, strains and tensions in society. I suggested, for instance, that contemporary concerns about swarming or gang violence in schools reflect broader fears about immigration and the shifting racial composition of Canadian society.

I also suspect that both the problems and reactions to them are heightened because of Canada's proximity to the United States. To some extent, and largely through the cross-border influence of American media outlets, we have imported American racial fears into Canada.

Young people are overrepresented in moral panics because their present bad behaviour is seen a portent for an even more troubling future. Deviant episodes—particularly if they involve public displays of violence and aggression—are understood as a sign that the passage to responsible adulthood is being mismanaged or breaking down due to failures on the part of the family or the educational system.

Public anxieties have been worsened by the emergence since the 1980s of a significant—and very real—problem of social exclusion. As more young people are made marginal by the process of economic restructuring, voices of alarm have been raised about the consequences for social order, concerns epitomized, perhaps, by street youth in general and squeegee kids in particular.

However, most young people say and do very little to justify these fears. Most, in fact, are and always have been, fundamentally conservative in their social attitudes, more like their parents than different from them—despite their long historical reputation for rebellion and defiance of adult authority. Research consistently shows that while young people do spend more time with their peers as they enter their teens, this is not necessarily at the expense of parental influence. The findings indicate that friend and parents are sovereign in difference areas—peers more influential in fashion choices and musical tastes, parents in directing educational and career decision making.

Nor are most young people enthusiastic participants in the forms of youth deviance most likely to be regarded by the community as serious. Both official statistics and unofficial self-report studies reveal that the bulk of adolescent deviance involves minor property offences (breaking and entering, shoplifting, and so on).

Most of these offences are unsophisticated in design and execution, and the offenders, by and large, do not become adult career criminals. Although I do not wish to underestimate the trauma and material loss of having your home broken into or your car stolen, these are not the kind of infractions most likely to generate debates about the state of the nation's youth.

Such moral panics are far more likely to be created by the more spectacular, but unrepresentative, acts of collective deviancy (see Chapter 2). It is quite evident that the most serious forms of deviant behaviour attract little more than a minority of the poorest and most disadvantaged in the youth population. At the same time, many more young people engage in less serious acts of deviance at some time or another during the transition to adulthood. Much of this behaviour in the American literature falls under the rubric of teenage culture.

Particularly in its more sanitized conventional versions, deviant adolescent behaviour is unlikely to interfere with the smooth integration of youth into society. This was recognized some time ago by Bennett Berger:

> Many, and probably most young persons, while they experience the classic problems of adolescent psychology described in the textbooks, seem to make their way through to full adult status without grave cultural damage, without getting into serious trouble, without a dominating hedonism, and without generalized attitudes of rebellion toward parents and the world. (Berger, 1973, p. 309)

But what of that minority of youth who do more regularly engage themselves in behaviours or adopt styles of dress and music regarded as serious or threatening or dangerous? In understanding persistent instrumental and expressive patterns of youth deviance, I have made that strand of sociological criminology called subcultural theory my starting point.

Subcultural theories are more concerned with youthful misbehaviour than they are in reactions to that misbehaviour. In Stanley Cohen's parlance, they concentrate on the folk devils rather than the moral panics. Throughout this book, we have encountered a number of these folk devils: street youth, squeegee kids, bike gangs, punks, dropouts, and skinheads.

Some of these deviant youth groups are of recent vintage and are unlikely to remain with us long; others have been more durable. Street gangs, for instance, have been around since the end of the nineteenth century. The first generation of American criminologists centred at the University of Chicago sought to understand and explain their origins and enduring significance in downtown areas.

Their successors in the post–Second World War years advanced the idea that group-based delinquency was not merely a response to inner-city problems of disadvantage and poverty in both the school and the street, but a solution to those problems as well. A newer generation of largely British Marxist-inspired theories have built on this basic insight, and have explained deviant youth subcultures as a form of expressive resistance to the key institutions and agents of capitalist society.

Most of the focus of subcultural theory and research has been on the behaviour of males. The archetypal folk devil, in addition to being either working-class and/or a racial minority, is male. Both British and American subcultural theorists pay scant attention to questions of female deviance. Where are the girl delinquents? When female delinquents have not been ignored, they have been viewed as isolated sexual offenders—promiscuous or prostitutes. Neither view is accurate. Both official statistics and self-report studies indicate that female delinquency is both common (though not as common as male delinquency) and not characterized by its sexual content. Theories of female delinquency have increasingly sought to explain the greater conformity of girls than boys in the gendered nature of the controls placed on adolescents and the different opportunities afforded them to deviate. Society reacts differently toward female delinquents than it does to their male counterparts. Whereas male street-corner youth get in trouble because they break the criminal code, female youth acquire a deviant status when they break the moral code that regulates female behaviour, particularly female sexual behaviour.

At various points in this book I have emphasized that much of the thinking about delinquency and the problem of youth is characterized by its cyclical nature. With regard to delinquency theory, various perspectives, approaches, and explanations fall in and out of favour. For instance, biological and psychological theories, very popular from the late nineteenth to the first part of the twentieth century, were gradually superseded by the sociological accounts that stressed the importance of the social environment. Subcultural theory grew from this starting point and remained very influential in North America until the 1970s and 1980s when it was replaced by other approaches, such as control theory, most notably, and by a return to psychological and, in particular, biological theories. Only recently, in light of growing concerns about unemployment, homelessness, and poverty—what European sociologists and policymakers refer to as the problem of social exclusion—has subcultural theory been revived in its American homeland. Likewise, there is an ebb and flow to the amounts of attention that street and school receive as sites of delinquent action. Streets kids are now very much a matter of concern, just as they were at the turn of the nineteenth century. But at mid-twentieth century, it was the high school that was at the epicentre, identified as a major source of adolescent rebellion. This focus has reemerged in contemporary concerns about safety in schools.

However, it is in responding to deviant youth that the cyclical character of public debate on problematic youth behaviour is most apparent. Many of the researchers whose work has figured most prominently in this book—Stanley Cohen, James Gilbert, Geoffrey Pearson, Thomas Bernard—have all emphasized the fact that societies like our own suffer from periodic outbursts of intense concern about delinquency. As a consequence, juvenile justice policies often oscillate between goals. Whereas rehabilitation had once been the priority of the juvenile justice system, that goal has increasingly been replaced by concerns with retribution and punishment.

Today young offenders are increasingly viewed as hardened criminals rather than reformable delinquents. It is this view that informs and drives most of the criticisms of the Young Offenders Act and that probably explains why the term juvenile delinquent sounds increasingly quaint and old-fashioned. In both official and popular discourse, the problem of delinquency has now become the problem of youth crime (Bernard, 1992, p. 55). As the current debate shows, moral panic often leads to moral crusades that focus on the introduction of more punitive measures for dealing with young offenders: boot camps, lowering of the age of criminal responsibilty, the "naming and shaming" of young offenders, zero-tolerance campaigns, police in high schools, and so on. Most of these initiatives are rooted in the assumption that all crime by youth originates in personal malice or, at best, personal inadequacy, rather than, as in the case of its more serious forms, a response to poverty, homelessness, and unemployment—socially structured disadvantage.

POLICY IMPLICATIONS

Finally, and briefly, I want to consider some of the implications for social policy of the account of youth and deviance offered in this book.

The first point that needs to be stressed is that young people break more rules than adults and that any judical policies premised on the assumption that juvenile delinquency is ever likely to be completely eliminated are utopian and doomed to failure. To some extent, we have to come to terms with the fact that adolescents are prone to behaviours that adults find unsettling.

Second, the system of juvenile justice is more successful at dealing with young offenders than it is generally given credit for. Moreover, its success derives from an emphasis upon treatment rather than punishment.

Third, get-tough policies—the Scared Straight approach, boot camp, longer prison terms—do not work: indeed, they are likely to turn naive risk-takers into rational calculators, drifters into desperadoes, serious juvenile delinquents into serious adult criminals.

However, in the current political climate—with right-of-centre thinking about criminal justice matters in the ascendancy—it is unlikely that my defence of the rehabilitative ideal and the treatment-oriented programs that it has spawned will go unchallenged. They are not what most people outside of academia want to hear, they are not ideas that are likely to sell (Bernard, 1992).

Youth justice policies are driven by political ideology, not criminological research. Unless research findings happen to coincide with the convictions of the government of the day, they are likely to remain ignored. Much of the vitriolic opposition to the Young Offenders Act, for instance, is independent of research documenting its failings. Conversely, little of the continuing enthusiasm for boot camp is diminished by negative evaluations of its effectiveness. Policies about young people and crime are formulated by elected politicians, responding to public opinion (or at least that portion of the electorate that votes for the party that they represent) and interest groups.

Fear of crime shows no sign of abating. Indeed, as the population ages, it is increasing, despite the best available evidence cataloguing an ongoing decline in crime rates, including youth crime rates. What is particularly disturbing is the obvious willingness of aspiring politicians to exploit these fears for their own electoral purposes. So instead of conceding the point and trying to identify which of the possible factors responsible for the downward trend policymakers might have some control over (unemployment rates, participation of young people in formal and informal learning), and trying to improve on them, we have the spectre of politicians seeking election, or reelection, on law-and-order agendas.

Ultimately, therefore, I am not optimistic about the development of more moderate views and policies on juvenile justice. There will continue to be, in Canada and elsewhere, episodic concerns about the problem of youth and periodic claims that we are in the middle of a youthful crime wave without historical precedent, that things are worse now than they ever have been in the past, and that increasing permissiveness, declining social controls, and insufficient punishment is responsible for the problem. New scapegoats will be found and new anti-crime campaigns launched. In particular, politicians will be under increasing pressure to tighten up the yet to be finalized youth justice act. In the process, more juveniles will find themselves in the net of the juvenile justice system, thus confirming—in higher arrest rates and custodial sentences—the original fears about a growing problem of youth crime. And so the cycle of concern and punitive response will continue.

REFERENCES

Acland, C. (1995). *Youth, murder, spectacle.* Boulder: Westview Press.

Addario, F. (1993, September 6). Teenagers increasingly under the gun. *Globe and Mail.* A3.

Adler, F. (1975). *Sisters in crime.* New York: McGraw-Hill.

Ageton, S. (1983). The dynamics of female delinquency, 1976–1980. *Criminology.* 21, 555–84.

Agnew, R., and Peterson, D. (1989). Leisure and delinquency. *Social Problems.* 36(4), 332–50.

Anderson, E. (1990). *Streetwise: race, class and change in an urban community.* Chicago: University of Chicago Press.

———. (1994, May). The code of the streets. *Atlantic Monthly.* 80–94.

Anderson, S., Kinsey, R., Loader, I., and Smith, C. (1994). *Cautionary tales: young people, crime and policing in Edinburgh.* Aldershot: Avebury.

Apple, M. (1985). *Education and power.* Boston: Ark.

Archambault, O. (1991). Foreword to *The Young Offenders Act: a revolution in Canadian juvenile justice,* A. Leschied, P. Jaffe, and W. Willis, eds. Toronto: University of Toronto Press.

Aries, P. (1962). *Centuries of childhood.* New York: Random House.

Armstrong, G., and Wilson, M. (1973). City politics and deviancy amplification. In *Politics and deviance,* I. Taylor and L. Taylor, eds. Harmondsworth: Penguin.

Asbridge, M. (1995). Hip hop subculture and style: a critique. Unpublished paper. Department of Sociology, University of Toronto.

Asbury, H. (1927). *The gangs of New York.* New York: Capricorn.

Ashton, D. (1988). Sources of variation in labour market segmentation: a comparison of youth labour markets in Canada and Britain. *Work, Employment and Society.* 2(1), 1–24.

Bachman, J. G., Green, S., and Wirtanen, I. D. (1971). *Youth in transition III. Dropping out—problem or symptom?* Ann Arbor, MI: Institute for Social Research.

Bachman, J. G., O'Malley, P. M., and Johnston, J. (1978). *Youth in transition VI. Adolescence to adulthood.* Ann Arbor, MI: Institute for Social Research.

Bala, A. (1988). The Young Offenders Act: a legal framework. In *Justice and the young offender in Canada,* J. Hudson, J. Hornick, and B. Burrows, eds. Toronto: Wall and Thompson.

Baron, S. (1989a). Resistance and its consequences: the street culture of punks. *Youth and Society.* 21(2).

———. (1989b). The Canadian West Coast punk subculture: a field study. *Canadian Journal of Sociology.* 14(3), 289–316.

———. (1994). Street youth and crime: the role of labour market experiences. Unpublished Ph.D. dissertation. University of Alberta.

———. (1997). Canadian male street skinheads: street gang or street terrorists. *Canadian Review of Sociology and Anthropology.* 34, 125–154.

Baron, S., and Hartnagel, T. (1997). Attributions, affect and crime: street youth's reactions to unemployment. *Criminology.* 35(3), 409–434.

Barrat, D. (1986). *Media sociology.* London: Tavistock.

Bean, P., and Melville, J. (1989). *Lost children of the empire.* London: Unwin Hyman.

Beck, U. (1992). *Risk society: towards a new modernity.* London: Sage.

Becker, H. (1963). *Outsiders: studies in the sociology of deviance.* New York: Free Press.

Bell, S. (1994). An empirical approach to theoretical perspectives on sentencing in a young offender court. *Canadian Review of Sociology and Anthropology.* 31(1), 35–64.

Ben-Yehuda, N. (1986). The sociology of moral panics: toward a new synthesis. *Sociological Quarterly.* 4, 495–513.

Bennett, A. (1999). Rappin' on the Tyne: white hip hop culture in northern England—an ethnographic study. *Sociological Review.* 47(1), 1–24.

Berger, B. (1963). Adolescence and beyond. *Social Problems.* 10(Spring), 294–408.

———. (1973). On the youthfulness of youth cultures. In *The sociology of youth,* H. Silverstein, ed. New York: Macmillan.

Bernard, T. (1992). *The cycle of juvenile justice.* New York: Oxford University Press.

Bernard, W. (1949). *Jailbait.* New York: Green.

Best, J. (1989). *Images of issues: typifying contemporary social problems.* New York: Aldine de Gruyter.

Bibby, R. (1985). *The emerging generation: an inside look at Canada's teenagers.* Toronto: Irwin.

Binder, A. (1993). Constructing racial rhetoric: media depictions of harm in heavy metal and rap music. *American Sociological Review.* 58, 753–67.

Black, D., and Reiss, A. (1970). Police control of juveniles. *American Sociological Review*. 35, 63–77.

Blackledge, D., and Hunt, B. (1985). *Sociological interpetations of education*. Kent: Crook Helm.

Boehnke, K., Hagan, J., and Hefler, G. (1998). On the development of xenophobia in Germany: the adolescent years. *Journal of Social Issues*. 54(3), 585–602.

Bordua, D. (1961). Delinquent subcultures: sociological interpretations of gang delinquency. *Annals of the American Academy of Political and Social Science*. 38, 119–36.

———. (1969). Recent trends: deviant behaviour and social control. *Annals of the American Academy of Political Social Science*. 338, 119–136, 369, 149–63.

Boritch, H., and Hagan, J. (1990). A century of crime in Toronto: gender, class and patterns of social conduct. *Criminology*. 28(4), 567–99.

Box, S. (1981). *Deviance, reality and society,* 2nd ed. London: Holt, Rinehart and Winston.

———. (1983). *Crime, power and mystification*. London: Tavistock.

———. (1987). *Recession, crime and punishment*. Basingstoke: Macmillan.

Box, S., and Hale, C. (1982).Economic crisis and the rising prisoner population in England and Wales. *Crime and Social Justice*. 17, 20–25.

Braithwaite, J. (1981). The myth of social class and criminality reconsidered. *American Sociological Review*. 46, 36–37.

———. (1989). *Crime, shame, and reintegration*. Cambridge: Cambridge University Press.

Brake, M. (1985). *Comparative youth culture*. London: Routledge and Kegan Paul.

Brannigan, A. (1986). Mystification of the innocents: comics and delinquency in Canada. *Criminal Justice History*. 3, 111–44.

———. (1987). Moral panics and juvenile delinquency in Britain and America. *Criminal Justice History*. 8, 181–91.

Brown, P. (1987). *Schooling ordinary kids: inequality in unemployment and the new vocationalism*. London: Tavistock.

Burman, P. (1988). *Killing time, losing ground: experiences of unemployment*. Toronto: Thompson Press.

Burrows, B., Hudson, J., and Hornick, J. (1988). Introduction to *Justice and the young offender in Canada,* J. Hudson, J. Hornick, and B. Burrows, eds. Toronto: Wall and Thompson.

Campbell, A. (1984). *The girls in the gang*. New York: Basil Blackwell.

———. (1990a). *The girls in the gang*. 2nd ed. New York: Basil Blackwell.

———. (1990b). Female participation in gangs. In *Gangs in America*, R. Huff, ed. Newbury Park, CA: Sage.

Campbell, E. (1969). Adolescent socialization. In *Handbook of socialization theory*, D. Goslin, ed. Chicago: Rand McNally.

Canadian Crime Statistics. (1993). Statistics Canada: Canadian Centre for Justice Statistics. Cat. No. 85–205.

Canadian Journal of Criminology. (1994). 36(2).

Carrière, D. (2000). Youth court statistics 1998/1999. Highlights. *Juristat*. 20(2). Statistics Canada: Canadian Centre for Justice Statistics.

Carrington, P. (1995). Has violent youth crime increased? Comment on Corrado and Markwart. *Canadian Journal of Criminology*. 35(1), 61–73.

———. (1999). Trends in youth crime in Canada, 1977–1996. *Canadian Journal of Criminology*. 41(1), 1–32.

Carrington, P., and Moyer, S. (1994). Trends in youth crime and police responses, pre- and post-Y.O.A. *Canadian Journal of Criminology*. 36(1), 1–28.

Cavender, G. (1981). "Scared straight": ideology and the media. *Journal of Criminal Justice*. 34, 430–40.

Cernkovich, S., and Giordano, P. (1979). A comparative analysis of male and female delinquency. *Sociological Quarterly*. 20, 131–45.

Chesney-Lind, M. (1997). *The female offender: girls, women and crime*. Thousand Oaks, CA: Sage.

Chesney-Lind, M., and Sheldon, R. (1992). *Girls, delinquency and juvenile justice*. Belmont, CA: Brooks/Cole.

Chibnall, S. (1977). *Law and order news*. London: Tavistock.

Christie, J., and Macleod, R. (1995). Midnight basketball, considered for inner-cities. *Globe and Mail*. (n.d.).

Clark, A. (1986). Summary—public hearing proceeding: background report, Royal Commission on Employment and Unemployment. St. John's, NF: Queen's Printer.

Clarke, J., Hall, S., Jefferson, T., and Roberts, B. (1975). Subcultures, cultures and class. *Working Papers in Cultural Studies*. 7(8) (Summer), 9–74.

Clarke, J., and Jefferson, T. (1976). Working-class youth cultures. In *Working class youth culture*, G. Mungham and G. Pearson, eds. London: Routledge and Kegan Paul. 138–58.

Cloward, R., and Ohlin, L. (1960). *Delinquency and opportunity: a theory of delinquent gangs*. New York: Free Press.

Cohen, A. (1955). *Delinquent boys*. Chicago: Free Press.

Cohen, P. (1972). Subcultural conflict and working-class community. *Working Papers in Cultural Studies*. 2 (Spring), 5–55.

Cohen, S. (1973). *Folk devils and moral panics*. London: MacGibbons and Kee.

———. (1980). Signs of troubles. Introduction to *Folk devils and moral panics,* 2nd ed. London: Martin Robertson.

Coleman, J. (1961). *The adolescent society*. New York: Free Press of Glencoe.

Conway J., (1992). Teenage victims of violent crime. *Juristat*. 12(6). Statistics Canada: Canadian Centre for Justice Statistics.

Corrado, R. (1994). The need to reform the Y.O.A. in response to violent young offenders: confusion, reality or myth? *Canadian Journal of Criminology*. 36(3), 343–78.

———. (1999). Review of "Mean Streets." *Canadian Journal of Sociology*. 24(4) (Fall), 563–566.

Corrado, R., and Markwart, A. (1992). The evolution and implementation of a new era of juvenile justice in Canada. In *Juvenile justice in Canada: a theoretical and analytical assessment,* R. Corrado, N. Bala, R. Linden, and M. LeBlanc, eds. Vancouver: Butterworths.

Corrigan, P. (1979). *Schooling the smash street kids*. London: Macmillan Press.

Coupland, D. (1991). *"Generation X": tales from an accelerated culture*. New York: St. Martin's Press.

Cowie, J., Cowie, V., and Slater, E. (1968). *Delinquency in girls*. London: Heinemann.

Crick, N., and Grotpeter, J. (1995). Relational aggression, gender and social psychological adjustment. *Child Development*. 66(3), 710–22.

Cullen, F., Golden, K., and Cullen, J. (1979). Sex and delinquency. *Criminology*. 7, 301–10.

Dahrendorf, R. (1959). *Class and class conflict in industrial society*. Stanford, CA: Stanford University Press.

Datesman, S., and Aickin, M. (1985). Offense specialization and escalation among status offenders. *Journal of Criminal Law and Criminology*. 75, 1246–75.

Davies, J. (1990). *Youth and the condition of Britain*. London: Athlone Press.

Davies, L. (1984). *Pupil power: deviance and gender in school*. London: Falmer Press.

Davies, S. (1994a). In search of resistance and rebellion among high-school dropouts. *Canadian Journal of Sociology*. 19(3), 331–50.

———. (1994b). Class dismissed? Student opposition in Ontario high schools. *Canadian Review of Sociology and Anthropology*. 31(4), 422–45.

DeFleur, L. (1975). Biasing influence on drug arrest records. Implications for deviance research. *American Sociological Review*. 40, 88–101.

Domm, G. (1993, June 12). Victims strike back. *Globe and Mail*.

Doob, A., and Meen, J. (1993). Exploration of changes in dispositions for young offenders in Toronto. *Canadian Journal of Criminology*. 35(1), 19–30.

Doob, A., and Sprott, J. (1999). Commentary. The pitfalls of determining validity by consensus. *Canadian Journal of Criminology*. (October), 535–543.

Downes, D. (1966). *The delinquent solution*. London: Routledge and Kegan Paul.

Downes, D., and Rock, P. (1995). *Understanding Deviance*, rev. 2nd ed. New York: Oxford University Press.

Easterbrook, M. (1999, July/August). Taking aim at violence. *Psychology Today*. 32(4), 52–56.

Eckert, P. (1989). *Jocks and burnouts: social categories and identity in the high school*. New York: Teachers College Press.

Eisenstadt, S. (1956). *From generation to generation*. Glencoe, IL: Free Press.

Elliott, D. S. (1966). Delinquency, school attendance and dropout. *Social Problems*. 13, 307–14.

Elliott, D. S., Hamburg, B., and Williams, K. (1998). *Violence in American schools: a new perspective*. Cambridge University Press.

Elliott, D. S., and Voss, H .L. (1974). *Delinquency and dropout*. Lexington, MA: D.C. Heath.

Empey, L. (1982). *American delinquency: its meaning and construction*, rev. ed. Homewood, IL: Dorsey Press.

Evans, J., and Himelfarb, A. (1987). Counting crime. In *Criminology: a Canadian perspective*, R. Linden, ed. Toronto: Holt, Rinehart and Winston.

Everett, P. (1986). *You'll never be 16 again*. London: BBC Publications.

Everhart, R. (1983). *Reading, writing and resistance*. Boston: Routledge and Kegan Paul.

Falkenstein, W. (2000). Hip hop subculture?: limitations and contributions of British subcultural theory—the Birmingham CCCS. Unpublished paper. University of Toronto.

Farrington, D. P., Gallagher, B., Morley, L., St. Ledger, R. J., and West, D. J. (1986). Unemployment, school leaving, and crime. *British Journal of Criminology*. 26, 335–56.

Fasiolo, R., and Leckie, S. (1993). *Canadian media coverage of gangs: a content analysis*. Ottawa: Solicitor General of Canada.

Felson, M. (1998). *Crime and everyday life*. Thousand Oaks, CA: Pine Forge Press.

Ferdinand, T. (1967). The criminal patterns of Boston since 1849. *American Journal of Sociology*. 73, 84–99.

Figuiera-McDonough, J. (1984). Feminism and delinquency. *British Journal of Criminology*. 24: 325–42.

Finchenauer, J. (1982). *Scared straight! and the panacea phenomenon*. Englewood Cliffs, NJ: Prentice-Hall.

Fine, G., and Kleinman, S. (1979). Rethinking subculture: an interactionist analysis. *American Journal of Sociology*. 83(1), 1–20.

Finestone, H. (1976). Victims of change. Westport, CT: Greenwood Press.

Fishman, M. (1978). Crime waves as ideology. *Social Problems*. 25(5), 531–63.

Foster, J. (1990). *Villains: crime and community in the inner city*. London: Routledge and Kegan Paul.

Frith, S. (1978a). *The sociology of rock*. London: Constable.

———. (1978b). The punk Bohemians. *New Society*. 43(805), 535–36.

———. (1985). The sociology of youth. In *Sociology: new directions*, M. Haralabos, ed. Ormskirk: Causeway Press.

Furlong, A., and Cartmel, F. (1997). *Young people and social change: individualization and risk in late modernity*. Buckingham: Open University Press.

Gabor, T. (1999). Trends in youth crime: some evidence pointing to increases in the severity and volume of violence on the part of young people. *Canadian Journal of Sociology*. (April) 385–397.

Gaetz, S., O'Grady, B., and Daillancourt, B. (1999). Making money. The Shout Clinic Report on Homeless Youth and Employment Central. Toronto Community Health Centre.

Gaines, D. (1991). *Teenage wasteland: suburbia's dead end kids*. New York: Pantheon Books.

Garland, D. (1990. Frameworks of inquiry in the sociology of punishment. *British Journal of Sociology*. 14(1), 1–19.

Gaskell, J. (1985). Course enrolment in the high school: the perspective of working-class females. *Sociology of Education*. 8, 48–59.

Gelsthorpe, L. (1986). Towards a skeptical look at sexism. *International Journal of Sociology of Law*. 14, 125–52.

George, N. (1992). *Buppies, b-boys, baps and bohos: notes on post-soul black culture*. New York: Harper Collins.

———. (1998). *Hip hop America*. New York: Penguin.

Gilbert, J. (1986). *A cycle of outrage*. New York: Oxford University Press.

Gillis, J. (1974). *Youth and history*. London: Academic Press.

Giordano, P., Cernkovich, S., and Pugh, M. (1986). Friendships and delinquency. *American Journal of Sociology*. 91, 1170–1202.

Gold, M. (1970). *Delinquent behaviour in an American city*. Belmont, CA: Brooks/Cole.

Goldstein, J. (1986). *Aggression and crimes of violence*, 2nd ed. New York: Oxford University Press.

Gottfredson, G. D., and Gottfredson, D. C. (1985). *Victimization in schools*. New York: Plenium.

Gottfredson, M., and Hirschi, T. (1990). *A general theory of crime*. Stanford, CA: Stanford University Press.

Gove, W. (1975). *The labelling of deviance: evaluating a perspective*. New York: Sage.

Granovetter, M. (1985). Economic action and social structure: the problem of embeddedness. *American Journal of Sociology*. 91, 481–510.

Griffen, C. (1985). *Typical girls? young women from school to the job market*. London: Routledge and Kegan Paul.

Griffiths, C., and Verdun-Jones, S. (1994). *Canadian criminal justice*, 2nd ed. Toronto: Harcourt Brace.

Gurr, T. (1989). Historical trends in violent crime: Europe and the United States. In *Violence in America*, T. Gurr, ed. Newbury Park, CA: Sage.

Hackler, J., Garadon, C. F., Frigon, C., and Knight, V. (1987). Locking up juveniles in Canada: some comparisons with France. *Canadian Public Policy*. 13, 477–89.

Hagan, J. (1985). *Modern criminology: crime, criminal behaviour and its control*. New York: McGraw-Hill.

———. (1991). Destiny and drift: subcultural preferences, status attainments and the risks and rewards of youth. *American Sociological Review*. 56, 567–87.

———. (1993). The social embeddedness of crime and unemployment. *Criminology*. 13(4), 465–91.

Hagan, J., Gillis, R., and Simpson, J. (1979). The sexual stratification of social control: a gender-based perception on crime and delinquency. *British Journal of Sociology*. 30(1), 25–38.

———. (1985). The class structure of gender and delinquency. *American Journal of Sociology*. 90, 1151–76.

———. (1987). Class in the household: a power-control theory of gender and delinquency. *American Journal of Sociology*. 92, 788–816.

Hagan, J., Hefler, G., Classen, G. G., Boehnke, K., and Merkens, H. (1998). Subterranean sources of subcultural delinquency: beyond the American dream. *Criminology*. 36(2) (May), 309–342.

Hagan, J., and Leon, L. (1977). Rediscovering delinquency: social history, political ideology and the sociology of law. *American Sociological Review*. 42, 587–98.

Hagan, J., and McCarthy, B. (1992). Streetlife and delinquency. *British Journal of Sociology*. 43(4), 533–61.

———. (1997). *Mean streets*. Cambridge University Press.

Hagan, J., Merkens, H., and Boehnke, K. (1995). Delinquency and disdain: social capital and the control of right-wing extremism among East and West Berlin youth. *American Journal of Sociology*. 100(4), 1028–57.

Hagan, J., Rippl, S., Boehnke, K., and Merkens, H. (2000). The interest in evil: hierarchical self-interest and right-wing extremism among East and West German youth. *Social Science Research*. 28(2) (June).

Hagedorn, J. (1988). *People and folks: gangs, crime and the underclass in the Rustbelt City*. Chicago: Lakeview Press.

Hall, S., and Jefferson, T., eds. (1976). *Resistance through rituals*. London: Hutchinson.

Hamm, M. (1993). *American skinheads*. Westport, CN: Praeger.

Hargreaves, D. (1967). *Social relations in a secondary school*. London: Routledge and Kegan Paul.

Hartnagel, T. (1990). Under/unemployment and crime among youth: a longitudinal study of recent high school graduates. Discussion paper 23. Centre for Criminological Research, Department of Sociology, University of Alberta.

————. (1992). Correlates of criminal behaviour. In *Criminology: a Canadian perspective,* 2nd ed. R. Linden, ed. Toronto: Harcourt, Brace, Jovanovitch.

————. (1998). Labour market problems and crime in the transition from school to work. *Canadian Review of Sociology and Anthropology.* 35, 435–460.

Hartnagel, T., Krahn, H., Lowe, G. S., Tanner, J., and Walter, L. (1986). Labour market experience and criminal behaviour among Canadian youth: a longitudinal study. Research Report for Solicitor General Canada. Population Research Laboratory, Department of Sociology, University of Alberta.

Hartnagel, T., and Tanner, J. (1982). Class, schooling and delinquency: a further examination. *Canadian Journal of Criminology.* 24(2), 155–71.

Hawkins, D., Farrington, D., and Catalano, R. (1998). Reducing violence through the school. In *Violence in American schools,* Elliott et al. 188–216.

Hebdige, D. (1979). The meaning of mod. Working Papers in Cultural Studies. *Resistance through rituals,* S. Hall and T. Jefferson, eds. London: Hutchinson.

Hill, G., and Atkinson, M. (1988). Gender, familial control and delinquency. *Criminology.* 26, 127–49.

Hindelang, M., Hirschi, T., and Weis, I. (1979). Correlates of delinquency: the illusion of discrepancy between self-report and official measures. *American Sociological Review.* 44, 995–1014.

————. (1981). *Measuring delinquency.* Newbury Park, CA: Sage.

Hirschi, T. (1969). *Causes of delinquency.* Berkeley: University of California Press.

————. (1975). Labelling theory and juvenile delinquency. In *The labelling of deviance: evaluating a perspective,* W. Gove, ed. New York: Sage.

Hirschi, T., and Gottfredson, M. (1983). Age and the explanation of crime. *American Journal of Sociology.* 89, 552–84.

Hobsbawm, E. (1963). *Primitive rebels.* Manchester: Manchester University Press.

Hood, R., and Sparks, R. (1970). *Key issues in criminology.* New York: McGraw-Hill.

Horowitz, R. (1990). *Honor and the American dream.* New Brunswick, NJ: Rutger University Press.

Hudson, J., Hornick, J., and Burrows, B. (1988). *Justice and the young offender in Canada.* Toronto: Wall and Thompson.

Huff, R. (1990). *Gangs in America*. Newbury Park, CA: Sage.

_____. (1996). *Gangs in America*, 2nd ed. Thousand Oaks, CA: Sage.

Hylton, J. (1994). Get tough or get smart? Options for Canada's youth justice system in the twenty-first century. *Canadian Issues in Criminology, Journal of Criminology*. 36(3), 229–46.

Jacobs, M. (1990). *Screwing the system and making it work: juvenile justice in the no-fault society*. Chicago: University of Chicago Press.

Jahoda, M. (1982). *Employment and unemployment: a social-psychological analysis*. Cambridge: Cambridge University Press.

James, J., and Thornton, W. (1980). Women's liberation and the female delinquent. *Journal of Research in Crime and Delinquency*. 17, 230–44.

Jankowski, M. (1991). *Islands in the street: gangs and American urban society*. Berkeley: University of California Press.

JarJoura, G. R. (1993). Does dropping out of school enhance delinquent involvement? Results from a large scale national probability sample. *Criminology*. 31(2), 149–71.

Jenkins, P. (1992). *Intimate enemies: moral panic in Great Britain*. New York: Aldine de Gruyter.

Jensen, G., and Brownfield, D. (1986). Gender, lifestyles and victimization: beyond routine activity. *Violence and Victims*. 1, 85–99.

Jensen, G., and Eve, R. (1976). Sex differences in delinquency. *Criminology*. 13, 427–48.

Jensen, G., and Thompson, K. (1990). What's class got to do with it? A further examination of power-control theory. *American Journal of Sociology*. 95, 1009–73.

Jefferson, T. (1975). Cultural responses of the Teds. *Working Papers in Cultural Studies*. 7(8), 81–86.

Juristat. (1992). Female young offenders, 1990–1991. Vol. 12(11). Statistics Canada: Canadian Centre for Justice Statistics.

Juristat. (1992). Youth property crime in Canada. Vol. 12(14). Statistics Canada: Canadian Centre for Justice Statistics.

Juristat. (1994). Trends in criminal victimization: 1988–1993. Vol. 13(3). Statistics Canada: Canadian Centre for Justice Statistics.

Juristat. (1995). Public perceptions of crime. Vol. 15(1). Statistics Canada: Canadian Centre for Justice Statistics.

Juristat. (1995). Youth court statistics. Vol. 15(3). Statistics Canada: Canadian Centre for Justice Statistics.

Juristat. (2000). The justice factfinder, 1998. Vol. 20(4). Statistics Canada: Canadian Centre for Justice Statistics.

Kanter, R. (1977). *Men and women of the corporation.* New York: Basic Books.

Kelling, G., and Coles, C. (1997). *Fixing broken windows.* The Free Press: New York.

Kennedy, L., and Baron, S. (1993). Routine activities and a subculture of violence: a study of violence on the street. *Journal of Research in Crime and Delinquency.* 30(1), 88–112.

Kett, J. (1971). Adolescence and youth in nineteenth century America. In *The family in history,* T. Rabb and R. Rothberg, eds. New York: Harper & Row.

———. (1977). *Rites of passage.* New York: Basic Books.

Kingery, P., Pruitt, B., and Heuberger, G. (1996). A profile of rural Texas adolescents who carry handguns to school. *Journal of School Health.* 66, 18–22.

Krahn, H., and Lowe, G. (1997). School-work transitions and post-modern values: what's changing in Canada? In *From education to work: cross-national perspectives,* W. Heinz, ed. Cambridge and New York: Cambridge University Press.

Krahn, H., and Lowe, G. S. (1998). *Work, industry and Canadian society,* 3rd ed. Scarborough: Nelson Canada.

Lab, S., and Clark, R. (1997). Crime prevention in schools: individual and collective responses. In *Crime prevention at a crossroad,* S. Lab, ed. Cincinnati, OH: Anderson.

Lagrange, T., and Silverman, R. (1999). Low self-control and opportunity: testing the general theory of crime as an explanation for gender differences in delinquency. *Criminology.* 37(1), 41–72.

Laub, J., and Lauritsen, J. (1998). The interdependence of school violence with neighbourhood and family conditions. In *Violence in American schools,* Elliott et al. 127–155.

Lauritson, J., Laub, J., and Sampson, R. (1992). Conventional and delinquent activities: implications for the prevention of violent victimization among adolescents. *Violence and Victims.* 7, 91–108

Lawrence. R. (1998). *School crime and juvenile justice.* New York: Oxford University Press.

Leblanc, M., Valliers, E., and McDuff, P. (1993). The prediction of male's adolescent and adult offending from school offence. *Canadian Journal of Criminology.* 33(4), 459–78.

Lees, S. (1986). *Losing out: sexuality and adolescent girls.* London: Hutchinson.

Leong, L. (1992). Cultural resistance: the cultural terrorism of British male working class youth. *Current Perspectives in Social Theory.* 12, 29–59.

Leschied, A., and Jaffe, P. (1988). Implementing the Young Offenders Act in Ontario: critical issues and challenges for the future. In *Justice and the young offender in Canada,* J. Hudson, J. Hornick, and B. Burrows, eds. Toronto: Wall and Thompson.

————. (1991). Dispositions as indications of conflicting social purposes under the J.D.A. and Y.O.A. In *The Young Offenders Act: a revolution in Canadian juvenile justice.* A. Leschied and W. Willis., eds.

Leschied, A. W., and Willis, W., eds. (1991). *The Young Offenders Act: a revolution in Canadian juvenile justice.* Toronto: University of Toronto Press.

Liska, A. (1987). *Perspectives on deviance,* 2nd ed. Englewood Cliffs, NJ: Prentice-Hall.

Lombroso, C., and Ferrero, W. (1895). *The female offender.* New York: Philosophical Library.

Loy, P., and Norland, S. (1981). Gender convergence and delinquency. *Sociological Quarterly.* 22, 275–83.

Lundman, R. (1993). *Prevention and control of juvenile delinquency,* 2nd ed. New York: Oxford University Press.

MacKenzie, D. (1995). Boot-camp prisons and recidivism in eight states. *Criminology.* 33, 34–41.

MacLeod, J. (1987). *Ain't no makin it.* London: Tavistock.

Macmillan, R. (2000). Adolescent victimization and income deficits in early adulthood: rethinking the costs of criminal violence from a life course perspective. *Criminology.* 38(2).

Marchak, P. (1981). *Ideological perspectives on Canada.* Toronto: McGraw-Hill Ryerson.

Markwart, A., and Carrado, R. (1995). A response to Carrington. *Canadian Journal of Criminology.* 35(1), 74–82.

Marquard R. (1998). *Enter at your own risk: Canadian youth and the labour market.* Toronto: Between the Lines.

Marron, K. (1992). *Apprenticed in crime.* Toronto: McClelland & Stewart.

Martinson, R. (1974). What works? Questions and answers about prison reform. *The Public Interest.* 35 (Spring), 22–54.

Matza, D. (1961). Subterranean traditions of youth. *Annals of the American Academy of Political and Social Sciences.* 338, 102–18.

————. (1964). *Delinquency and drift.* New York: John Wiley & Sons.

Matza, D., and Sykes, G. (1961). Juvenile delinquency and subterranean values. *American Sociological Review*. 26, 712–19.

Mawby, R. (1980). Sex and crime: the results of a self-report study. *British Journal of Sociology*. 31, 326–543.

McCarthy, B., and Hagan, J. (1991). Homelessness: a criminogenic situation? British Journal of *Criminology*. 4 (Autumn), 393–410.

———. (1992). Mean streets: the theoretical significance of situational delinquency among homeless youths. *American Journal of Sociology*. 98(3), 597–627.

McCormack, A., Janus, M., and Burgess, A. (1986). Runaway youths and sexual victimization: gender differences in an adolescent runaway population. *Child Abuse and Neglect*. 10, 387–93.

McLaren, P. (1986). *Schooling as a ritual performance*. London: Routledge and Kegan Paul.

McRobbie, A. (1981). Settling accounts with subcultures: a feminist critique. In *Culture, ideology and social process*, T. Bennett, G. Martin, C. Mercer, and J. Woollacott, eds. London: The Open University.

———. (1994). Post modernism and popular culture. London: Routledge and Kegan Paul.

McRobbie, A., and Garber, J. (1975). Girls and subcultures: an exploration. In *Resistance through rituals*, S. Hall and T. Jefferson, eds. London: Hutchinson.

Melly, G. (1970). *Revolt into style*. London: Penguin.

Merchant, J., and MacDonald, R. (1994). Youth and the rave culture, ectasy and health. *Youth Policy*. 45 (Summer), 16–38.

Merton, R. (1938). Social structure and anomie. *American Sociological Review*. 3, 672–87.

———. (1968). *Social theory and social structure,* 2nd ed. New York: Free Press.

Messner, S., Krohn, M., and Liska, A., eds. (1989). *Theoretical integration in the study of deviance and crime*. Albany: State University of New York Press.

Messner, S., and Rosenfeld, R. (1994). *Crime and the American dream*. Belmont, CA: Wadsworth.

Miller, W. B. (1958). Lower class culture as a generating milieu of gang delinquency. *Journal of Social Issues*. 14(3), 5–14.

Monahan, T. (1970). Police dispositions of juvenile offenders. *Phyhon*. 31, 91–107.

Montgomery, R. (1976). The outlaw motorcycle subculture. *Canadian Journal of Criminology and Corrections*. 18, 332–42.

—————. (1977). The outlaw motorcycle subculture II. *Canadian Journal of Criminology and Corrections.* 19, 356–61.

Moore, D. (1994). *The lads in action: social process in an urban youth sub-culture.* Aldershot: Arena Publications.

Moore, J., and Hagedorn, J. (1996). What happens to girls in the gang? In *Gangs in America,* 2nd ed., C. Ronald Huff, ed. Thousand Oaks, CA: Sage. 205–218.

Moore, J. W. (1991). *Going down to the barrio: homeboys and homegirls.* Philadelphia: Temple University Press.

Morash, M. (1986). Gender, peer group experiences and seriousness of delinquency. *Journal of Research in Crime and Delinquency.* 23, 43–67.

Morash, M., and Rucker, L. (1990). A critical look at the idea of boot camp as a correctional reform. *Crime and Delinquency.* 36 (April), 204–22.

Morris, A. (1987). *Women, crime and criminal justice.* Oxford: Basil Blackwell.

Morris, R. (1965). Attitudes toward delinquency by delinquents, non delinquents and their friends. *British Journal of Criminology.* 5, 249–65.

Morrison, B. (1997). *As if: a crime, a trial, a question of childhood.* New York: Picador U.S.A.

Morrison, P. (1988, May 29). Ounce of prevention vs. weight of gang influence. *Los Angeles Times,* 25–26.

Muncie, J. (1984). *The trouble with kids today: youth and crime in postwar Britain.* London: Hutchinson.

Mungham, G., and Pearson, G. (1976). Introduction: troubled youth, troubling world. In *Working class youth culture,* G. Mungham and G. Pearson, eds. London: Routledge and Kegan Paul.

Murdock, G. (1974). Mass communication and the construction of meaning. In *Reconstructing social psychology,* N. Armstead, ed. Harmondsworth: Penguin.

—————. (1982). Mass communication and social violence. In *Aggression and violence,* P. Marsh and A. Campbell, eds. Oxford: Blackwell.

Murdock, G., and McCron, R. (1976). Youth and class: the career of confusion. In *Working class youth culture,* G. Mungham and G. Pearson, eds. London: Routledge and Kegan Paul.

Murdock, G., and Phelps, G. (1973). *Mass media and the secondary school.* London: Macmillan.

Musgrove, F. (1964). *Youth and the social order.* London: Routledge and Kegan Paul.

Nelsen, R. (1987). Books, boredom and behind bars. an explanation of apathy and hostility in our schools. In *The political economy of Canadian education*, T. Wotherspoon, ed. Toronto: Methuen.

Norland, S., Wessel, R., and Shover, N. (1981). Masculinity and delinquency. *Criminology*. 19, 421–33.

O'Grady, B., Bright, R., and Cohen, E. (1998). Sub-employment and street youths: an analysis of the impact of squeegee cleaning on homeless youths. *Security Journal*. 11(2–3), 315–323.

O'Grady, W. (1991). Crime, violence and victimization: a Newfoundland case. In *Crime in Canadian society*, 4th ed., R. Silverman, J. Teevas, and V. Sacco, eds. Toronto: Butterworths.

Owram, D, (1996). *Born at the right time: a history of the baby boom generation*. Toronto: University of Toronto Press.

Padilla, F. (1992). *The gang as an American enterprise*. New Brunswick, NJ: Rutger University Press.

Parker, H. (1974). *View from the boys: a sociology of downtown adolescents*. Newton Abbot, UK: David and Charles.

Parsons, T. (1942). Age and sex in the social structure of the United States. *American Sociological Review*. 7, 604–16.

Pearson, G. (1976). "Paki-bashing" in a North East Lancashire cotton town: a case study and its history. In *Working class youth culture*, G. Mungham and G. Pearson, eds. London: Routledge and Kegan Paul.

———. (1983). *Hooligan*. London: Macmillan.

Pearson, P. (1998). Sugar and spice and veins cold as ice: teenage girls are closing the gender gap in violent crime. *B.C. Report*. 9(20), 26–27.

Piliavin, I., and Briar, S. (1964). Police encounters with juveniles. *American Journal of Sociology*. 70, 206–14.

Pilkington, H. (1994). *Russia's youth and its culture*. London, New York: Routledge.

Platt, A. (1969). *The child-savers*. Chicago: Chicago University Press.

Polk, K., and Schafer, W. (1972). *Schools and delinquency*. Englewood Cliffs, NJ: Prentice-Hall.

Polk, K. (1972). Class, strain and rebellion among adolescents. In *Schools and delinquency*, K. Polk and W. Schafer, eds.

Polk, K., and Halferty, D. (1972). School cultures, adolescent commitment and delinquency. In *Schools and delinquency*, K. Polk and W. Schafer, eds.

Polk, K., and Pink, W. (1971). Youth culture and the school: a replication. *British Journal of Sociology*. 22(2), 160–91.

Pollock, J. (1978). Early theories of female criminology. In *Women, crime and the criminal justice system,* L. Bowker, ed. Lexington, MA: D.C. Heath.

Porteous, M., and Colston, N.J. (1980). How adolescents are reported in the British press. *Journal of Adolescents.* 3, 197–207.

Power, M. J., Benn, R. T., and Morris, J. A. (1972). Neighbourhood, school and juveniles before the courts. *British Journal of Criminology.* 12(2), 111–32.

A profile of youth justice in Canada. (1998). K. Stevenson et al. S. Besserer, ed. Ottawa: Canadian Centre for Justice Statistics.

Pronovost, L., and Leblanc, M. (1980). Transition statutaire et delinquance. *Canadian Journal of Criminology.* 22, 288–97.

Rankin, J. (1980). School factors and delinquency: interaction by age and sex. *Sociology and Social Research.* 64, 420–34.

Reid, S., and Reitsma-Street, M. (1984). Assumptions and implications of new Canadian legislation for young offenders. *Canadian Criminology Forum.* 7(1), 1–19.

Reid-Macnevin, S. (1988). Implementing the Young Offenders Act. In *Ontario: critical issues and challenges for the future,* J. Hudson, J. Hornick, and B. Burrows, eds. Toronto: Wall and Thompson.

———. (1991). A theoretical understanding of current juvenile-justice policy. In *The Young Offenders Act: a revolution in Canadian juvenile justice,* A. Leschied, P. Jaffe, and W. Willis, eds. Toronto: University of Toronto Press.

Reinarman, G., and Levine, H. (1989). The crack attack: politics and media in America's latest drug scare. In *Images of issues: typifying contemporary social problems,* J. Best, ed. New York: Aldine De Gruyter.

Reiss, A. (1960). Sex offences: the marginal status of the adolescent. *Law and Contemporary Problems.* 25, 309–33.

Reitsma-Street, M. (1993). Canadian youth court charges and dispositions for females before and after implementation of the Young Offenders Act. *Canadian Journal of Criminology.* 35(4), 437–58.

———. (1999). Justice for Canadian girls: a 1990s update. *Canadian Journal of Criminology.* 41(13), 335.

Reynolds, S. (1999). *Generation ecstasy: into the world of techno and rave culture.* New York: Routledge.

Riley, D. (1987). Time and crime: the link between teenager lifestyle and delinquency. *Journal of Quantitative Criminology.* 3, 339–54.

Roberts, J., and Doob, A. (1990). News media influences on public views on sentencing. *Law and Human Behaviour.* 14, 451–68.

Roe, K. (1983). Mass media and adolescent schooling: conflict or co-existence. Stockholm, Sweden: Almquist and Wiksell International.

———. (1987). The school and music in adolescent socialization. In *Pop music and communication,* J. Lull, ed. Thousand Oaks, CA: Sage.

Roncek, D., and Lobosco, A. (1983). The effect of high schools on crime in their neighbourhoods. *Social Science Quarterly.* 64, 598–613.

Rosenbaum, J., and Prinsky, L. (1991). The presumption of influence: recent responses to popular music subcultures. *Crime and Delinquency.* 37, 528–35.

Rutter, M., Maughan, B., Mortimore, P., Ouston, J., and Smith, A. (1979). *Fifteen thousand hours.* London: Open Books.

Sacco, V., and Kennedy, L. (1994). *The criminal event.* Toronto: Nelson.

———. (1998). *The criminal event,* 2nd ed. Toronto: Nelson.

Sandhu, H., and Allen, D. (1969). Female delinquency: goal distribution and anomie. *Canadian Review of Sociology and Anthropology.* 5, 107–10.

Savoie, J. (1999). Youth violent crime: *Juristat.* 19(13). Statistics Canada: Canadian Centre for Justice Statistics.

Schafer, W., Olexa, C., and Polk, K. (1972). Programmed for social class: tracking in high school. In *Schools and delinquency,* K. Polk and W. Schafer, eds. Englewood Cliffs, NJ: Prentice-Hall.

Schafer, W., and Polk, K. (1967). Delinquency and schools. the president's commission on law enforcement and administration of justice, Task Force Report: Juvenile Delinquency and Crime. Washington, DC: Government Printing Office.

Schissel, B. (1993). *Social dimensions of Canadian youth justice.* Toronto: Oxford University Press.

Schreiber, D. (1963). The dropout and the delinquent. *Phi Delta Kappan.* 44, 215–21.

Shaw, C., and McKay, H. (1942). *Juvenile delinquency and urban areas.* Chicago: University of Chicago Press.

Sheley, J., and Wright, J. (1993). *Gun acquisition and possession in selected juvenile samples.* Washington, DC: U.S. Office of Juvenile Justice and Delinquency Prevention.

Shepherd, M. (1998, October 26). *Toronto Star.* B1

Shoemaker, D. (1990). *Theories of delinquency.* New York: Oxford University Press.

Short, J. (1989). Exploring integration of theoretical levels of explanation: notes on gang delinquency. In *Theoretical integration in the study of deviance and crime,* S. Messner, M. Krahn, and A. Liska, eds. Albany, NY: State University of New York Press.

Short, J., and Strodtbeck, F. (1965). *Group process and gang delin-quency*. Chicago: University of Chicago Press.

Shover, N., Norland, S., James, J., and Thornton, W. (1979). Gender roles and delinquency. *Social Forces*. 58, 162–75.

Shroud, C. (1993). *Contempt of court: the betrayal of justice in Canada*. Toronto: Macmillan.

Siegel, L., and Senna, J. (1994). *Juvenile delinquency: theory, practice and law,* 5th ed. St. Paul, MN: West Publishing Co.

Silverman, R. (1990). Trends in Canadian youth homicide: some unan-ticipated consequences of a change in law. *Canadian Journal of Criminology*. 32(4), 651–56.

Silverman, R., Teevan, J. Jr., and Sacco, V. (1991). *Crime in Canadian society,* 4th ed. Toronto: Butterworths.

Simon, R. (1975). *Women and crime*. Lexington, MA.: Lexington Books.

Simpson, J. E., and Van Arsdol, M. D. Jr. (1967). Residential history and educational status of delinquents and nondelinquents. *Social Problems*. 15, 25–40.

Singer, S., and Levine, M. (1988). Power-control theory, gender and delinquency: a partial replication with additional evidence of the effects of peers. *Criminology*. 26: 627–47.

Singh, R. (2000). North American rave: A case for the re-evaluation of subcultural theory. Unpublished paper. University of Toronto.

Smith, D. (1982). Street level justice: situational determinants of police arrest decisions. *Social Problems*. 24, 69–73.

Solomon, P. (1992). *Black resistance in high school: forging a separatist culture*. Albany: State University of New York Press.

Spergel, I. (1964). *Racketville, slumtown and haulberg*. Chicago: University of Chicago Press.

Sprott, J. (1996). Understanding public views of youth crime and the youth justice system. *Canadian Journal of Criminology*. 38(3), 271–91.

Sprott, J., and Doob, A. (1998). Is the quality of youth violence becoming more serious? *Canadian Journal of Criminology*. (April), 185–94.

Stinchcombe, A. (1964). *Rebellion in a high school*. Chicago: Quadrangle Books.

Strange, C. (1995). *Toronto's girl problem: the perils and pleasures of the city, 1880–1930*. Toronto: University of Toronto Press.

Stroud, C. (1993). *Contempt of court: the betrayal of justice in Canada*. Toronto: Macmillan.

Sugarman, B. (1967). Involvement in youth culture, academic achievement and conformity in school. *British Journal of Sociology*. 18(2), 15–64.

Sullivan, M. (1989). *Getting paid: youth crime and work in the inner city*. Ithaca, NY: Cornell University Press.

Surette, R. (1992). *Media, crime and criminal justice: images and realitites*. Pacific Grove, CA: Brooks/Cole.

Sutherland, N. (1976). *Children in English-Canadian society: framing the twentieth-century consensus*. Toronto: University of Toronto Press.

Sykes, G. (1958). *Society of captives—a study of a maximum security institution*. Princeton: Princeton University Press.

Tanner, J. (1978a). Youth culture and the Canadian high school: an empirical analysis. *Canadian Journal of Sociology*. 3(1), 89–102.

———. (1978b). New directions for sub-cultural theory: an analysis of British working-class youth culture. *Youth and Society*. 19(4), 343–73.

———. (1981). Pop music and peer groups: a study of Canadian high-school students' response to pop music. *Canadian Review of Sociology and Anthropology*. 18(1), 1–13.

———. (1990). Reluctant rebels: a case study of Edmonton high-school dropouts. *Canadian Review of Sociology and Anthropology*. 21(1), 79–94.

———. (1992). Youthful deviance. In *Deviancy, conformity and control in Canadian society,* 2nd ed., V. Sacco, ed. Scarborough, ON: Prentice-Hall.

Tanner, J., Davies, S., and O'Grady, B. (1999). Whatever happened to yesterday's rebels? Longitudinal effects of youth delinquency on education and employment. *Social Problems*. 46(2), 250–74.

Tanner, J., Hartnagel T., and Krahn, H. (1995). *Fractured transitions from school to work: revisiting the dropout problem*. Toronto: University of Toronto Press.

Tanner, J., and Krahn, H. (1991). Part-time work and deviance among high-school seniors. *Canadian Journal of Sociology*. 1693), 281–302.

Tanner, J., and Wortley, S. (2000). Youth, leisure and crime: preliminary findings. University of Toronto.

Taylor, I. (1982). Moral enterprise, moral panic and law and order campaigns. In *The sociology of deviance,* M. Rosenberg, R. Stebbins, and A. Turowetz, eds. New York: St. Martin's Press.

Thomas, W. I. (1928). *The unadjusted girl*. Boston: Little, Brown.

Thompson, H. (1967). *Hell's angels*. New York: Ballantine.

Thompson, K. (1998). *Moral panics*. London and New York: Routledge.

Thorne, B. (1993). *Gender play: girls and boys in school*. New Brunswick, NJ: Rutgers University Press.

Thornberry, T. P., Moore, M., and Christenson, R. L. (1985). The effect of dropping out of high school on subsequent criminal behaviour. *Criminology*. 23, 3–18.

Thornton, S. (1995). *Club cultures; music, media and subcultural capital*. Cambridge: Polity Press.

Thrasher, F. (1937). *The gang*, 2nd revised ed. Chicago: University of Chicago Press.

Tittle, C., and Meier, R. (1990). Specifying the S.E.S./delinquency relationship. *Criminology*. 28(2) 271–99.

Tittle, C., and Villenez, W. (1978). Social class and criminology. *Social Forces*. 56, 474–502.

Tittle, C., Villenez, W., and Smith, D. (1978). The myth of social class and criminality: an empirical assessment of the empirical evidence. *American Sociological Review*. 43, 643–56.

Tracy, P. (1987). Race and class differences in official and self-reported delinquency. In *From boy to man: from delinquency to crime*, M. Wolfgang, T. Thornberry, and R. Figlis, eds. Chicago: University of Chicago Press.

Tracy, P., and Kempf-Leonard, K. (1996). *Continuity and discontinuity in criminal careers*. New York: Plenum Press.

Tracy, P., Wolfgang, M., and Figlio, R. (1985). Delinquency in two birth cohorts. Washington, DC: U.S. Department of Justice.

Tremblay, S. (2000). Crime statistics in Canada, 1999. *Juristat*. 20(5). Canadian Centre for Justice Statistics.

Vallee, B. (1997). *Edwin Alonzo Boyd: The story of the notorious Boyd gang*. Doubleday Canada Limited Toronto

Vaughan, C. (1990). Everything old seems new again, to teens. *Globe and Mail*. (n.d.)

Vaz, E. (1966). Self-reported juvenile delinquency and socio-economic status. *Canadian Journal of Criminology and Corrections*. 8, 20–27.

Vigil, J. (1990). Cholos and gangs: culture change and street youth in Los Angeles. In *Gangs in America*, C. R. Huff, ed. Newbury Park, CA: Sage.

Visher, C. (1983). Gender, police arrest decisions and notions of chivalry. *Criminology*. 21, 5–28.

Waddington, D. (1992). *Contemporary issues in public disorder*. London and New York: Routledge and Kegan Paul.

Waddington, P. (1986). Mugging as a moral panic: a question of proportion. *British Journal of Sociology*. 37(2), 245–59.

Watson, J. M. (1980). Outlaw motorcyclists: an outgrowth of lower class cultural careers. *Deviant Behaviour*. 2, 31–48.

Weber, T. (1999). Raving in Toronto: peace, love, unity and respect in transition. *Journal of Youth Studies*. 2(3) (October), 317–36.

Weinstein, D. (1991). *Heavy metal: a cultural sociology*. New York: Lexington Books.

Wertham, F. (1953). *Seduction of the innocent*. Port Washington, NY: Kennikat Press.

West, D., and Farrington, D. (1973). *Who becomes delinquent?* London: Heinemann.

West, W. G. (1978). The short-term careers of serious thieves. *Canadian Journal of Criminology*. 20(2), 169–90.

———. (1979). Serious thieves: lower class adolescent males in a short-term deviant occupation. In *Crime and delinquency in Canada*, E. Vaz and A. Lodhi, eds. Toronto: Prentice-Hall.

———. (1984). *Young offenders and the state*. Toronto: Butterworths.

Whyte, W. (1955). *Street corner society: the social organization of a Chicago slum,* 2nd ed. Chicago: University of Chicago Press.

Wiatrowski, M., Hansell, S., Massey, C., and Wilson, D. (1982). Curriculum tracking and delinquency. *American Sociological Review*. 47, 151–60.

Widom, C. (1988). Child abuse, neglect and violent criminal behaviour. Unpublished manuscript. Cited in Chesney-Lind, 1997.

Wilkins, L. (1964). *Social deviance*. London: Tavistock.

Williams, T. (1989). *The cocaine kids*. New York: Addison-Wesley.

Willis, P. (1976). *Profane culture*. London: Chatto and Windus.

———. (1977). *Learning to labour: how working-class kids get working-class jobs*. Aldershot: Gower Publishing.

Wilson, J., and Kelling, G. (1982, March). Fixing broken windows. *Atlantic Monthly*. 29–38.

Wolf, D. (1991). *The rebels*. Toronto: University of Toronto Press.

Wolfgang, M., Figlio, R., and Sellin, T. (1972). *Delinquency in a birth cohort*. Chicago: University of Chicago Press.

Wortley, S. (1996). Justice for all? race and perceptions of bias in the Ontario criminal justice system—a Toronto survey. *Canadian Journal of Criminology*. 38(4), 439–68.

Yablonsky, L. (1962). *The violent gang*. New York: Macmillan.

Young, K., and Curry, L. (1997). Beyond white pride: identity, meaning and contradition in the Canadian skinhead subculture. *Canadian Review of Sociology and Anthropology*. 34(2), 176–206.

Young, M., and Wilmot, P. (1957). *Family and kinship in East London*. London: Routledge and Kegan Paul.

Zatz, M. (1987). Chicano youth gangs and crime: the creation of a moral panic. *Contemporary Crisis*. 11(2), 129–58.

NAME INDEX

Parsons, Talcott, 31, 274
Pearson, Geoffrey, 3, 4, 91, 98, 234, 252, 256, 262, 273, 274
Pearson, P., 186, 274
Pepler, Debra, 188
Peterson, D., 204, 259
Phelps, G., 108, 128, 201, 273
Piliavin, I., 212, 274
Pilkington, H., 180, 209, 274
Pink, W., 108, 274
Platt, Anthony, 29, 274
Polk, Kenneth, 101, 102, 108, 165, 274, 276
Pollock, J., 181, 274
Porteous, M., 5, 274
Power, M. J., 100, 275
Prinsky, L., 18, 276
Pronovost, L., 166, 275
Pruitt, B., 125, 270
Pugh, M., 201, 202, 266

Rabb, T., 270
Rankin, J., 198, 275
Reid, S., 223, 275
Reid-Macnevin, S., 223, 275
Reinarman, G., 19, 231, 275
Reiss, A., 44, 45, 211, 212, 261, 275
Reitsma-Street, Marge, 179, 214, 223, 275
Reynolds, S., 152, 275
Riley, D., 202, 204, 275
Rippl, S., 148, 149, 267
Roberts, B., 262
Roberts, J., 11, 275
Rock, P., 264
Roe, K., 111, 112, 275
Roncek, D., 275
Rosenbaum, J., 18, 276
Rosenberg, M., 278
Rosenfeld, R., 82, 98, 272
Rothberg, R., 270
Rucker, L., 240, 273
Rutter, M., 100, 247, 276

Sacco, V., 12, 38, 93, 274, 276–78
Sampson, R., 52, 270
Sandhu, H., 195, 276
Savoie, J., 41, 46, 49, 52, 276

Schafer, W., 102, 165, 274, 276
Schissel, B., 227, 276
Schreiber, D., 165, 276
Sellin, T., 244, 280
Senna, J., 65, 277
Shaw, Clifford, 70, 142, 171, 178, 242, 276
Shaw, Henry, 69
Sheldon, R., 182–84, 194, 197, 262
Sheley, J., 125, 276
Shepherd, Michelle, 5–7, 20, 276
Shoemaker, D., 206, 276
Short, J., 77, 82, 276
Shover, N., 197, 273, 276
Shroud, C., 276
Siegel, L., 65, 277
Silverman, R., 93, 207, 270, 274, 277
Simon, R., 186, 277
Simpson, J. E., 165, 204, 267, 277
Singer, S., 205, 277
Singh, R., 152, 277
Slater, E., 181, 263
Smith, A., 100, 247, 276
Smith, C., 45, 259
Smith, D., 56, 212, 277, 279
Solomon, P., 118–21, 277
Sparks, R., 54, 56, 68, 268
Spergel, I., 77, 277
Sprott, J., 5, 11, 49–51, 264, 277
St. Ledger, R. J., 247, 265
Stebbins, R., 278
Steinberg, Laurence, 127
Stevenson, K., 275
Stinchcombe, Arthur, 117, 128, 198, 277
Strange, C., 209, 210, 277
Strodtbeck, F., 77, 276
Stroud, Carsten, 225, 277
Sugarman, Barry, 107, 108, 277
Sullivan, Mercer, 61, 79, 98, 140–42, 162, 171, 277
Surette, R., 9, 11, 250, 277
Sutherland, N., 26, 27, 29, 278
Sykes, G., 74, 169, 235, 271, 278

Tanner, J., 45, 53, 106, 110, 115, 118, 166, 168, 174, 268, 278